KEYNOTES
IN
LIFE AND WORK

BY THE SAME AUTHOR

KEYNOTES
IN
LIFE AND WORK

PERSPECTIVES GAINED
FROM A LIFE
WORKING IN STEINER EDUCATION

BRIEN MASTERS

First published in 2009 by Perevale Publications
© 2009 Brien Masters
Brien Masters
Friar's Ash
Priory Road
Forest Row
East Sussex RH18 5HP
England

ISBN 978 0 9564 126 0 7

Printed in Great Britain by Cpod, Trowbridge, Wiltshire.

Contents

3. viii. 11

Dear Heidi,

I deeply appreciated the 80th birthday outing to the prom last week — such an exhilarating performance, and the chance to experience Norrington one last time. Many thanks for planning the event and taking care of all the arrangements.

Enclosed, a copy of Dr Páleš' book for you and a recent publication of mine which includes a study on Oliphant (who cropped up in our conversation) — both with my best wishes.

With warm regards,

Brian

Acknowledgements

The eleven essays in this work are the result of paths that have crossed my own life's path with various others. In some cases those who have trodden the other path are implicitly identifiable. Here, however, I wish to be more explicit by expressing gratitude as follows:

To the editors of the *Golden Blade 2009* for permission to reprint the article 'About time too: Beethoven and the scherzo—a symptom of the consciousness soul'; to Sevak Gulbekian, chief editor of Temple Lodge Publishing, for permission to reprint the article 'The Spirit or the Letter: on whose side is the teacher of literacy fighting?' in *The Future is Now: Anthroposophy at the New Millennium*; to Dr Richard House, Senior Lecturer at Roehampton University, for his highly professional input on the transcript of the lecture 'School-readiness and Child Development: A Framework for Understanding and Decision making', first given at the Norwich Steiner School; to Christine Polyblank of the Ringwood Waldorf School, for making available the transcript of the lecture 'The senses and the modern child', given at the Easter Conference of the National Association of Steiner Schools, Easter 2007; to colleagues at the Harduf Waldorf School for inviting me to become Senior Academic Consultant on Waldorf Education, a position which led to the request from the Ministry of Education in Israel for the paper on 'Distinctive Features of Waldorf Education and their Relevance For or Bearing On Assessment'; to Dr Ken Gibson and his Humanities Section of the School of Spiritual Science team who organised the historiography conference in summer 2006 which formed the basis for the article on 'Crowns with but a Single Trunk: Enigmas in the Life and Karmic Background of Laurence Oliphant'; to David Lowe, organiser of the Tuesday public lecture series at Rudolf Steiner House, London, whose unfailing encouragement and enthusiasm led to the lectures on which the articles 'What are we fighting for now? A perspective on how Shakespeare's use of language supports us on our way to becoming human' and 'On the Sands with Printless Foot: The Work of the Elements in the Landscape' are based; to the late Misses M. Bridger and M. Buckeridge, co-founders of Perevale Home, Nutley, without whose indefatigable dedication the present Nutley Hall would not have been established; to the late Dr Jean Mierowska, music teacher and adjudicator, for companionship over more than half a century and for her unfailing and rigorous recognition of what *is* music and *why*, both as regards standards of composition and performance; to Josie Alwyn, Dr Christopher Houghton-Budd and Dr Richard House, Trustees of the London Waldorf Teacher Training Seminar, for their continued support over many years; to the Hermes Trust for its support in this publishing venture; to Paul Breslaw and Inge Tombs for invaluable technical support and assistance; to William Bishop, author, for advice on self-publishing; to Aaron Breslaw for generous assistance in preparing the front cover.

Proem

The image on the front cover, reproduced here with the parent's kind permission, is of a 6-year-old child's drawing. On being delicately questioned as to its content, the child's reply was: "It's to thank the tooth fairies,"—which referred to the recent loss of an incisor. Without the child's at all intending it, of course, the questioner definitely felt an arrow of child wisdom penetrate the eager target of his soul. As when in archery the arrow, drawn from the quiver, speeds from the strung bow and quivers for a split moment as it makes its mark, the child's reply shuddered in the questioner's consciousness, bringing awe, awakening, insight, humility, a touch of amusement, warm flowing love for the child and the never-ceasing astonishment that whizzes through the spiritual space that constitutes human childhood. It's hard to imagine what a future dentistry might make of the dental arches of Neanderthal Man—but those worlds are surely closer together than the moribundity of average modern adult consciousness and that of the child 'thanking the tooth fairies'.

The great self-portraitists—Rembrandt, van Gogh and Leonardo, for instance—veil their inmost being behind the totally visible image they place on the canvas. (And you would need to be wealthier than a bonus-pocketing banker during an economic recession to have such a canvas in your personal possession!) By contrast, young children's drawings, no doubt worth less than the paper they're drawn on at Sotheby's, whatever 'label' the child may attach to it, are a portrait of self, not veiled behind external likenesses but uninhibitedly revealing a catalogue of open secrets at any given moment in their incarnation.

Looking at the drawing on the front cover (with or without one's tooth-fairy hat on!) one is struck by the firm stance of the figures beneath the 'apple tree', complemented by the unhesitating fullness of the colours. This lack of hesitation despite their not being in the assertive red end of the spectrum. To watch a child drawing and see the little hand go straight to the right place in the crayon box—like Joan of Arc making a beeline for the disguised Dauphin in the mingling crowd of courtiers resident at Chinon—is to witness 'sure-footed' spirituality at work.

The clues to the child's inner being (self-portrait), which are perhaps the most pregnant here, are the uprightness of the trunk of the tree and the triangular headgear that the figures are wearing. These are complementary. The storm-defying uprightness portrays ever growing inner certainty, ego strength, which is still able to reach upwards to a harvest of cosmic fruit. The triangular motif, according to experts who have studied children's drawings, signifies that the child, while having arrived at a firm inner point in incarnation (the base of the triangle) still has access to its spiritual origin, the upward pointing apex of the (usually isosceles) triangle—unlike the 'top hats' which often occur in drawings done by children at the Rubicon stage of development (see page 32).

Nowadays, when biographical workshops and biographical counselling have become so widespread, even if there is a modicum of self-indulgence entailed in the process, we may surely welcome the insight that this may engender into the human being's prenatal nature. The understanding of childhood can be seen as a springboard to what lives beyond the ephemeral and yet is reflected in it, or what lives beyond the sensible and yet is somehow sense-supersensibly revealed.

Every human countenance, it could be said, is a front cover. We all wear unliftable veils, whether we are Arabic-chatting wives buying a sprig of parsley at the local market or iron-visaged Japanese emperors watching an execution; whether we are Catherine the Greats commanding nations or Toms, Dicks and Harrys commanding cockney accents; whether we are Salome writhing on a psychologically stained dance floor or Parzifal eagerly emerging from his thick forest of doubt; or whether we are Teresas awaiting canonization or unknown soldiers awaiting burial in a Belgian grave.

> Lifting corners of veils is one of the aims of the present work
> veils woven of the fabric of time
> time that has stridden through one self-portrait
> a self-portrait drawn with septennial brush strokes
> the hand guided by the sure-footedness of destiny
> or simply poised in questioning gesture;
>
> And alongside each colour
> selected from the crayon box of memory
> are thoughts arising from hindsight and later experiences
> experiences that bring the hues of the past to the fore
> colouring the sea- and mountain-scapes of life
> as the sun arches towards its patient horizon.

Brien Masters
Christmas 2008

Introduction

The circle consisted of all the teachers and children of The Waldorf School of La Palma, housed in a beautiful district on the western side of the island, the greenest of the Canaries and the one which boasts the greatest number of volcanic craters within historic times. Dramatic postcard views of Teneguia in eruption convey the awe and natural power of the island's most recent such event (26 October 1971).

The children had prepared several things to welcome the English visitor. In the circle, each one introduced him- or herself *in English*, however recently they had begun to learn the language, with: 'My name is ...; I am ... years old; I come from ... [surprisingly international]; and I am in Class ...' As we went round the circle the teachers joined in. I think one 'cover' teacher had never spoken even that much English before. And clearly, as it came to my turn, the expectation mounted; and at the mention of an age of 77 a gasp (of 'can that be?') burst forth, creating a crater, might one say, of warmth in which the welcome was complete.

The essays gathered here together in one volume, have essentially two origins. The first was advice from one of my publishers as to 'time-sensitive' material and publishing, and the problematic fact that not all time-sensitive works are proving commercially viable titles in the present cultural and economic climate. The second follows from that. It was the advice of a friend: to follow what so many are doing today (in view of our cultural malaise and the effect of the internet on the book trade) and self-publish, with print runs according to need, however small, using electronic methods.

The confluence of these pieces of advice seemed to meet what I saw as urgent needs in one quarter of society or another. However, on sharing my ideas with the friend, he thought that they might prove electronically too ambitions for a 'beginner' and suggested a volume that consisted of as much plain text as possible (which is how this has panned out) with the fleeting memories of 11 x 7-year phases providing a unifying factor.

After all, beyond a certain age, every day in life seems time-sensitive! So the composition of the book comprises essays of varying genres (and even slightly varying formats, according to the documents' origin) that reflect the cultural sensitivity—if that is not too euphemistic a way of describing the situations in which we find ourselves—of the time in which we live, preceded by an introductory piece in which I mostly try to look at each topic in the light of some biographical perspective.

The 'exercise' has proved to be one in which the subjects (personal life events) in being objectified, have often gained in the sense that it encouraged them to stand at the thresholds of memory, seemingly with new significance.

So for the present circle of readers, however small: 'My name is Brien Masters; I have lived through 11 septennial phases, and you will hear some of the keynotes of my life and work, and where I am 'coming from' in the following pages.'

1931-1938

The earliest memory that I have been able to access readily is of being in a wood near what was usually referred to as 'the family watermill'. It was on the south side of the River Aln in Northumberland, from which both the county town of Alnwick and the tiny harbour at the river's estuary, Alnmouth, take their names. Kathleen Raine, in her *Autobiographies*, enables the reader to enter into a mode of consciousness, certainly a mood, that I can clearly identify with in what happened in that wood. The consciousness of *I am an 'I'* arose within a nature setting that was to colour my childhood as has no other occurrence that I am aware of. Even if I could emulate her magnificent yet tender, participative style, it is not my present purpose, though I expand inwardly with sheer gratitude when I realise that it was nature, especially with her abundance of summer flowers, sharp north-easterly air and swift, soothe-cool river currents that would seem to have affirmed whatever higher authority ordained: *it is time to incarnate.*

I could easily trace that connection with nature through eleven seven-year phases, wherein an echo of that first memory thankfully lingers on. Often, too, the echoing has spilt into ink, and identifying just where would be part of the tracing. But here I wish, rather, to begin by paying tribute to people who have touched my life—more than touched—in a way that has resulted in an unfading interest in and an unending search into Shakespeare—his language, his enquiring mind, and his plumbing the depth of the human heart.

It was a school friend of my mother's in Alnwick who, when I was a boy, gave me as a birthday present a copy of Shakespeare's complete works. Yet despite my being evacuated during the Second World War to the bard's birthplace and being ferried to school over the River Avon every morning beside the church where his tomb rests, and despite there being Reynolds on my father's side of the family and Hathaways related by marriage to that same family

stream (both names that crop up in research that delves into
Shakespeare's Warwickshire connections), and despite my good
fortune in having English teachers at grammar school who flamed
with rare enthusiasm for his writing (the one who would lash out
with reams of Shakespearean vituperative instead of droning dry
reprimands for miscreants who hadn't done their homework, making
all of us itch with delight and admiration; and the other who strode
up and down between the desks chilling our blood as she
gesticulated madly and ranted and raved with red hair tangled and
tossing in a Lady Macbeth fashion *during exam-preparation
lessons!),* and despite playing bassoon in a performance of Vaughan
Williams' *Sir John in Love* in Stratford-on-Avon during the Festival
of Britain celebrations in the presence of the composer, and despite
being roped into a performance of *The Tempest* (as Caliban: my first
and last appearance on the Shakespearean stage) in a village which
bore the name of Hampton-in-Arden and was, indeed, part of the
Forest of Arden in which *As you like it* is set, and despite ... despite
... it was not until I heard A.C. Harwood lecture in the early 60s on
the development of human consciousness as mirrored in English
literature, that Shakespeare's full stature began to dawn. It was in the
days before English money became metric—there were 240 pennies
in the pound—and Harwood's lectures made all the pennies drop for
me in one great avalanche of mental clatter. But it was only after
much avid work on Shakespeare, and some 33 years later, that the
thinking of Owen Barfield—through his books and through
conversations I had with him at the Wallhatch in Forest Row during
the last phase of his long life—made it clear to me what that literary
stature really meant for the consciousness of humanity in general.

Thus, I can, with some degree of certainty, recognise that what
Barfield termed *participative consciousness* enjoyed by humans
before (Western) rationality got the upper hand during the last four
hundred years, was (a) what children in general recapitulate in their
early years; and (b) what impressed itself on my own experience of
life during those first seven years, particularly in connection with

nature, becoming one of the very first stepping stones on which Brien Masters set his foot when crossing over from whatever went before May 1931 to whatever came after.

The essay that follows is, apart from anything else, a tribute to those who drew aside the curtains which allowed me a glimpse into Shakespeare's world, while dealing with what I perceive to be something in his style—a tessera in the vast mosaic of his oeuvre— that pinpoints his contribution to the evolution of consciousness, showing the way, as I believe, that looks back at 'original participation', looks fully and profoundly into 'the now', and looks forward to the long journey that lies before us towards 'final participation'. What his genius brought forth is surely a significant stepping stone between those two banks—though I refrain from looking for any biographical symbol (of a family-watermill-on-one-bank-of-the-river kind) in connection with the potent image.

What are we Fighting for Now?
A perspective on how Shakespeare's use of language supports us on our way to becoming human

There were three veterans—each well over a 100—attending the ceremony at the cenotaph in Whitehall this year (November 2008), as the world reflected on the 70th anniversary of the cessation of hostilities of the war that would purportedly 'end all wars' (1914-1918). The Sunday newspapers ventured the comment: What have we to fight for now? No mention, however, of the inner hostilities that beset us in our effort to become, or even remain, human in the modern world. William Blake's well-known "I will not cease from mental fight, / Nor shall my sword sleep in my hand. / Till we have built Jerusalem / In England's green and pleasant land," though often unfortunately rousing sentimental or nationalistic feelings, points in the direction of 'mental fight', a direction I wish to pursue here with the help of an aspect of Shakespeare's use of language.

For the vast majority of the time nowadays we see and use language, both in its spoken and written forms, as the conveyor of meaning. Furthermore, it is meaning that mostly can be gleaned from language through our rational intellect. In Shakespeare's *Hamlet*, the audience—but only the audience—has been party to the pang of conscience that smites the soul of Hamlet's uncle, who has murdered his brother the king in order to gain the Danish throne and the hand of Hamlet's mother, his brother's widow. Despite his dark-as-hell treachery, the audience may well feel some compassion for his situation as he kneels at his prayers seeking absolution, or at least comfort, but finding none. With euphemistic simplicity he agonises, "My words fly up, my thoughts remain below; / Words without thoughts never to heaven go." Shakespeare thus allows us, in two astonishingly plain-worded rhyming lines, to zoom-lens into the usurper's tempestuously tattered state of soul.

Language, as shown here, in the hands of the supreme poet, enables the soul to live on more than one plane—with the use of some poetic devices (figures of speech, assonance, rhythms, rhyming schemes and so on)—to live on the super-rational plane rather than merely on the plane of straightforward, intellectually-gleaned meaning. There are, of course, many shades of enhancement of meaning, from the rational to the super-rational, which are found in abundance in a variety of literary art forms which we need not elaborate here. Still 'higher', perhaps, is the use of language in mantric formulae, which, it could be argued, Shakespeare at least approaches in his *deus ex machina* moments, especially in the last plays (*Pericles, Cymbeline, A Winter's Tale* and *The Tempest*), which, whilst being important 'for the record', is not the immediate matter of our present enquiry.

The bard incarnated at a time of Rubicon-like change in Western consciousness. From the early 16th century more and more of the mind's attention was directed towards the earthly plane and the laws which 'explained' the physical phenomena visible (audible etc.) to the five senses. Although reference to Medieval correspondences abound in his works—from which it would follow that his hearers, groundlings included, must have been au fait with them—poignant moments in *Hamlet* make it clear that this form of (super-rational) consciousness was fast fading. In his feigned madness, Hamlet, in derisive mood, flings the tragic fading into Ophelia's face, increasing her disbelief and consternation at the change that has apparently come over him. Earlier, we have been given a glimpse into the source of his madly construed words in one of Hamlet's famous soliloquies:

> I have of late—but wherefore I know not—lost all my mirth, foregone all custom of exercises; and, indeed, it goes so heavily with my disposition that this goodly frame, the earth, seems to me a sterile promontory; this

> most excellent canopy, the air, look you, this brave
> o'erhanging firmament, this majestical roof fretted with
> golden fire, why it appears to me no more than a foul and
> pestilent congregation of vapours.

Hamlet is merely voicing, of course, what is already apparent in
the ebbing tide of Medieval/Renaissance consciousness (as evident
in the thinking of Galileo, Copernicus and those of like mind)—a
tide which on its turn is destined to flood swiftly, via the intellect of
Bacon and Newton, amongst others, into every bay on the coast of
Western civilisation, from the invention of the Newcomen-Watt
steam engine in the 18th century into our present time with the latest
nuclear developments and achievements in genetic engineering.

Time and again, Rudolf Steiner emphasises the evolutionary
necessity of what we term materialism, the fruit of such intellect,
while at the same time pointing towards the equal necessity of
developing *counter-forces* if civilisation is not going to be engulfed
in matter at all costs. I believe that those counter-forces exist in that
poetic use of language which reminds the rational mind that 'all that
glisters is not gold', and that there is meaning beyond the sense-
perceptible phenomenon—anticipating perhaps the recent research
that is beginning to value the part played by the brain's right
hemisphere in the evolution of consciousness.

It is perhaps significant that, squeezed in between their Roman
Catholic past and their Puritanical future, Shakespeare's
contemporaries were avid theatre-goers—and by and large it is *his*
plays that, from among the many playwrights of his day, which we
still see performed on stage. A glance at the music of Galileo's
'Italy' and Shakespeare's England may illuminate a facet of our
theme. True, madrigalists were prolific in late Renaissance Italy, but
it is the canon of Palestrina's ecclesiastical compositions that stands
out as a beacon of 16th century achievement. Prolific, astonishingly
pure, and unparalleled in contrapuntally creative flow, the ability to
emulate Palestrina's style represented, so to speak, the *sine qua non*

for aspiring composers right down to modern times. Indeed there are those who hold the opinion that Baroque, Viennese Classicism, and Romanticism, the three great musical styles born of the diatonic system, are mere degenerations of what Palestrina and his illustrious contemporaries achieved. Be that as it may, the texts of this vast output of ecclesiastical music are in Latin. This flourishing was superseded—which is not to say bettered—by the sudden outburst of Italian opera, starting with Peri and Caccini and coming quickly into its first full flowering with Monteverdi's *Orfeo*, first performed in Mantua in 1607. Opera texts were in the vernacular: Italian. If Latin somehow preserved a lingering, non-rational form of participative consciousness (because a foreign language to the majority of the population), the new genre, opera, must have come as a shock to the system, albeit, judging by its crescendoing popularity, a pleasant one. Nevertheless, it seems that the baton that Galileo was to hand on was thrust into the hands of the nation destined to cradle the Industrial Revolution (in England's green and pleasant land!) rather than the generation of opera lovers who were on his doorstep.

There was, of course, a wealth of ecclesiastical music in England, too, the composers of the day setting both English and Latin texts, seemingly thus avoiding falling between the last Tudors' two religious stools. But in the present context it is the English madrigal school which I wish to highlight. When Edmund Fellowes was engaged in his pioneer work of putting the genre onto the map of people's awareness, he did not stop short at bringing out comprehensively edited sets of the music, but also published a volume of madrigal texts. Thomas Campion is known for having been both poet and composer, but the poets chosen by other madrigalists, Fellowes clearly felt, must take their fair share of acclaim in that remarkable outpouring which continued well into the Jacobean first quarter of the 17th century. This outpouring was surely part of the counter-force to the descent of the imaginative consciousness of earlier times into the materialistically-bent intellect that we all enjoy and are spiritually challenged by today.

One of the most basic of human inventions is the *step*. It makes the outer gradient more manageable for the foot and the energy forces of the traveller. The phenomenon to which I am referring could be seen as the inner equivalent—the step, constructed by the genius of one human being, becoming an asset for those who use it to ascend the inner gradient—*Gradus ad Parnassum*, as referred to in classical times. In England, after the so-called 'Golden Age', genius was to express itself through language rather than music, Purcell's genius notwithstanding.

Everyone, no doubt, will have cause to be grateful to different steps that destiny has given them personally. The pun—amongst other figures of speech—in Shakespeare's oeuvre, seems to me to epitomise the enormous step that his style offers the striving Ego of our present epoch. The word pun itself actually only appeared after Shakespeare's death, the Classical term for this figure of speech being *paronomasia,* a play on words. However, of all figures of speech it has suffered a strange fate, q.v. the groan with which it is often received by the modern intellect, with the punner as often as not apologising in advance. Shakespeare occasionally puns at this elementary, often groin-groaning, level, too. For our present purpose, we can discount this degradation of what, not so long ago, was a valued literary tool—certainly nothing to be ashamed of.

One of the outstanding insights of the Shakespearean scholar, James Shapiro, who teaches at Columbia University in New York, is evident in his comment on Shakespeare's use of the less-known figure of speech: *hendiadys*, meaning 'two in one'. It is particularly prevalent in *Hamlet*. "The book and volume of my brain" (I v), "Angels and ministers of grace" (I iv), "a fantasy and trick of fame" (IV iv), "though I most potently and powerfully believe" (II ii), "a foul and pestilent congregation of vapours" (II ii) are a few examples. It has been suggested that the English language lends itself well to hendiadys, in that its vocabulary, containing strata from different foreign eruptions into its cultural massif, is endowed with words of almost identical meaning. The Anglican Prayer Book is often linked with this assertion, e.g. "We have erred and strayed from thy ways like lost sheep; and have followed too much the devices and desires of our own hearts." But this does not explain Shakespeare's use of the figure of speech, which avalanches into his plays in c.1599 and almost disappears after five years. *Hamlet* furnishes 65 examples and *Othello* 28. Shapiro connects it with the intensity of meaning that bursts into human consciousness at this time through *Hamlet* (and plays that follow)—for further evidence of which he cites the painstaking work of Alfred Hart who counted 600 words that the bard introduced into the work, which he had never used before (only one third of which he was to use again), and 170 of which are words or phrases coined or used in new ways. (Compare this with how many of us coins even one new word in a whole life-time!) Even allowing for the fact that Shapiro appears to assume that the Elizabethan playgoers had only the consciousness of the average person of 2005—the date of the book's publication—we could readily go along with his observation that the audience must at times have found it taxing to follow.

Shapiro's further insight, "The more you think about examples of hendiadys, the more they induce a kind of mental vertigo," (*1599 A Year in the Life of William Shakespeare* p.321) takes us closer. Vertigo is a complaint suffered by those who find altitudes difficult. They don't have 'a head for heights'. The language of the poet attempts, in expressing the heights (be they of feeling or thinking), to convey something of that region to his readers—or, particularly as in this case we are referring to a playwright, to his *listeners.* Moreover, they are heights which, if we become oblivious to them, no longer support us in overcoming the obstacles we encounter (developing the counter-forces) in our striving to become human.

Commentators on Shakespeare's art of language have observed how it goes through three main phases. His early style is so pregnant with the richness of linguistic life that the meaning can be burdened by it. The meaning in his last plays, albeit something of a quality that requires a feat of imagination if the listener is going to scale its imaginative heights, somewhat subdues the richness of his language to which we are accustomed—needless, to say, the subduing is only comparative. In the middle plays, the wealth of language and the meaning play an equally exalted partnership. Measured by this, *Hamlet* with its density of language and its profundity of meaning, rises to the heights—heights from which Shakespeare goes to enormous lengths to convey the breakthrough that is occurring in the development of human consciousness (the 'spectator consciousness' that the bard hinted at after 1599 in switching from calling the play-going 'auditors' to calling them 'spectators')—*but at the same time* in making the literary demands that he did, gives the spectators what they needed in order to achieve the dizzy heights that he, as lead climber was able to reach and in which he was thoroughly at home. We could say: the wherewithal to conquer mental vertigo and ultimately to enjoy and take in the benefits of higher consciousness.

In the way that the fully-in-the-know spectator (in the audience) watches Hamlet—who with spectator consciousness (born of the loss of a father and the promptings of that father's ghost) watches the king, his stepfather who, conscience-plagued, is easy prey to be ensnared by the spectacle of the play within the play which he is watching—each one in the audience is witnessing and participating in one of the most poignant moments of the delivery and birth of spectator consciousness in history. It is as if its pregnancy is terminated at one and the same moment as its coming of age. But it is not the spectator consciousness of the mindless football hooligan swayed by his fellow supporters in the modern Olympic stadium, though this is also a phenomenon of the fifth Post-Atlantean epoch. It is the consciousness which, while gazing into the depths which open up in our age of materialism, is prevented from being dragged down and trapped there—merely gazing vapidly and gawping at those depths—by the birth of a counter-force: the highest, newly-acquired level at which the mind of the bard is arriving and exploring, the level to which he gives expression firstly in the poetic pre-eminence of his language (which has been in place, of course, from the beginning), secondly in the coinage of new words, phrases and new meanings that are an increasingly evident hall-mark of the middle plays, thirdly with the density of metaphor, fourthly with the mind-spiralling hendiadys that we have noted, and fifthly with the pun (which we are fast approaching). All this becomes the consciousness platform from which Shakespeare launches the resurrection-like scenes that are the culmination of the last four 'comedies'.

Now the pun, (properly: paronomasia, the Greek term it audaciously expunged!) is also a 'two-in-one' brother of hendiadys. But in Shakespeare's hands, particularly in the way in which he uses it at climacteric moments and nodal points in the plot, it is as if the 'one' of the two-in-one becomes the eye of a needle through which the mind is enabled to pass and expand (to whatever degree of consciousness the listener is able to muster) onto a higher plane than either of the original plane of the 'two', or, indeed, on a higher plane than the two-in-one of the hendiadys had achieved. The pun, moreover, often gains effect through its home-hitting brevity. (Somewhat in stark contrast to my eye-of-a-needle effort to diagnose what is going on!) When the eyes of Richard II's soul are turned inward—he has been captured and imprisoned in Pontefract castle—not, alas, through his uncle's prophetic warning early in the play, the tidal wave of his self-knowledge breaks on the shore of his by now inescapable political situation with, "I wasted time; and now doth time waste me" (V v). Not that Shakespeare leaves it at that. In grand soliloquy style, that he was hardly to surpass until *Hamlet*, he continues:

> "For now hath time made me his numbering clock: / My thoughts are minutes; and with sighs, they jar / Their watches on unto my eyes, the outward watch, / Whereto my finger, like a dial's point, / Is pointing still, in cleansing them from tears." (ibid.)

These last words before Richard is assassinated, act as a sort of counterbalance to the earlier scene in which his uncle has warningly implored him to mend his unwantonly extravagant ways. In reply to the king's: "How is it with aged Gaunt?" the puns begin: "O, how that name befits my composition! / Old Gaunt, indeed; and gaunt in being old: Within me grief hath kept a tedious fast; / And who abstains from meat that is not gaunt? / For sleeping England long time have I watch'd; / Watching breeds leanness, leanness is all gaunt: / The pleasure that some fathers feed upon / Is my strict fast [...] / Gaunt am I for the grave, gaunt as a grave, / Whose hollow womb inherits naught but bones." (II i) And as if to give the speech the status of *locus classicus*, Richard replies: "Can sick men play so nicely with their names?"

Orienting our way through the literary thick forest of Hamlet, we come across puns at many significant moments in the play. Some examples follow.

1. At one of the first moments that Hamlet shares (in an aside) his suspicion concerning the cause of his father's death, to the king's greeting he replies: "A little more than kin and less than kind."

2. To the king's invitation to Hamlet's mother to leave Hamlet's brooding presence: "No jocund health that Denmark drinks today / But the great cannon to the clouds shall tell;" (I ii), Hamlet responds when the court has left him alone: "O, that this too, too sordid flesh would melt, / Thaw and resolve itself into a dew! / Or that the Everlasting had not fix'd / His canon 'gainst self-slaughter." And as with loathing he remembers the queen, the encapsulated pun seems to conjure up the very 'sin' of Eve and Adam in Eden: "Heaven and Earth! / Must I remember? Why, she would hang on him / As if increase of appetite had grown / By what it fed on:" (ibid.)

3. The Ophelia part of the tragedy is marked by a conversation

between daughter and father (Polonius). She confirms what she believes to be Hamlet's feelings for her with: "He hath, my lord, of late made many tenders / Of his affections to me." Polonius: "Affection! Pooh! [...] Do you believe his tenders as you call them? [...] I'll teach you: think yourself a baby; / That you have ta'en these tenders for true pay, / Which are not sterling. Tender yourself more dearly; / Or,—not to crack the wind of the poor phrase, [Is Polonius anticipating by some 300 years the low esteem with which the pun has come to be held?] Wronging it thus—you'll tender me a fool." And as Ophelia's heart clings to hope: "My lord, he hath importuned me with love / In honourable fashion," Polonius scorns: "Ay fashion you may call it; go to, go to." (I iii)

4. In the ghost scene, Shakespeare hasn't finished with his canon of puns. Hamlet's first sight of the ghost provokes an avalanche: "Angels and ministers of grace defend us! / [...] I will speak to thee: I'll call thee Hamlet, / King, father, royal Dane: O answer me! / Let me not burst in ignorance: but tell / Why thy canonized bones, hears'd in death, / Have burst their cerements." (I iv)

5. We learn of Hamlet's feigned madness first from Ophelia. Again she is speaking to her father, describing, and trying to make head or tail of Hamlet's peculiar behaviour. In response to Polonius' question: "Mad for thy love?" she tells of his gestures, "He took me by the wrist and held me hard; / [...] And with his other hand thus o'er his brow," and of the only sound he makes: "He raised a sigh so piteous and profound / That it did seem to shatter all his bulk / And end his being:" But it is his manner of exit that gives the audience more than a hint of his 'absent' state of mind—the 'ended being' and senselessness of the madman: "That [being] done [...], With his head over his shoulder turn'd, / He seemed to find his way without his eyes; / For out o' doors he went without their help." (II i)

6. Nor is Shakespeare above using the pun at its most featherweight. After the dialogue between himself and the understandably interfering Polonius ends with the latter drawing a blank, he retires from the scene with, "My honourable lord, I will most humbly take my leave of you," at which Hamlet brusquely retorts: "You cannot, sir, take from me anything that I will more willingly part withal," (II ii). In fact, the lightness of the pun seems to add poison to the sting in the tail.

7. As we are made aware of the impending dénouement of the tragedy, when, finally dispelling all Hamlet's doubt about his uncle's guilt, he witnesses the murderer's disturbed reaction to the (re-)enacted crime in the orchard, Hamlet concludes with "the play's the thing / Wherein to catch the conscience of the king." (II ii) There are half a dozen other verbs that Shakespeare could have used instead of 'catch' but none would have punned so nicely with 'play' and at the same time struck an alliterative note with 'conscience'.

8. Particularly harrowing is the scene between Hamlet and his (as he now deems) whore of a mother. Shakespeare opens several curtains onto these most racked feelings of Hamlet's. The first is through the eyes of the king. Polonius makes a seemingly innocent remark, during the discussion between himself, his daughter, the king and the queen. Following the queen's, "Ophelia, I do wish / That your good beauties be the happy cause / Of Hamlet's wildness," which appears to be absolutely genuine, Polonius, having given Ophelia a book "to colour her loneliness," goes on with some of his well-meaning waffling: " with devotions visage / And pious action we do sugar o'er / The devil himself". At which the king bares his troubled soul again: "How smart a lash that speech doth give my conscience! / The harlot's cheek, beautified with plastering art / Is not more ugly to the thing that helps it / Than is my deed to my most painted words:" (III i) He has prostituted his humanity. The

second reference to the harlot's cosmetics is in the grave-digging scene. Hamlet is holding the skull of his father's jester whom he loved and remembers from his childhood. From the sweet memories of the jester's jibes, gambols, songs and "flashes of merriment that were wont to set the table on a roar," the taste becomes bitter, 'abhorred', as the happy vision fades and the deathly reality of the skull stares him in the face. With the utmost irony he jabs, "Now get you to my lady's chamber and tell her, let her paint her face an inch thick, to this favour she must come;" (V i). Thirdly (though actually earlier in the play than the grave-digging scene), at the smartest, salt-in-the-wound moment in the scene between Hamlet and the queen, i.e. between mother and son, after the latter has thrown off the cloak of his madness and, goaded by the king his father's ghost, he exhorts his mother to change her ways and forsake "mine uncle's bed," for 'rank corruption infects unseen', climaxing with "Mother [...] confess yourself to heaven; / Repent what's past; avoid what is to come; And do not spread the compost on the weeds, / To make them ranker." (III iv) It is yet another passage, lofty in language, saturated with metaphor and spiralling into paronomasia, after which, when the queen finally breaks down with, "O Hamlet, thou hast cleft my heart in twain," Shakespeare impels the audience through the crusted ceiling of pedestrian reason to the heights of compassion.

With these examples, I submit that, quite apart from the effect of the *content* of the play on the soul of the 'spectator', it is the style and manner of the playwright's use of language that perform a central task in the schooling of the mind of the person borne forward on the racing current of the modern Consciousness Soul. It is Shakespeare's well-targeted puns that are strengthening for the muscles of the mind, so to speak, that is jettisoned into the fray of materialism—a 'mental fight' that not only copes with materialism but also, through developing the necessary counter-forces, is able to conquer that materialistic power which would use the advent of rational thinking in evolution to prevent us from becoming human, thereby dulling the *thinking*, stifling the *feeling* and mechanising or nullifying the *will*. For it is in our inner hostilities that we draw on the schooled strength of these three veteran soul forces—veteran, yet always needing to be 'fighting fit'.

1938-1945

The memories that people have of school amaze me. My only memory of the first school I attended (though I can recall its name) is of lying under a blanket on a camp bed. Was it some hidden streak of phlegma which records moments of comfort in a sea of otherwise unpalatable discomfort? More as a picture, I also recall striding along the top of a roadside bank on the way to school one morning—but this is only an isolated incident in the picture gallery, an incident which I suspect hasn't faded because on that occasion I was accompanied by my cousin George—one of his rare visits, on leave from his time in the Royal Horse Guards, then stationed at Windsor Castle. On a return visit with my mother, it was the horse which had been trained to carry the kettle drums when the military band went on parade that left an impression. Many has been the stable in which that impression has been re-conjured through the pungent smell.

Another distinct, if not strong, memory is of a school playground in the country somewhere near Wolverhampton. Muddy it was, too, like the trampled area around a five-barred gate where cattle congregate at milking time. It was a brief visit with a school friend whose parents had a holiday cottage in the village. Why I was there during school time I can only speculate—perhaps to afford me a memory of the local children's vigorous team play: the elated and abandoned chorusing voices, the mud-splodged knees, the concertinaed socks, the trailing shoelaces, my friend himself who seemed to be the only child wearing spectacles and the incessant break-time movement. Oh yes, and at some point a slate was put into my hand, cool smooth, and a soft, sombre grey. But as to its possible link to the acquisition of literacy or numeracy I am oblivious. Yet by this time I had acquired a fair degree of music literacy.

A series of events resulting from the slump in the 1930s caused my father's firm to close. This, following his decision not to be involved in the manufacture of ammunition (which was the direction his next firm was taking as part of the 'war effort') meant the family moved to Hollyfields, a large sports club belonging to the Birmingham Gas Corporation where father was appointed warden. School was literally round the corner.

At age 10/11 a few things began to register in the mind. I think I would be able to pick out on a school photograph the teachers of the two classes and of the headmistress. As to lessons: it stands to common sense they must have happened, but the occasion that remains vivid in the memory was one in which I demonstrated— solo—the sailors' hornpipe at an assembly to the senior school. Bizarre, I know, but that's the way it is. How to reconcile the dreamy boy that must have meandered through each school day with the fact (a) that he passed the entrance examination to the grammar school; and (b) that he was awarded a school prize (*Lamb's Tales from Shakespeare!*) for "being voted most popular boy", as the inscription clearly states, is beyond me.

School-readiness and Child Development
A Framework for Understanding and Decision Making

Good evening to you all:[1] first may I thank the organisers for giving me this opportunity of speaking on a theme that is very vibrant and very pertinent, not only to your community, but also in the educational climate of today. I think that the concept of school-readiness must be very new (I cannot imagine that it actually existed 80 years ago in 1919).

If you think back all those years to the established practice on the continent, your children would have gone to school when they were seven years of age—still the case in many countries. That was an established practice. Steiner certainly built on that, children being, by and large, seven by Easter and ready to enter the first class of the school in the following autumn.

Last Saturday, I bumped into an old colleague whom I didn't recognise—he is thirty years older than he was when we first met—though he *did* recognise me. He had become rather gnarled and wise! When his class from Basle in Switzerland came over on an exchange visit in Class 8, he asked me if I would teach them music. I remember some half of his class being boys who could sing bass and tenor parts—Class 8! In those days, in the English Class 8s that I knew, practically no boys had broken voices. This indicates a big difference between the continental approach to school-readiness and the English approach. If one enters into school proper at the age of 6 or 7, this already implies something which is a keystone of Waldorf education—namely, that the chronological age of the child is considered to be very important. This is a central issue. I think that it is generally agreed that, of all the famous educationalists who adopt

---

[1]   This is a transcript of a lecture given at the Norwich Steiner School, with expert editorial input from Dr Richard House who, at that time, ran the Playgroup.

or develop a developmental approach to childhood and to education, Steiner has taken it further than anyone else and gone into enormous depths, looking at what child development implies, what it embraces, what it entails—and building the whole of pedagogy and the curriculum precisely on that.

If we look perhaps at the social setting of what I have just referred to, that children enter into Class 1 at the age of seven (very different from what our chairperson was saying at the beginning, where we are wheedled, cajoled, made to believe, that early approaches to education are a good thing)—if we look into that, then we see that it was intrinsically coupled with the mother's role in society at the turn of the last century (1900); and in particular the mother's role in the family (now superseded of course). This meant that the children, in phase one of their lives (and I will be referring, when we speak of a Steiner Kindergarten, to that phase one mode of *learning*)—in that first phase, the children lived in the home environment, and the home environment was a busy place. There were by no means all of the gadgets that we are privileged to have today, which cut down the work and which have liberated us from many of the tasks that were performed then. It was hard work to run a home—you had to be extremely organised the whole year round; and the children imbibed this atmosphere as they grew up in their early years.

But when the first Steiner school began (September 1919) a radically changing social setting was taking place. The first World War had just ended; the women folk had had not only to run their homes but run them on less than a shoestring in many cases, and keep the war effort going at home as well, whether in this country or on the continent. Following the cessation of hostilities, the sad fact had to be faced that both sides of the conflict were confronted with a future without millions of their men folk, it impressing itself upon family life—and, therefore, upon the lives of children. Now although the first Steiner school did not open with a Kindergarten, and didn't have one for some time, Steiner fully recognised that this would become necessary; and he also saw that the change in the woman's role in society—the mother's role in the family—was something that had come to stay and that could develop positively into the future.

Presumably weighing against that positive future and its effect on children, Steiner also gave *sufficient* knowledge and wisdom for those who felt motivated to run Kindergartens, playgroups, toddler's groups and so forth. They were then able to develop that body of knowledge so that the education of young children—no longer in the home setting but in a more formal setting, away from the home—could be carried out, based on an insight into the needs of pre-school children.

There is something else which is very pertinent to Steiner school-readiness. As well as recognising that society is changing very rapidly, for whatever reason, Steiner also saw the Kindergarten teacher as having equal status to that of all other teachers. This was profoundly radical at that time: the qualifications you needed at that point to run a nursery were miles apart from the qualifications you would have needed to prepare children for common entrance or matriculation (or the German equivalents). But despite the difference in the qualifications and the knowledge that was expected from different teachers, Steiner saw the nursery teacher and the Kindergarten teacher as having equal professional status and equal salaries to the qualified teacher with many years of experience, head of department and so forth. This fact has not been brought out very much, certainly not in the specifically Waldorf literature. I emphasise it here because it means that *Steiner saw what was happening in the Kindergarten or in the playgroup as being of absolutely equal value* (some might say more), but I will not enter into that contentious issue now!)—equal educational value to what took place later on in school. You could say: 'Well, if the Kindergarten arranges a structured day where you have 12 or 16 children, it is different from the home.' You have a more *organised* situation and the day has to be structured. Nevertheless, a big component in that day is a kind of *home from home*—I am putting it very simplistically. The Kindergarten teacher will be mending an apron, podding peas, winding wool … or whatever might be required by the Kindergarten, in a homely way with the children doing 'their thing' around and about. You would probably observe, 'the children are playing'—and so they are. (In fact, it was due to the voice of Waldorf, that when the provision for Early Years education was discussed by our present government in its previous term of office, at least some reference to play got included in their prescription for nursery work—which is of course good news. I won't go into the anomaly of what kind of good news it was—rather miserable good news! …) So the children would be playing; and play and experiential learning activities, pure activities, formed—I think one can affirm quite ardently—the *main ingredient* of the Kindergarten day.

Now there were other educationists who were contemporary with Steiner (and it has always puzzled me why he never made any reference to them)—people like Montessori, for instance. I am no expert on Montessori, but my friends who are tell me that Montessori also placed play very high on the educational agenda, but that she saw it as a *means to intellectual learning*. Steiner never encapsulated how he saw play in the Kindergarten, but I think one could state that for Steiner, play wasn't a *means* for learning; *play was in itself learning: play is learning.*

What does that mean? What does it mean that the person who is presiding over play has equal status because that kind of experiential learning is *just as important* as someone sweating away doing a maths paper at the age of 17? This is integral to Steiner's approach to education, and a major factor in what we are considering this evening. So it wasn't until the children became school-ready that learning changed its mode from being, let us say, 'hands on' to another mode of learning—the kind that you get in Steiner schools in Class 1.

Now if one looks at the course that education took during the 20th century, you will see that a certain 'star' arose in the educational firmament—a star which became brighter and brighter, and which seemed to outshine all other stars. (I'm not now speaking about Steiner education but generally about the educational scene.) This star was *the star of the intellect.* All forms of education gradually got directed towards this preoccupation, and it eclipsed all other stars in the educational sky. Because of this brightness of the intellect and the attraction that it had for educators, it became that which guided people—which was, generally speaking, the 'be all and end all' of education: the main aim.

To put it radically, one could say that this aim of developing the intellect blinded adults to other values, the other diverse and rich i that children possess. It was Professor Howard Gardner in the 1980s who pointed out that children have intelligences *other than* the intellect! It is only very recently, then, that this furrow has been ploughed. But with adults having been blinded to this, childhood gradually became undermined. Some commentators—writers like Neil Postman, for example, who has been very outspoken about this whole issue—would make strikingly dramatic remarks like 'childhood has disappeared'—annihilated by the pressure that has been put upon educationalists to develop the intellect at all costs, and never mind if the cost is childhood itself.

So the antidote to this cultural trend must be: If childhood is going down that slippery slope, then we must do what we can to *preserve* childhood, to prevent that slippage from happening. One of Steiner's greatest admirers (and the admiration was mutual) was the English educationalist Margaret Macmillan, and her sister Rachel, who also ran a Kindergarten with very different aims from Montessori. She also had as one of her aims that of preserving childhood. This does not mean to hold children back, an important point to emphasise; it means preventing the atrophying of childhood, the undermining of it, and *allowing children to be children, and go in a mature way through each phase of their development.*

Steiner went into this in great detail. Nevertheless it is a fact that intellect in the educational firmament so took hold of people that parents in particular began to vie with one another and proclaim, 'Oh, my child has done *so and so* within one year or at the age of *so and so'*. The implication of this way of thinking was, 'Your child is so many months late going through that hoop'. I don't know whether you saw the cartoon (I think it was in *Punch*) which showed two parents, and one of their children shaking a rattle while the other parent's child (a 4-year-old) was sitting with his nose in a book. The caption read: 'My child is reading but your child only plays with a rattle.' The next drawing was of the same parents 14 years later with the child that had had his nose in a book, wielding a rattle and wearing a football supporter's scarf, while the other one is studiously reading Plato (or sometime like it). So the other parent says, 'Oh, yes, my child is reading and yours is shaking a rattle'! That parents vied with one another, of course, gave educationalists the opportunity to take this bit of the intellect between their teeth and gallop off with it.

Today, all this is irritated and compounded to the nth degree by the Government introducing laws about league tables and what have you —what we are all living through, and our children are the sufferers. It is a situation which *guarantees* 29 children out of 30 not to be in first place in the class, and all the psychological and emotional consequences that go with that through the twelve plus years of their school careers.

With parental ambition, then, fuelled by fear, if you want to go in the opposite direction to preserve childhood and yet not wanting your child to miss out, then you need to have something in place that is very strong. Something that you believe in so firmly that you can stand through thick and thin, say, with the grandparents coming along and saying, 'Doesn't Henry read yet? He's age 5!' 'Oh, no, he goes to the Steiner Kindergarten.' *'Steiner Kindergarten?'*: What's that?—it sounds rather foreign.' And on it goes … You have to be very, very firm in your resolve. So I would like to describe or characterise some of the components that are part of the Steiner view on school-readiness, which I think can help empower one to be firm and authoritative in one's beliefs.

First let me briefly speak about a conversation I had in the Ministry of Education in Israel. Some years ago I was appointed there as Senior Academic Consultant on Waldorf Education. The Education Department in Israel had done a survey of university students and had discovered that a high proportion of students were dropping out in their first year of university. With the kind of thinking that probably only Jews have—such tremendously *honest* thinking that can look the most awful of scenarios in the face—the education minister said, 'Well, if this is happening, our system must be wrong. We must be starting wrongly and we're ending up in this dire situation.' This realisation then led to his question, 'So how do *you* do it in Waldorf? You don't have all these assessments and evaluations and external examinations. How do you evaluate your pupils' progress in Waldorf? You get them to university, don't you: they do very well at the academic level, don't they? You've got statistics that were carried out by the German Government to prove it—and so forth. How do you do it?' We need so to rationalise how we do it that the rational approach to education is enough to help our resolve on the right course of action.

The answer lies in Steiner's view of *the whole child.*

School-readiness is not something that's a kind of tick-list—though you *can* do it that way: actually write down a check-list and tick off various criteria, going through the list and finding out if the child is school-ready in Steiner terms. Rather than that, I'm going to go through what Steiner's view of the whole child was; but as it is extremely complicated, I'm going to whittle it down to four components.

What you see in front of you is clearly just the external physiology of the child—you see the child's countenance and the rest of the *physical* body—that's the first component. Second component—which not many people consider as a component in its own right: that is the *life* that makes that physical body function. These are life forces. Children have their ups and downs like we adults do; they feel better on some days than on others, and so forth—that's life! Third component—the psyche, *the soul*, whatever you like to call it. And the fourth component, *the individuality*. Steiner saw the individuality as something very significantly separate from the psyche. I would like to look at each of these four components in turn, and give an example that relates to each one of them which will contribute to determining whether a child is school-ready.

Starting with the *physical make up of the child,* think back to when your child was two days old, blissfully sleeping in the cradle, head a little bit on one side, perhaps, and the arms—the upper arm is coming straight up from the shoulder, a bit like an epaulette. The fingers hardly reach to the ear. Gradually, this proportion—which is already head-heavy in embryo—this proportion changes in relation to the limbs and the head. So a very good indication that the limbs have reached the proportion that is a mark of school-readiness is when the arm has grown so long that, not only does it go up to the ear as on day one, but it can reach over the head and touch the opposite ear. I won't ask you all to do that—it could be embarrassing! You see that is pure proportion, it isn't *how* you do it; it's the fact that the child *can* do it. I said I'd give one example for each of these four components of the whole child; and that is very objective. There will be other valid criteria that people use which I'm leaving on one side.

Now to the *life forces*. I'm going to couple this with an indication of Steiner's which might be surprising for people who haven't heard about it before. Steiner frequently spoke about the second teeth—the eruption of the second teeth and how they push out the milk teeth. Children change their teeth at different ages and it goes on a long time. The last molar to come through might only happen in the teenage years, so this does surprise people. Why *was* Steiner so emphatic about this being an indication of school-readiness?

These teeth, which are changing from the milk teeth to the permanent teeth, are an indication that the life forces are strong to the point of being in the process of recycling all the cells in the body: a process which goes on throughout life, being roughly seven year rhythms. The teeth are so hard that they can't be changed like the other cells, such as your nose cells, your little toe cells or your liver cells etc. These are just part of the life forces' task of changing and replacing them. And then, of course, those cells are excreted through the system once they have been replaced; but that can't happen with the teeth. So the life forces have to be strong enough actually to *change* the teeth.

Thirdly the psyche. In looking at the behaviour of the psyche that indicates school-readiness I'd like briefly to focus on the element of play. Earlier I mentioned play as an important part of the Kindergarten or playgroup structure of the day. Now Steiner divided childhood into 3 x 7 years, so that by the time you're collecting your first degree, your bachelor's degree, you are completing your third seven-year period. Equally, those seven-year periods can also be divided into threes. So if one divides the first seven years into three you will find the first 2⅓ years consist of a time when children can be very happy just, shall we say, exploring: they've got to crawl, they've got to sit up, they've got to find their upright position, find their feet (physically and metaphorically), start walking, and so forth … and then starts the adventure of life—all the exploring. It is truly amazing—I don't know of anyone who has grown up in a toy-free house, but my guess is that, if that were the case, as two-year-olds they wouldn't feel deprived—they would adventure so much into your kitchen cupboard and your ironing cupboard—you name it— that life would be full of interest, never a dull moment, certainly never a dull moment for the parent!

So a child of that age, in their play, is following the hands-on exploration. Take that beautiful red garnet brooch that you're wearing for the first time: your one-year-old will suddenly find a way of getting it into his mouth, and it will be beautifully embalmed with saliva! Now what is this hands-on approach to play, as far as the psyche is concerned? Steiner was quite content to use vernacular terms for this. He said, 'That's *will;* the child is exploring the world through will.' Will, for Steiner was part of the psyche; part of the soul's experience of the world, just as feeling and thinking are part of the psychological experience of the world.

When the child gets a little older, then another faculty is formed, a faculty which we usually refer to as 'fantasy'. The child will find a kitchen spoon or something equally utilitarian, and that spoon, through fantasy, will *become* something that the child has experienced—the mast of a little boat that he saw when he went down to the Broads, or the gear lever of the taxi or the bus—it could be anything. But the thing in itself, and the gesture of the physical object which is in the child's hand, are now met with equal measure by the child's ebullient fantasy. That, in essence, is the sparking point for the child's play during this middle period.

The psyche changes again in the last third of this pre-school time when the child is moving towards school readiness. It's *the thinking element* that emerges, but expressed in a young form—a fantasy-like form. The child will come into your playgroup, sitting room or your kitchen, with *an idea!* For example, the coalman has just delivered ten bags of coal; and every cushion in the house will be ransacked and the kitchen table hijacked, with the latter becoming a coal lorry. The fantasy now *directs* the play and everything is subject to it. This, then, is school-readiness from the psychological point of view.

Now, finally—how about *the individuality?* When does the individuality of the child tell you that it is ready for school? In this case, probably one of the best ways of discerning that is to look at children's drawings. Their *free* drawing—not the kind of drawing produced when you sit down and say, "Draw me a picture for Auntie Florrie's birthday." These drawings are largely self-portraits, right from the early years, and this has been wonderfully documented by various people. My favourite reference in this respect is Michaela Strauss's *Understanding Children's Drawings*. Right from the first little scrawls and scribbles and spirals and so forth, where it doesn't look much like a drawing (you couldn't even sell it off as a Picasso!), to later drawings, you will see how the child's inbred individuality expresses itself in these self-portraits. Thus, the windows in the house that they draw become the portrait of the child's individuality—looking out through the senses, more strongly, more consciously. The chimney acquires smoke as the individuality brings a new kind of warmth into the habitation of the physical body. And without here going through all of the stages, the last stage is often referred to as 'the triangle'. The child draws triangular shapes usually with its base horizontal and the acute angle pointing upwards. Experts who have gone into this talk of a stage where the child experiences a very firm base. The triangle is as isosceles as a child will make, and of course that means a very firm base. But at the same time, it is not cut off like the top hats that nine-year-olds draw; it's still in touch with what's up there—the home of the individuality, the spiritual home. And this form appears in all sorts of guises in children's drawings. You can see what is going on—the point which the individuality has reached in inhabiting its tiny body, which is growing, changing its proportions, establishing itself as a basis for life.

Four things on your 'checklist' then and, of course, you are looking for them to be more or less harmonious: you won't want three of these criteria to be at the school-readiness stage and the other one way out.

I would like to say one last thing to conclude before we take our refreshments, and that is that the second consideration on the checklist is of paramount importance at age seven; that is to say, *the readiness of the life forces*. Was it St Paul, when he wrote to the Corinthians, who spoke of 'Faith, hope and love'—a famous passage. Well, for the child who is coming to the school-readiness stage, you have got your checklist on the physical body, the life forces, the psyche and the individuality; but I would like to suggest that the greatest of these at this stage is the life forces. It's almost like a second birth. Steiner regarded the maturity of these life forces at this six- or seven-year stage as being of paramount importance because it is those very forces which are transformed from the task they had previously, to that which now becomes their task when formal schooling begins. As described earlier, previously their task was to *fashion* the physical body.

That fashioning is a vital task of the life forces in these early years. Now *surplus* life forces become available and are transformed into what it takes to learn, to remember... This explains why Steiner thought that premature learning, which has been proven by researchers as not actually giving children much of a head start anyway, was not very advantageous. In fact it is *disadvantageous* for the child, because the forces that are being used are the very ones that actually have another task in those early years. And it's only after this stage of school-readiness that they are then liberated—that they become available. 'Here are my surplus life forces, dear parents and teachers, now it's *your* turn'.

So the greatest of these four components in Steiner education at school-readiness stage is the life forces. On that note, let's exercise our life forces by eating some of those mouth-watering cookies and cakes!

1945-1952

At the beginning of this third septennial phase, I took up organ lessons. After having been a somewhat stockily-built junior, my sudden spurt of adolescent growth enabled my legs to reach the pedal-board of the organ. Seeing this, a curate invited me up into the organ loft, amusing himself by pulling out stops at irreverent random while I played *The Teddy Bears' Picnic*, and at the same time labelling me with the nickname Paddle-Steamer Beethoven. Fortunately he was the only person who availed himself of the divine inspiration!

At the same time, the choirmaster of the church where I sang took a much more sober course of action, putting my parents in touch with Russell Green, conductor of the Birmingham Festival Choral Society (of *Elijah* fame—Mendelssohn was acclaimed as having written his masterpiece for the choir in the 'Victorian' heyday of Birmingham's music festival). So I got off to a good start, crossing the city to the so-called old church, Edgbaston once a week for an organ lesson.

It took a tram and bus journey to get there from home, followed by a walk to the beadle's house, his clematis-entwined trellis-porched front door sporting a ship's bell, the dangling rope of which needed a lusty tug, and coloured lamps to port- and star-b'd. There, I picked up the keys for the vestry that clanked on a colossal iron ring, making one feel like some jailer out of a 19th century rescue novel. For some reason that has slipped my mind, there were occasions when the keys didn't need returning. Instead, after practice, I let myself out through the only self-locking door that the church boasted, which led from the bell-ringing chamber into the graveyard. This necessitated negotiating one's way down the pitch black nave from the sanctuary (where the organ console stood and the light switches were boxed) to the west end, where, with idle bell ropes eerily brushing one's cheek as one fumbled for the tiny exit, one finally emerged to be greeted not by outside lamps but by ancient, marble headstones, gaunt in the darkness at various rather tipsy angles of repose. Many was the occasion when I wished for a full moon.

The diet of the first year or two's organ lessons consisted of Bach, nothing less, certainly leaving the flippancy of *The Teddy Bears' Picnic* high and dry on the shore of the young fresh-from-Cambridge curate's sense of adolescent humour. It doesn't take much to become addicted to Bach, once your legs and feet have thundered out the subject of a fugue on the magnificent diapasons of a full-voiced, three-manual church organ, and you are the sole occupant of a vast, sacred building in the dead of night, making its rafters shudder and its aisles echo with the voice of the 'king of instruments' as Mozart enthusiastically referred to it. Night life, might one call it? Added to this were the Town Hall performances in due season of the St Matthew Passion and the B minor Mass in which Ferrier sang. She gave the heart, the spine, the whole mind and spirit of the adolescent a gift for life—the gift of *experiencing* what *was* music. We didn't listen to recordings; it had to be the diva herself (whom of course we adored like a hero). It carried pain, too, the pain of realising how small was the oasis of true music, whilst having consciously to consign *so* much trash to the desert of the very culture in which one was growing up. And being adolescent, tolerance was out of the question, as was the avoidance of falling into the trap of musical snobbery.

Around the moon node (18+ years) of this septennial phase, two further events confirmed for me that I was on the right path: I became an undergraduate, reading musicology at the University of Birmingham, and I landed an organist and choirmaster position at St Leonard's Marston Green. I had been trying to find an organ job for some time, but without success (no-one wanted a young upstart) when Marston Green found me. One of my failed auditions was at Sheldon Parish Church, after which it transpired that the Rural Dean there had handed my name and details to the vicar of a neighbouring parish who, coincidentally (if there is such a thing), was seeking a new organist. This was the Rev. H.R. Sproule (Roy) whose savvy and position as incumbent, boosted by the enthusiasm of an extended family of choristers, apparently over-rode the church authorities' unanimous opinion that it would be ill-advised and too risky to appoint an adolescent to such a central office. I don't know whether the authorities' opinion changed greatly, but my connection with the church happily lasted for six years (two periods of three years each, in between which was wedged a post-graduate year in London and two years' National Service in the Royal Artillery). Moreover, the members of the choir became lifelong friends and it was there, through Roy, that I was introduced to the work of Rudolf Steiner.

In my book published for the Mozart 250th birth celebrations (*Mozart: his musical style and his role in the development of human consciousness*) I have outlined my everlasting indebtedness to Anthony Lewes, Professor of Music at the Barber Institute of Fine Arts. Through his insight into musical style, other composers became admitted into my musical oasis—not hoards!—and the adolescent intolerance and snobbery were slowly transformed and guided into other musical directions. The essay which follows (published in the current *Golden Blade*) represents one of two main directions—which are: music in education, and music as a valuable tell-tale in my unending search into the evolution of human consciousness. 'About time too' (the essay), though it only apparently addresses the latter, does, in fact, supply some grist to the mill for music in education, insofar as Steiner pointed out how beneficial musical humour is for the budding idealism of adolescence. How this comes about will entail research, still to be pursued—maybe during the twelfth septennial phase...

About Time Too
Beethoven and the Scherzo: A Symptom of the Consciousness Soul[1]

The article on the Scherzo in Grove's *Dictionary*[2] written by Hugh MacDonald gives prominence to the fact that Haydn's string quartets op.33 (1781) are the works which proclaim the "scherzo's decisive admission to the canon of movements in regular Classical usage"; and in the same breath adds the intriguing fact that the scherzo in no.3 is "decidedly serious, even sombre, in colour". Looking at what followed, we could easily take Haydn's placing the scherzo on the musical map as something of a Marco Polo gesture and Beethoven's voyaging round the entire scherzo-globe as a Magellan gesture.

At the same time, if we note that, alongside the Haydnesque sombre, serious nuances, the scherzo in Beethoven's 5th Symphony has something of a macabre character (other unusual or even bizarre examples may come to the reader's mind), we have no alternative but to assume that in this remarkable Classical phenomenon there is more than superficial playfulness (*scherzare* = to jest). Here, I am enquiring into what that 'more than superficial playfulness' might be. Why the *third* movement of the symphony and of so many other Classically designed works? Why preceded by the *minuet* (after all, sarabandes, gigues, gavottes and half a dozen other dance forms were there in the ubiquitous Baroque suites, still the bread and butter of musicians in Haydn's boyhood)? Why—if we see 'papa' Haydn as setting the precedent—did he single out *scherzo* as the title for a movement which (may I rub in) *could be sombre in his hands* when, at the mere tilt of a wig, he could romp into exquisitely playful

---

[1]   The substance of this article is based on a lecture, given by the author on the same theme, to the Anglo-German Club of Abingdon nr. Oxford, in June 2008.

[2]   *The New Grove Dictionary of Music and Musicians,* London: Macmillan, 1980 edition.

musical jesting—almost anywhere, but most exuberantly in his last movements—as no other composer had (or has?) succeeded in doing? Why...? Why...? Why...?

Let us jump! In what is often published as the first of the Grimm's *Fairy Tales,* there appears near the beginning of the tale a frog—no less. The princess has dropped her golden ball into a well and the frog retrieves it for her *with certain conditions.* Fast-forwarding through agenda that Freud would no doubt have imputed as being in the frog's mind, I have observed, in telling the tale countless times, that, at the point in the story where the frog appears, children invariably find him amusingly attractive, an attitude which remains throughout the story—increases in fact, when he is heard hopping slip-slop up the palace steps where the princess lives, and when he causes her distress and provokes considerable disgust as he eats off her dinner plate etc.

His transformation into the shining prince (interpreted as humanity's future state; the emergence of the Ego's higher nature) seems to be telling us that our present 'amphibious' ugliness—the wanton destruction of Amazonian forests, the plastering of urban square mileage with inhuman living quarters, the alarming increase in knife crime and child suicides, and so on—is hideously *incongruent with our ultimate human potential.* At the same time, we have to acknowledge that incongruity is the spice of humour—at all levels. 'Seeing the funny side' of humanity's amphibian nature—slimed with materialism, culturally slobbering and ground-hugging, sunk in wells close to despair, yet ready to be flung against the threshold of transformation—is surely the only way, so to say, that the gods can cling with positivity to the place they saw for man in their cosmic design. Indeed, their *ideal.*

That potential lies in the *will.* In the will there is hope. In the

Oberufer Paradise Play,[3] which depicts the triumph of Lucifer in
bringing about the 'Fall of Man', the angelic being who acts on
God's command, reflects at the end of the play: "Blame not our will
but our lack of wit." Ostensibly it is a comment on the actors (and
they were amateurs all, ordinary villagers) and any shortcomings
their performance may have disclosed. Seen in the context of
evolution, however, it is the lack of wit—latterly over the last
millennium: the one-sidedness of wit, wit fed by insatiable greed,
the advance of wit at the expense of ethics etc.—that brings about
the continuing 'Fall of Man'. The answer lies in the will—the will to
set things right, the will to learn from self-knowledge, the will that is
the sincere response to the feeling of retribution-pricked conscience,
the will that wants to nail its colours to a resurgence of culture.
'Blame not our will...'

So in what way does human will relate to music? Below we shall
glance at earlier styles, though here our sights are directed towards
the second half of the 18th century, the hinterland of the port from
which Beethoven embarked. If the first movement of the Classical
symphony addresses the thinking capacity within the soul (often
through a wonderfully sonata-form-structured interplay of themes
and motifs),[4] and the second movement emphasises the soul's
feeling quality, then the third movement evokes that soul element in
which redemption lies: the will. We are most human there—not only
when we succeed and triumph but also when we succumb to our
fallibility (where we are 'only too human'). Hence the perfect niche
for the scherzo.

The tempo of the scherzo originated as three beats in a bar—
simply, it would seem, following the pattern of the minuet, its
predecessor in symphonic design. On the other hand, the *speed*

---

[3]   See *Christmas Plays from Oberufer*, Translated by A.C. Harwood, Sophia
       Books, 2007 pp.19-41.
[4]   See Masters, B., 2006 *Mozart: his musical style and his role in the development
       of human consciousness,* Forest Row: Temple Lodge, pp.61, 85-97 for thoughts
       on sonata form, related to the present context.

usually exceeds that of most minuets, denying any feeling of triple
time—the lift, carry, place of the eurythmist's threefold walk. In
fact, the speed of the scherzo calls for a decisive *one* beat in a bar.[5]
The (frog-legged!) effort that goes into the first beat of the bar
provides the lift that carries right through the other two beats. Thus
one could say, underlying man's macabre or sombre moods (both
adjectives ending in ... *re!*) or, for that matter, underlying his over-
the-top jollity, there is the lifting drive, the first-beat-in-the-bar
aspiration—which provides the momentum—which the gods
perceive as the *hope* in the spectacle of hideous or humorous,
helpless or harrowing, hindering or hallucinating, human
incongruity and the whole shambles and hullabaloo that we have
made of Creation.

In Greek mythology it was at the bottom of Pandora's box that
hope remained, something that would glimmer encouragingly in the
future provided, surely, humanity was vested in unbound energy,
pure will, determined drive and creative confidence to change for
the better. These are qualities that are vested endemically in the
scherzo. But what about the gods perceiving hope? This is
something that can be read between the lines of evolution, and at
this point it will further my case if I turn to look at some musical
milestones in the evolution of human consciousness, more
specifically in relation to *time*.

The musical ingredients which we find in compositions can of
course be enumerated at great length. Here we shall stop short at
what the layman could be expected to be at ease with: melody,
rhythm and harmony. The earliest plainsong that has come down to
us from the 4th century AD has no harmony and no rhythm, certainly
no beat. To see the priest in a Russian orthodox church service
standing reverently in front of the reredos conducting the
congregational chanting is to realise that his function is one of

---

[5]   In Beethoven's 9th Symphony the composer deliberately jests by swinging from
      phrases of four bars (what audiences would have found conventional) to
      phrases of three bars, and is explicit about it: *ritmo di tre battute* etc.

ensuring that the musical part of the service serves the divine-communal or communally-divine, so that it is in keeping with the mystical enactment of the sacrament. His use of the gently outstretched hand to beat time is as far away from Lully's use of his time-beating stick (the French must have had a word for it!) as Saturn is removed from the Moon—his death was caused by the thump which he gave on the first beat of a certain bar, which landed not on the podium as intended, but tragically on his foot, causing gangrene to set in! In ancient plainsong the musical experience is one in which the soul is 'lifted' into divine heights. Podium striking, or the baton wagging of the modern conductor are altogether on another planet.

However, when this experience—of music being essentially beyond the confines of measured time, and human consciousness being transcendentally heightened as a result—when this experience became increasingly difficult for humanity to access, as the incarnating spirit became more deeply embedded in *physical* existence, one final attempt to cheat matter of this triumph, so to speak, is to be found in Gothic style. The barrel vault of the Romanesque basilica was raised. Rose windows appeared in north and south transepts and at the west end, where the added height of the roof permitted. Other features, too, all of which enabled the church-going worshipper entering the building to 'take heaven by storm'.

Notwithstanding, the *human element* had already made its incursion into music by this time—Chartres cathedral, in which Gothic first fully flowered, was (re-)built in 1196-1221.[6] We know this human element as the added second voice in *parallel organum* and, still more independent, as the second voice in *free organum,* these two developments occurring in the 9th and 11th centuries respectively.[7]

Nevertheless, the free flow of the music—essentially with little

---

[6]   Grodecki, L., 1963 *Chartres,* Paris: Draeger, pp.44ff.

concern for any tonal centre (musical perspective, so to say) or any rhythmical shape to the melodic contour (short and long notes)— still prevailed. Herein was manifest the *eternal*. When a child, ensconced in her 'den' under a shady bush in the garden one sunny day in June is 'as happy as the day is long', she is oblivious of time —needs to be called out of her dream world for tea. It is a state of mind similar to the opening phrase 'Once upon a time—when was it, when was it not?' of the fairy tale. The three sets of circumstances bear a certain resemblance. No wonder that those who experienced being lifted into eternity by the plainchant regarded the composers as saints: St Ambrose (c.339-397), St John Chrysostom (c.347-407), St Gregory the Great (c.540-604). The preservation by religious denominations of plainsong chanting and similar over so many centuries bears witness to their spiritual origin. Similarly: in the cloisters, the copyist had the same attitude towards them as towards the gospels.

The *human* element brought rhythm into this early (musically-induced, if you like) quasi-paradisal state of mind. Eternity 'fell' into time. Greater self-consciousness entered the process of composition. Note lengths started seeping into the seemingly endless and beginningless 'once-upon-a time' drift of the plainchant. Through the Middle Ages, through the Renaissance, the seeping continued as the human element gradually overrode the divine. The scales of planetary origin were superseded by the diatonic scale. Bar lines crept into music as performers lost their innate ability to sing and play out of a kind of rhythmically united, dream-like super-consciousness which was the guarantee, one might say, for cohesion.

Meanwhile we continued to distance ourselves from our divine origin. The cosmos is full of rhythm but humans do not have an arithmetic to express it exactly. We bumble along contentedly enough with our calendar adjustments every leap year and so on—

---

[7]   See Davidson, T.D. and Apel, W., 1950, *Historical Anthology of Music: Oriental, Medieval and Renaissance Music,* London: Oxford University Press, pp.10-22.

but only by supplanting consciousness of cosmic rhythm with measured time. Cosmic memory once possessed by humans has helter-skeltered, albeit via sundials and sandglasses, into Swiss railway timetables, itemised phone bills and Wisden-recorded record-breaking. The carrier pigeon has fallen lifeless into the latest speed of broadband.

The incongruity of the human state was experienced as a poignant climax by the 17th century metaphysical poets, with its most pivotal symbol being the birth of the Jesus child. William Drummond of Hawthornden (1585-1649) expressed several dimensions of the contrast in his sonnet *The Angels for the Nativity of Our Lord*: "A saviour there is born more old than years, / Amidst heaven's rolling heights this earth who stayed;" and the spatial equivalent of this temporal contrast: "There is he, poorly swaddled, in a manger laid, / To whom too narrow swaddlings are our spheres." There is also Richard Crashaw's (c.1613-1649) well-known Chorus from *The Flowering Heart*: "Welcome all wonders in one sight! / Eternity shut in a span." The last lines of the first stanza are even more pertinent to our present argument: "Great little one! whose all-embracing birth / Lifts earth to heaven, stoops heaven to earth." Finally, let me cite a complete stanza from George Herbert's (1593-1655) *Easter-Wings* (the format is his).

> Lord, who createdst man in wealth and store,
> Though foolishly he lost the same,
> Decaying more and more,
> Till he became
> Most poore:
> With thee
> O let me rise
> As larks, harmoniously,
> And sing this day thy victories:
> Then shall the fall further the flight in me.

Even Herbert's rhythmic pattern is indicative of the loss of something higher than the prosaic—where, within five lines, the iambic pentameter of line one dwindles into the thud-thud of a single spondee (Most poore)—followed, through reversing the rhythmic sequence, by the regaining of that 'something higher' through divinely-derived *yet human* forces.

If Beethoven's mimicry of Maelzel, the inventor of the metronome, is anything to go by—the former wrote a round in which he clearly scorned the metronomic slavery into which musical time could only too readily subside—he despised (rather than regretted) the loss of eternity. That is certainly in keeping with the choler that is deeply bound up with his nature. Yet (another incongruity, already alluded to) despite this he nearly always chose a one-beat-in-a-bar tempo for his expression of the liberty-restoring potential of the human will in his scherzi. What, we might ask, is therefore his antidote to 'beat-slavery' that he incorporates in his style?

One antidote is the use of *sforzandi* in places where the tyranny of the beat at the beginning of each bar is denied. This device, however, is by no means confined to his scherzi. How could it be? *All* his music celebrates the Schillerian freedom of the human spirit. It is thus a musical ingredient which crops up throughout his oeuvre, also in various guises, the more obvious of which are as follows.

- An accentuated note in a bar other than the first note.
- An accentuated first note in a bar where the conventional phrasing would suggest otherwise.
- Irregularly accentuated notes (in the above sense) in a passage where the melodic element has been minimised in favour of allowing the harmony to be the main vehicle for the rhythm.
- In the overall design of a movement the insertion of a

section of music which is unanticipated, i.e. unlike the *cadenza* in a concerto, but is thrust upon the listener contrary to the expectations aroused by the composer through the course of the music. In terms of design this would be the equivalent to a so-called interrupted cadence[8] —not, in some ways, unlike the punch line in a good joke.

- The positioning of the scherzo prominently as the second movement, as in the 9th symphony, instead of the traditional third (taken up by Bruckner)—cf. *The Frog Prince* where the incongruency is brought close to the beginning of the story so that the remainder of the story can deal with how the problem is resolved of transforming amphibious man— who looks so comic when viewed from the eternal plane of divine beings—into his higher nature.

- There is also the melodic feature which provides not so much an *outer* dynamic but an *inner* impression on the listener for its effect. This is through an unexpected note or harmony. The C sharp of the opening theme of the *Eroica Symphony* (bar 7) or the A natural on the second beat of bar 7 in the slow movement of the *'Pathétique' Piano Sonata* are examples.

The other antidote I would like to bring here lies in his musical humour. If Mozart, through using the fortepiano, heralded the human ensoulment of music, Beethoven—instant monarch of the pianoforte[9]—surely embodied the descent of spirit into matter in his masterly strokes of (musically humorous yet *still aesthetically satisfying*) incongruity.

---

[8] The Penguin *A New Dictionary of Music,* 1958, defines a cadence as "a progression of chords (usually two) giving an effect of closing a 'sentence' of music", and points out that the interrupted cadence is unique amongst the different types of cadence in that it leads *away* from the expected progression— rather than bringing the musical sentence to a close.

[9] See Masters, B., op. cit. p.107 for further background to this phenomenon.

Beethoven *Piano Sonatas* Op. 2 nos. 1, 2 & 3.

The three sonatas[10] which Beethoven published as opus 2 (1795)
were dedicated to Haydn. All of them have four movements. In op.
2/1 the third movement is marked Menuetto and has little to indicate
the scherzo nature of things to come at this point in the sonata (and
symphony etc.), though in bars 9-10 the music suddenly steps out of
its lyrical and rather tranquil *piano* with *forte* repeated notes (a) and
the up-beat of the last phrase before the double bar is marked
sforzando (b), pointing, as it were, to the future.

In op. 2/2 the third movement no longer subscribes to the Classical
minuet tradition. It is not only entitled Scherzo, its theme and the
handling of it show signs of maturing skittishness. The basic
building block consists of a zig-zaggy rising motif (c) anchored by a
dense chord in the bass (d), the two together paying lip service to
sobriety.

---

10 A personal note. Having in mind the death last year of an old colleague, Nancy
     Hummel, who studied music in Edinburgh with Sir Donald Tovey, I am
     venturing in the following analyses to emulate his style of popular analysis,
     albeit without his vast spectrum of erudition. This is in the hope that the layman
     will be able to gain something which will help to substantiate the argument
     pursued in the article.

But this is thrown completely to the winds when the roles of right
and left hands are reversed (e). With the dense chords—now marked
forte and exploding into *fortissimo*—far from anchoring the gaiety,
they generate mounting excitement. Added to all is the slapstick-like
four-beat effect (instead of three, the tempo in the time signature) of
the final cadence, galumphing through bars 43-44 (f).

Beethoven's wit begins subtly in the scherzo of op. 2/3 with an
unaccompanied phrase which already combines opposites in
miniature—the upward-going surge of the first four notes (g) and
the downward-retreating scale of bars 2-4 (h).

The composer then quietly makes merry with the theme by
developing it into 3-voiced polyphony (3-7), with a half close in
bars 8-9 (i). There then follow six bars where the two motifs (g and
h) that were wedded at the opening, go their own ways: one ever

downward for 18 notes (j) and the other ever more flightingly
upward over a 6-fold sequence (k). Beethoven peppers the disputing
pair with sharps and flats before reaching the dominant key in bar
17.

Beethoven *Piano Sonata* Op. 14 no. 2.
The above three scherzi written during the years of the composer's
Sentient Soul phase (1791-98) demonstrate how the journey begins.
In his op. 14/2 he gains self-confidence in several respects. The
second movement is an original theme with variations. Even within
the theme, the last four bars display Beethoven's fiery defiance of
beat-tyranny with four *sforzandi* (l), the first three of which are on
weak beats (the second and fourth beats of the bar in quadruple
time). They culminate harmonically in the fourth *sforzando* which is
a long held note (m), in which the composer seems to enjoy the
rhythmic confusion caused. Then, to cap it all, after this chord dies
away, the last six chords end in an immaculately conventional
cadence, as if 'butter wouldn't melt' (n). However, the rests between
the very last (three) chords, do carry with them a hint of veiled
cockiness (o). Needless to say, whenever this part of the theme
comes out of the wings in the succeeding variations, there is an
abundance of musical clowning to go with it.

The third movement of the sonata is marked Scherzo, though the ear
doesn't need to see the indication. The first theme consists of three
rhythmically identical motifs written across the beat (p, q, r). The
tempo could easily be taken as being three medium (crochet) beats

—which would be the traditional third movement tempo. But by bar 3 the theme sits on a long note (s) which at the same time impishly discloses that the time signature is actually three quick (quaver) beats to a bar. The farce continues, which I shall leave listeners to enjoy for themselves when they get a chance to hear it. However, the climax of the hilarity comes *after* the last bar's squiggle has fluttered out of the air at the end of the movement. Beethoven isolates the three notes in bar 7 for this purpose (t)—whereupon the audience is waiting for the fourth movement to follow … when the pianist stands up, bows and exits, with the audience realising that the scherzo, highly successful *as* a scherzo, was, in fact, the finale. Even if the suspicion that this might be the case may have dawned in the discerning listener's mind—on realising that the structure of the movement is rondo (rather than scherzo and trio)—the anomaly is still entertainingly enjoyable.

Beethoven *Piano Sonata* Op. 28, Scherzo: Allegro vivace.

The second example from this phase of the composer's life (the Rational Soul, 1798-1805) occurs in the more orthodox 4-movement op. 28. The movement (in traditional third place) opens with a motif which dive-bombs into the bass clef through four octaves on F-sharp (bars1-4), a note which, however, proves *not* to be the keynote but the major 3rd, as the sharp-nosed busy-bodies of bars 5-8 are at nit-picking pains to point out. Beethoven hardly even listens to them with his second dive-bombing, now on the note A (9-12), which leads still not to the home key but to the dominant (16). The third and fourth sorties—which are emphatic *fortes*—state (like a pedant pulpit-thumping while denouncing an innocent joke and thus making a laughingstock of himself) the relationship between the two keys by adding (i) the tonic (17-20) and (ii) the mediant (25-28). After the double bar, the composer uses the descending octave motif to lead through a delightfully playful sequence of modulations (33-48).

The motif returns without accents (49-52), as though this irregular behaviour is perfectly normal, only to be overtaken with positively crashing triads in 1st inversion (57-60) with the left hand entering impetuously before it is due, which elicits a prolonging of the, by now, almost farcical spectacle of the nit-picking commentators to double its original length (61-69).

Beethoven *Symphony No. 3* Op. 55, Scherzo: Allegro vivace.
The third symphony contains a scherzo and trio as the third movement on the fullest Beethovenian scale, impelled throughout by his inimitable drive and humour. Some of the main landmarks are as follows. The first theme consists of strings (without double basses) busying themselves like a shoal of hungry trout darting hither and thither after mayflies on the surface of a lake, but otherwise getting nowhere—until the oboe enters after *an odd* 6 bars with a light-hearted theme, cheekily (seeing it is so near the beginning) in the dominant key. Its thematic material provides Beethoven with valuable motifs for juggling with later.

The process is repeated, though with the double basses pedantically

pointing out that the key *is actually* the dominant and not the home
key, and with the oboe counteracting their solemnity by jumping the
gun still earlier than the first time (entering on the equivalent of the
last note of bar 4). It is joined for its last bars by flute and bassoon
who are clearly hooked by all the jollity. A chromatic passage
follows in which the flute, far from being called to heel by the
double basses' harmonic gravity, flies off the harmonic handle still
further, with the theme *in the dominant of the dominant*—and this
after only 40 bars! The whole orchestra now gleefully toss their
shabby academic gowns around with a fugato based on motifs (w +
x), (x) being subtly and simply changed, with an accent appearing
where there was none before. The passage cuts into the
mesmerising, fish-flashing fussiness like a pike's dorsal fin slicing a
sheet of calm water, but disappears as quickly as it came—though
having impelled the shoal into the key of the minor mediant. The
violas try their hand at further distractive play, with a repeated D,
having also the impudence to shift the tempo into a three-bar beat,
not specifically indicated by Beethoven as in his 9th Symphony's
Scherzo, but there nevertheless. The cellos and basses will have
nothing to do with this escapade and come in again with anchored
pedantry, not yet however in the home key until, at bar 93, the
heavyweights (trumpets, timpani and French horns) are called in to
restore harmonic order, which they do blazingly successfully for
more than 20 bars. The strings, not to be outwitted, pull out a new
trump card, a theme which throws the listener, through its three
sforzandi on the *second* beat of each bar, completely off the
rhythmic scent (115-117).

This happens twice, setting the wind and strings off with (u),
gossiping as if somewhat scandalized at a cocktail party by what has

happened (119-130). At this point, Beethoven brings the result of his carefully crafted roller-coaster to a climax with a theme, suspiciously resembling the bars that had accompanied motifs (w) and (x), though now lacking every vestige of modesty. It carries the music with maintained momentum over 23 bars to reach its final cadence. The Trio, which follows after a repeat, begins with a bravura-like theme for three French horns (166-173), like a nobly, if rather pompously mounted hunt appearing from a forest onto a stretch of open country, their prancing hunting pink delighting all onlookers.

The wind and strings respond by chirping like a flock of excited sparrows hopping about in a hedgerow, inquisitive to know what the chase is all about, while the horses prance onward. Beethoven doesn't let on.

But if the object of the hunt is a fox, it leads them all a merry dance (199-216), leaving the hunting party high and dry on a somewhat bemused flattened 7th in the home key, before disappearing over a distant hill with their minds no doubt on the forthcoming noggin of whiskey rather than the ignominious chase. The Scherzo repeats, but Beethoven still has two white rabbits left in his topper. The first is at bar 381 when, instead of the repeat (y) there is a hilariously reprimanding change of tempo.

But it seems to have little effect on those of the party who are talking nineteen to the dozen, who continue as before. Finally we arrive at the Coda, just 18 bars long and ushered in by the kettle drums, who appear softly on the scene like a dark-clad pied piper. At first, no-one appears to take the slightest bit of notice—bizarrely the harmony just doesn't tally with what the drums are doing—until the French horns call the rest of the orchestra to order, all exuberantly joining in the festive alternating of tonic and dominant (431 et seq.) to fatten the concluding crescendo.

There follows a final bar's absolute silence—marked by Beethoven with a pause—which gives us cause to pause and reflect (inwardly smiling with the composer) on the rich funfair of life 'up with which' we have been caught. The Finale banishes any superficial comedy that may be in the air, with its first note (D—the note of the scale most foreign to the tonic chord we have just heard thundering) at which we are plunged into the Promethean-like, quasi-passacaglia that raises the funfair of life to the fanfare of higher life which is the ultimate task of the 4th movement of the symphony.

But in the end, it is not these kinds of devices that offer the modern Ego the antidote to materialism, which only Beethoven can provide in such rich measure, despite their importance and significance as a feature of his musical style: it is the *genius of*

Beethoven itself. Through being saturated in what his spirit embodies in the music, he brings to the Ego which has incarnated in the Consciousness Soul Age, not only the immersion in matter—and the pain of the experienced discordance that absolute opposites have to endure: spirit in matter[11]—he also brings that which can enable the spirit to rise above being nailed to the cross of metronomic time to a state—*without losing our necessary earthly focus*—which is every human listener's birthright, a state which exists on the plane of eternity.[12]

How other composers have followed this is another story—but at this point in history I would suggest that it is a matter of their following rather than superseding him. The outburst of applause after a Beethoven symphony—or after performances of his other major works—is surely testimony enough.[13]

In his *Songs of Experience*, the Romantic poet William Blake (1757-1827) stood (presumably metaphorically speaking?) before the tiger, and being precipitated—certainly metaphorically—into "the forests of the night" was awestruck by what he saw. At one point he can do no other than sink to his knees: "Did he who made the lamb make thee?" and "What immortal hand or eye dare frame thy fearful symmetry?" Today, much of the music that is in the air—mostly in the electronic air—leads us, like lambs to the slaughter, to the despotic dominance of the beat. It is in the 'burning bright' Beethoven, particularly in the scherzi and their significance in the

---

[11]   The pianoforte with its iron frame, so germinal in Beethoven's musical development, is itself an instrument that depends, so to speak, upon the performer to imbue its tone with soul cf. the *quality* of sound when the oboe gives the A for the orchestra to tune to and (as is the case when the item is a piano concerto) when the A for tuning up is played on the piano.

[12]   This vital aspect of the Consciousness Soul Age is discussed by Steiner in lectures published under the title *From Buddha to Christ,* 1978 Anthroposophic Press.

[13]   Whenever it is possible, to experience this fully it is worth actually *going* there. Being in the same space as that in which the music is re-created by the striving will of conscious human performers, unbamboozled by discographic obsession.

symphonic re-shaping of Classicism, that through his *immortal ear* we ordinary mortals of the Consciousness Soul Age can be reminded that our incongruity, though it often has its funny side, is actually no laughing matter. Increasingly so, in fact. It is as though, when his spirit lives in a performance of his music, each one present receives a rope ladder dangled down from the musical heights of his or her nobler self, up which the listener is not elevated to eternity— as in Gregorian plainsong—but for climbing which we are given new strength to follow the master *in the 4th movement* (the finale) towards that plane of eternity, whence the music flows, by ascending the ladder, even if we can only manage a rung or two to begin with.

Just as Beethoven himself dived ever anew into his material (q.v. for instance the difference that is discernible when one compares his original notebook jotting of a theme with how it transpires in the published opus)[14] and, as if in a royal mint, imprinted it with his eternal being, so can the performer and listener alike feel the continual piercing-into-eternity that vibrantly informs his style of composition, dissolving the *mechanical tick of the clock* into the *'magical' touch of the Cosmos*. Or as Crashaw so succinctly and eloquently put it: 'eternity shut in a span'.

If, as we learn from Greek mythology, Prometheus 'once upon a time' stole the fire of the Gods for humanity's sake (a jest on a cosmic scale?), the fire surely did not all meet its irrevocable and irrecoverable destiny in the blast furnaces of the 20th century and the rising price of a barrel of oil today. Some of it surely continues to burn with Beethovenian brightness—sweeping away accreditation paranoia to make room for creativity, disdaining surveillance culture that eclipses human trust and inspired initiative, and *cremating time towards eternity*.

---

[14]   See Miles, P., undated, *Beethoven's Sketches—An Analysis of his Style Based on a Study of his Sketch Books,* Dover Publications, passim.

1952-1959

These were my ' journeyman' years. From the family circle—closed and bordering on the clan-like—and the warm fireside of childhood, youth and 'coming of age' into the unknown, there was the post-graduate year in London, delving into 17th century manuscripts in the British Museum and mopping up diplomas in organ performance at the Royal College of Music and the Royal College of Organists. There were the two years of National Service—coming to terms with being trained as an internationally recognized professional murderer, so to say—with its four postings to Oswestry (on the Welsh border), Aldershot, the heavy anti-aircraft regiment on the Isle of White, and finally the posting overseas to the sleepy town of Celle in the British Zone of Germany.

It was there, essentially, that I determined to take up anthroposophical work after demobilisation, rather than continue with a career solely in music. This was despite the peripheral connection with Moeck Verlag and C.F. Peters, the farewell organ recital given in the Martin Luther Kirche in which I celebrated English composers alongside J.S. Bach, the musical beano of a week's leave from the Royal Artillery spent in the Ruhr Gebiet (hearing for the first time parts of Wagner's *Ring*, meeting the celebrated composer Siegfried Reda and various music critics in the area, viewing Verdi's *Othello* from the lighting box of Oberhausen's opera house and afterwards speaking with the singers and stage hands etc.

The journeyman journey ended at Hampton Manor and with my resuming the position of organist and choirmaster at Marston Green. But there, springing forward like a greyhound unleashed, began new work (music therapy, teaching basketry, gardening, bread baking, teaching weaving to beginners and the dozen and one tasks one takes up in curative education). To cap it all—was it a cap?—in April 1956 came marriage, with all its life lessons.

In Memoriam Jean Mierowska

She was christened Jean Elaine Nora Eccles.[1] We met at the University of Birmingham on the first day of the Freshers' Conference in 1949. The earliest really distinct memory that I can muster at the moment is of standing in the queue at the refectory waiting for lunch with the freshers. It was not love at first sight, but I certainly felt a connection which was not there with any of the other newcomers. I never discussed whether this was similar in any way for her.[2]

The most prominent feature in her external appearance that comes readily to mind was the expression in her eyes: something between somewhat introspective, quiet radiance and twinkle—I don't know how else to express this. Whenever I met her in recent years (not all that much: two fleeting visits, slotted into hectic South African schedules), the same expression shone through the ageing countenance. It was an expression which came out at its fullest brilliance when she was recalling appreciatively certain passages of music—or, even more so, savouring these *in the moment*, either when singing or at the keyboard or simply listening[3]—passages which we both very obviously related to in the same way. The latent twinkle then unmistakably shone out and predominated. This twin-soul connection that we had—the only words I can find which are

---

[1]   The parents returned from New York—I think they had married in the States—because of the pregnancy/birth. Nora was 'Nonie's' name; Elaine I don't know the origin of (perhaps some of the Celtic connection?); Jean suited her well provided you allow for the fact that she was the sort of person that hardly fitted into a name.

[2]   We often referred to 'old times', but were not in the habit or trawling over how we met and ogling over the minutiae which brought us close. Essentially, our footsteps brought us face to face, and circumstances ensured that we were often bound together into a bundle of two. Even the graduation journey from 1949 to 1952 was one which only the two of us trod in precisely the same way from beginning to end.

[3]   Gestures that she could hardly restrain, and the occasional guffaws of approval that would emerge. I imagine Berlioz must have been like that.

appropriate—was something which I have never found, even
remotely, in anyone else. Bear in mind, I am here talking about our
relation to and within music. It spanned the years, though the span
certainly faded, even went out of sight, when we parted, and only
reappeared when we reconnected through her reading of
anthroposophy—something which increased after the death of her
husband Henryk, who was a Christian Scientist.[4] Perhaps even the
term 'twin-soul' is not accurate enough: the connection is arguably
more in the spiritual sphere than that of the soul, though it filters
through to the latter. Nevertheless, with us it did filter through
sufficiently into the soul sphere to develop into love that was not
merely universally en-grailed in our shared musical (and other)
interests, but what eventually led to our marriage and the blessings
that our children, Alison and Richard, brought with such immense
and ever-wondrous richness to that.

But first some account of the 'filtering through'. The tracks which
brought about our meeting were in some ways unsurprising. Both
pathways (as far as the musical emphasis was concerned) clearly led
from the past, although her connection with music remained far
more central to her life than did mine—as evidenced firstly in her
very musical relatives,[5] secondly in her successful university life,
and thirdly in her striking out in her own right as a professional
musician in the 60s, right through to her last teaching days in the
Eastern Cape.

She was brilliant at school, attending the renowned 'public' girls
school in Solihull. She could have studied anything, I think, that she
put her mind to. She was especially gifted in languages, revelled in

---

[4] It seems that they had no difficulty in respecting one another's religious
persuasion.

[5] Her father had it in his finger tips; her 'Uncle Jack' his brother was by all
reports a financial genius and had built an organ in his house where he played
Bach's works 'for relaxation'; her grandfather was an organist and 'local'
conductor of opera, her beloved granny a singer of the 'gather the rosebuds
while ye may' order.

the Old High German and Faroese that she was studying as a 'subsidiary' subject (which we all were obliged to take—Italian being my lot, instead of the Geography which I had angled for), but was just as deeply entranced by philosophy or Scottish country dancing, to mention a couple of items that could be construed as featuring at the opposite ends of the cultural spectrum. However, despite all her multi-faceted gifts—which surely would have been qualification enough for university entrance—she had taken a year out after school (thus manoeuvring us into the same intake) to study music with Ian Parrott, a lecturer who became one of our tutors at the university. He was 'a dear'. He had fought at El Alamain (about which he wrote a tone poem for orchestra), he simply oozed music, propagated a rather unkempt, sub-tropical moustache on his upper lip, 'paddled' through town on a bicycle with raincoat 'tails' winging their way somewhere in the rear, and—his endearing trait as far as we cranky students were concerned—wore rubber galoshes which scrunched on the lino floors of the annexe where his tutorial room was. Moreover, if certain hints and remarks were anything to go by, he had divined that the two of us were somehow specially connected, at least as soon as we realised it ourselves, if not before. I have recently discovered that he had a strong Celtic streak which might suggest some premonitionary predisposition.[6]

Parrott taught her pure Renaissance counterpoint. She could compose this like a 16th century native—more like churning it out than having to sweat over it, as it seemed to a Bach- and Victorian-soaked musician like me! But she excelled in everything and at the end of the three years we were at Birmingham, it must have been difficult for the faculty to decide to which of the two of us to award the graduate prize of 'Barber Scholar'. There could surely have been no doubt that she also *deserved* it. That they chose me rather than her (and we both gained II.i.Hons) I don't completely understand.

---

[6] Three years ago she sent me a newspaper cutting of him, aged 83; earlier she had asked him if she could use his name as a referee, to which he warmly acquiesced. A photocopy of his reply was amongst her papers.

But it was typical of her that, as far as I know, she harboured no resentment. On the contrary, she was over the moon about all that went on in my life when I went to the Royal College of Music as Barber Scholar, something that we shared in copious correspondence at the time, as well as on the rare occasions when we met.[7]

The 'first years' in 1949 (so soon after the war, with not many people entering university compared with numbers now) did not comprise a huge intake. The whole music department would have fitted fairly neatly into the sitting room at Friar's Ash. We thus formed student ties fairly rapidly. It was during the performance of the first Gilbert and Sullivan opera that a significant bit of 'filtering through' took place. Jean already played the clarinet *and* the double bass(!) before she arrived at the university. I 'picked up' the bassoon through unique circumstances, acquired a teach-it-yourself book and quickly joined several orchestras. When recruits for the Students Union Opera Orchestra were required, most of the music students happily got themselves roped in,[8] especially the first years—student life and all that.[9] (We weren't into alcohol and I don't think drugs had been invented!! In any case, the 'highs' that came our way were high enough for our post-war appetites.) After the fourth or so performance I accompanied her on a very rainy and blustery black night to her train—she lived in Hampton-in-Arden, while I merely had to take a tram to the northern suburbs of the city—and it became clear as the train was about to depart that we were destined to have a

---

[7]   Not only over the moon: she devotedly typed up (sometimes lightly editing as she went) research that I had done in the British Museum and in the Ashmolean Museum in Oxford. The layout was professional to the extreme, an aspect of life in which she visibly rejoiced (she had taken some secretarial training on leaving school—just in case life caught her on the back foot). The same care for what had to be read could be observed in her musical handwriting, which was so clear that it was possible to sight-read her scores.

[8]   Not to mention that the revered Dr Parrott strongly recommended paying close attention to Sullivan's orchestral scoring.

[9]   So with our wind playing we found ourselves on neighbouring desks.

more personal connection than the rollicking companionship we already enjoyed. Nothing particularly overwhelming outwardly, but definitely an incisive moment in time—for me, readily recaptured even as I write—which was life-changing. We were then about 18.5 years, she being the elder by c.9 months.

I have to insert here that this presented, for me personally, a considerable dilemma. My girlfriend at the time—the only one I had ever had, both of us members of a large Youth Club—had led me to anthroposophy, though neither she nor I were remotely aware of the fact at that point. This will become obvious if I note that her geography teacher at school had just married the Rev. Roy Sproule and I was about to become—or had just been appointed: I have not looked up the exact dates—organist at his church, St Leonard's, Marston Green where she (Molly), *her* sister (Mary Barnett), *her* husband (Geoffrey), *his* brother (Francis) and *his* wife (Alice) were all leading choir members. My girlfriend and I went to different grammar schools, but all through the 6th form I had earned the reputation of holding strong views about geographical topics (a subject which I adored and took at the then equivalent of 'A' as well as Scholarship-Level) which concurred entirely with my girlfriend's geography teacher—whom she fondly referred to as 'Old Talamo'.[10] Thus, as you may well appreciate, it was not only the fact that Roy made the bread for the mass with his own hands that led me to Marston Green. The karmic nudges and shoves going on were pretty hefty.

But all this sounds too school oriented. The fact is that I deeply loved my girlfriend (as deep as youth goes—here manifestly not being the place to try and characterise this) and the dilemma of daily having to experience the *confluence* of this (though in a strange sense not *conflict*) with the feelings that were growing in me for

---

[10] Molly and Mary came from an East Anglian family, though the father must have had Italian in his background. The really 'old' Mrs Talamo, their dear mother, was still alive, an exceptional woman in whom deep wisdom and warm open-heartedness dwelt in peace-engendering harmony.

Jean was unbearable. I felt that the only honourable thing to do was formally to break off the 'relationship' with the former.[11] Both her family and my mother were terribly upset by this, not to mention the two of us for there was no real logic that the mind could offer to the heart. What in heaven's name, is an ethical principle when your eyes are smarting with tears? The upset all round was particularly compounded by the fact that my mother had not taken kindly to Jean —just the opposite of how her family had welcomed me with open arms (especially 'Granny-Christina', after whom Alison got her second name). However, despite the friction and awkwardness caused at home, I stuck to the future rather than clinging to the past. As far as I know, Jean remained oblivious of all this to the end.

She, I guess, from what I saw of it, was far better at organising her ongoing university assignments than I was. She marched off to her tutorials (still with Parrott) with a calm and determined step, whilst my memory of myself includes putting the finishing touches to set exercises all too hastily on public transport. What with my organ and choirmaster job, all the bassoon playing I did, my Secretaryship of both the University Music Society and Managership of the University Symphony Orchestra, my organ lessons ... what else could one expect? Added to this was the social life which we shared increasingly—theatre-going, concert-going, eating out (jellied eel and similar 'first-timers' barely within our means), visiting one another's homes as lovers then did, and, in the summer, long cycle rides, since we were both mad about nature. Her father never did believe that we scoured the countryside, aided by 1″ Ordnance Survey maps, searching for rare wild-flowers and tucked-out-of-the-way Norman churches!

But I feel sure, now, that she had a faint but firm remnant of what Barfield calls 'original participation' in her consciousness. I think my fairly large measure of it was natural—q.v. the fact that I can

---

[11]   Not that I did this in any formal written way, though goodness only knows this
        might have spared us from some soul-rending hours.

never remember anything of the indoors of the places where we lived, until about the age of 9. She also must have had it as part of her nature, but I suspect that it was prompted by the fact that she was such an intellectual high-flyer and that Nature therefore offered her an outlet, or balance, Hampton-in-Arden being midst some of the most beautiful of rural surroundings as far as the Midlands go— the Arden part of the village's name refers to the same Forest of Arden in which Shakespeare set *As You Like It*. It may also have been that nature had become something of a consolation for her dismally strained family relationships—but more of that later.

Then came 1952. What was I to do with my Barber Scholarship? Our professor, Sir Anthony Lewis as he became known when he left the Barber Institute Chair to take up Directorship of the Royal Academy of Music in London, proposed two possibilities: either I should go to Worcester cathedral and become articled to Sir David Wilcocks as a cathedral organist, or I should extend my studies by going to the Royal College of Music in London.[12] This choice, though, took me a long way from Jean, and I *think* (forgive my vagueness) that it was at this very serious point that we woke up to the longer-term reality of our relationship, though not yet becoming officially engaged. I can see her now, standing beneath the trail of billowing smoke issuing from the funnel of the ancient steam engine, at the edge of one of the woodland coppices near her home, waving to me as I went shooting by to London on a New Street to Euston express to take up my post-graduate studies. A figure in white and fairly long skirts—to the despair of her mother (somewhat amusing, we thought, irreverently, at the time) who was very

---

[12]   It was London for me, despite the attractive thought of being a recluse in a cathedral, a decision which was influenced by the possibility—actually I insisted on it—of studying composition with Dr Herbert Howells and organ with Dr George Thalben-Ball. The former was my organ teacher's hero, whose compositions I loved; the latter was one of our local heroes as City Organist— though, in fact, he was not at all local, being organist and choirmaster at the Temple in London and originally from Australia.

conscious of how she herself looked (clothes, make-up, perfume, jewellery, elegance, ultra but still dignified femininity, the latest sophistication in spectacle frames, weekly hairdo...), Jean rigorously and *scornfully* eschewed fashions, one of the unusual and refreshing externalities that I found attracted me to her.

At the end of this academic year, during which I was awarded my diplomas (ARCO in December, ARCM in June), I had to wait for my call up papers (National Service) to make their way through the bureaucratic sausage machine. Roy invited me to go along with him to an anthroposophical study group,[13] and at the same time introduced me (though inevitably the 'me' became 'us') to Hampton Manor. Had it not been *Hampton* Manor, I wonder if I would have been so drawn to it?[14] The Manor was literally ten minutes walk from the Eccles household. Despite initial misgivings, meeting the handicapped was certainly a turning point for me, sufficient on reflection for me to give up my ambition of a musical career and enter anthroposophical work through this door. (Nutley Hall was a continuation of that.) Jean must have had mixed feelings, though never, as far as I can remember, stated these in terms that looked anything like a danger-warning in our relationship. Nor do I know how her family looked upon this development in our careers. Was I asleep? Did she shield me from her family's views? Perhaps the grandiose environment of the Manor (built by a member of the

---

[13] This consisted of a bevy of priests from different denominations (excepting Roman Catholic and Eastern Orthodox). The study opened my eyes to Steiner's four or five lecture cycles on the Gospels. One of these was seldom absent from my kit bag during my artillery days.

[14] And had it not been Roy—for whom I had the most profound regard which did nothing but grow during the life-long length of our unique friendship—I wonder if I would have disdained(!) to go and help 'backward children' (as they were then colloquially but frequently and openly referred to) play the recorder, an instrument I'd only once come across, when a friend of Stan Beddowes had brought a class of children to squeak, abominably out of tune to the delicate and somewhat snobbish ear of a music student trained by Wishart in the University Motet Choir, in a workers' concert given in the Great Hall of the university.

famous Peele family, Sir Robert being the politician who reorganized the British police force and 'gave' the name *Bobbies* to police constables), right in the centre of *their* village, was a respectable enough credential.

This brings me to a painful episode. It was at about this time—I had to wait some six weeks after coming down from London for the conscription papers to sausage-machine their way through the bureaucratic system (Mid-November when I finally set off for Oswestry, my first station in the Royal Artillery)—that the following conversation between us took place. Jean and I had never had so much leisure. She, in fact, was about to take up a teaching post at a Quaker Foundation in North Yorkshire, so this must have been in the summer. It was during this relaxed time that she told me more about her family situation than I had been able to glean before. To say it had been far from happy is an understatement. I realised that her grandparents were a godsend to her outwardly and inwardly, but her story shed infinitely more light on why, apart, that is, from their inherent goodness.[15] For her only memories of her parents (those, at any rate, which apparently overshadowed all else) were of them continuously bickering. To put it more radically: her childhood home was permeated by an atmosphere of undiluted acrimony. It was, in fact, during her university days that her father could no longer stand the situation and left home, never to return. By this time she had considerable sympathy for him, though she clearly agonised over not letting this be evident at home, for her mother's sake. Well, a degree of this was more than self-evident during my visits, and I trust that my arrival on the family scene had done something to alleviate the situation: the bickering was much more pianissimo, I imagined, when 'visitors' were present than at other times—especially a visitor who brought all the *joie de vivre* that we

---

[15] She would call in there, it seemed, on every conceivable occasion. True, her Granny often provided her generously with spending money, but the motivation was obviously how she felt utterly at home there: a meal, a bed, a welcome at any time, a fund of family anecdotes of which she never tired.

as young students enjoyed and displayed unreservedly, and no doubt often thoughtlessly, not to mention the absolutely crazy things that we got up to.[16]

So far, so good—or rather, so painful. But then came Jean's most intimate confession. Up the road from where her family lived, close to the railway station, she had a school friend (Brenda Dutton) who, it transpired, had been something of a psychological life-line to her. Not so much personally, though the connection remained strong all their lives. But because of Brenda's family. There was an elder sister, Barbara, who became a teacher of art, and the four of them— father, mother and two daughters—seemed as though they were the perfect family. (It might help to add, that Jean's grandparents for all their homeliness and hospitality were not demonstrative in any way with their regard for one another. Happily there was no flagrant friction there, or anything approaching it, yet there was no *outer* sign of affection.) But it was the poignant way in which this lasting, ingrained impression of Brenda's family was first communicated to me that I want to convey here. "… I thought [had grown up to think] that people who loved one another *were odd*." This revelation left me dumbfounded. I still feel the shock sustained by my soul at that moment—as it reverberates on to this day. I came from exactly the opposite kind of family. Almost too much the other way. Clan-like. I thereupon resolved that, if possible, I would bring her something of what I had been privileged to bask in every day of my childhood —though externally all I did was to propose marriage. After a day or two considering the proposal, she accepted. We had more than two years to wait—I eventually was posted to Germany and she up in Yorkshire—but it was a time of varying degrees of elation and inner preparation.

1953-1955:   2nd   Lieutenant   R.B.   Masters,   R.A.;   then

---

[16]   Swapping bassoon and clarinet at the conversazione; inventing parts in the Gilbert and Sullivan to the visible delight of the Conductor Tim (Something); we even stayed out under the stars one especially balmy summer's night without letting our poor families know…

demobilisation, then the long preparations for the wedding. Jean was meticulous in all details. A wedding dress that truly reflected what was going on in her active mind, and, once again, no hesitation about treading on the toes of bland and blind followers of whatever fashion was paraded in the shops, or fear of what the wedding guests might think. Tradition and fashion were irrelevant: *we* were the pioneers. How adolescent! Yet it demonstrates how confident we felt that we were taking the right step. The world, after all, needs reform. Look at the ruination caused by the War…

Music was a big thing in the wedding service. I had got my job back at Marston Green (my successor had moved up the ladder and was on his distinguished way to becoming organist of Hereford cathedral) so we had a 'crack' choir at our disposal. My former organ teacher from grammar school and university days, Russell Green, played for us. He and Jean were very fond of each other, though they had only met once or twice. The choir in procession sang a modern chant which I had composed for the occasion to be sung to the colossal and celebratory Psalm 104. Today, I think I'd blush at the arrogance which might come across to a captive audience—er, sorry: an unsuspecting congregation. But we—and particularly she—revelled in it. Mark you, we revelled as much and just as sincerely in the 16th century Byrd or Tomkins as we did in Finzi or Vaughan Williams, our contemporary heroes, so it was not that we thought cultural life only began in the year 1930. We would never have become non-conformists. Nevertheless, any opportunity to inject a dynamic dash of the here and now into the Anglican tradition was worth its weight in gold—and here was a bit-between-the-teeth opportunity that would never recur. We were goaded on in this, to boot, by those younger members of the choir who lapped up 'modern' choral music.[17]

Her parents insisted on a sumptuous reception at a fashionable

---

[17]   The four Barnetts (though I'm not 100% sure whether Mary was included) all sang in the Birmingham City Choir—conducted by none other than Sir David Wilcocks prior to his salmon-leaping to King's College Cambridge!

hotel. Fair enough. She was not averse to this—champagne corks popping and what have you. Yes, let 'the oldies' have their bit of the fun. I think my humble family coped—and my mother had the Hartnell label to flash anyway (look at the wedding photographs and you'll see her silver fox fur). It was Easter Tuesday 3rd April 1956 (giving the parson a day's rest after his busiest day of the year). We had a few days 'off' incognito, using a borrowed car to drive to Northumberland via the Peak District; and then I plunged back again into Curative Education.

Every night after the 'children' at the Curative Home had been given evensong and were in bed, the staff met to study anthroposophy. Jean was not strictly a member of staff. (Not that I could boast any contract.) She had built up a small but enjoyable circle of music pupils in the village, but came to these regular staff meetings nonetheless. I am sure, on hindsight, that, through my eagerness for anthroposophy, and an equal eagerness to study it along with like-minded people (my army readings had been mostly completely solitary), I lingered thirstily at these discussions for too long into the evening and that this might have been the seed which grew, albeit out of sight, sending down roots that eventually split the rock of our foundation in twain.

I don't remember ever discussing children. We were full of life. Weekends were free—we'd scoot off on Saturdays clad in white crash helmets on our Vespa. And we 'lived in' in our own little flat —and didn't feel the lack of a family. Where would we have put a family anyway? But clearly that wasn't Alison's view! She arrived on 3 December 1958. Richard five and a bit years later.

1958. It was not only growing family life that caused our move away from Hampton Manor. Colleagues there were not happy about one aspect of the management. Notwithstanding the gardener's splendid efforts, the resentment showed most of all in food supplies: there was no attempt to provide *quality* that supported the inner spiritual life. Those who held the purse strings (the Directors of an independent Trust) no doubt had their hearts in the right place, but had not sufficiently penetrated anthroposophical insights to get their priorities right—or such was the staff's view—and we tried everything as a body to alter this (through discussions and many meetings) but to no avail.

So ties were loosening. Just before and in readiness for Alison's birth, we as a family had moved into two rooms in Quaker Ridge, Jean's mother's house (her father had departed, as I said earlier), and we stayed there for the winter months. I had meanwhile landed a teaching job at Uffculme Open Air School on the outskirts of Birmingham ('special education' increments attached to the salary), a school that had started in Victorian or Edwardian days, I think, founded by the philanthropic Cadbury family. This brought in money. Work at Hampton Manor was on the basis of £3 per week pocket money, so you didn't need much of a capacious pocket to accommodate it, even in those times; yet we also had our little flat and 'all found'. The capital thus amassed eventually enabled the move to Nutley to take place.

1959. When spring started warming up, we took the bold step of buying a caravan and putting it at Cherington Rectory in Roy's garden. What a happy summer that was—for us all. Exultant. I drove down in the bubble car on Friday evenings after school. On arrival, I got into my treasured pale blue tweed suit, hugged and hugged (and composed the occasional song for) my baby daughter, played the organ for Sunday services, and drove the couple of hours back to school through the early mists of Monday mornings. The mists, curling through the lush meadows, were external but also sometimes at that hour internal, till my class of 30 ultimately 'brought me down' with a bump!

Life in Cherington was idyllic for a tiny baby—and, I like to think, for a young mother 'without a care in the world': the Rectory led straight onto the most glorious, farm-and-hay-smelling Cotswold countryside. Larks abounded. That year there was glorious sunshine and the wild roses and elders blossomed in rare abundance. We made rose petal syrup and elderberry cordial etc. which took us through at least one winter.[18] Often at weekends the Barnett tribe would drive down and we felt all united again, socially, artistically, and in Roy's absolutely unique, totally unaffected and genuine style of religious worship (—bordering on the esoteric?). Geoffrey and Mary had their second child by this time, Catherine, and she and Alison were christened at the same service at the font in the picturesque old village church of St Nicholas on Whitsunday—with the most beautiful choral quartet you could wish for.

Meanwhile the hunt for the future was taking place. My former colleagues were looking for a property where we could work with the handicapped and run the place in accordance with the threefold social order as far as possible, feed the residents with bio-dynamic or wholefood produce, and form what we conceived to be a truly anthroposophical community. After hunting high and low for a property where this could take place, Nutley Hall came on the market. A parent at Michael Hall, known to the Rudels at Peredur, who was an accountant helped us acquire this. We idealistically sank all our harvested funds, down to the last penny, into the purchase, at which the accountant insisted that the substantial outbuilding be put in my name for security—foolish young things not to think of the future, type of reaction!! But how enormously grateful we became later for the financial foresight and good, common sense of that man. We renamed the place Perevale (reminiscent of the *Mabinogion,* in which the hero Peredur is the Celtic version of Parzifal), and 'opened shop' at the end of a hard-working summer in which we got the place refurbished and spruced up. I meanwhile had handed in my statutory term's notice at the Cadbury/State school where I was teaching in Birmingham, and the three Masters moved into the clockhouse—Morning Watch

---

[18]   The Whitsuntide choir at Nutley (1960), to celebrate our first such festival there (with Leaney and the Osbornes et al) were regaled at their weekly rehearsals with thirst-quenchers made on the Rayburn, which still had traces of those Cotswold delights.

Cottage[19]—after the end of term in December, in time to establish a corner where we could dress our first Sussex/Norwegian spruce and celebrate Christmas. But these blue skies were not to last for ever.

I have often wondered if it was fickle of me not to stay longer in the Curative work, and at the time suffered pangs of conscience, but after seven years of it I had become increasingly aware of the Age of Michaël and those young people who were incarnating into *this* age. It irritated me: What was I doing working with those whose contribution to evolution could only happen in a future incarnation? I thus embarked on the Michael Hall Teacher Training Course and started teaching at Michael Hall in 1963. For my poor colleagues at Perevale this was a wrench, but not for Jean. The move to Friar's Ash (which she had never seen until the day we moved in, with Richard in her arms and Alison holding my hand as we walked down the drive) gave her, I believe, a breath of independent air which had been entirely missing from her married life. It is a measure, I reflect now, of the trust that existed between us that such a thing could happen.

It also has to be said that not only was she not a feminist in the 'elegant' sense of the word, she was not a 'homemaker' in the traditional sense of *that* word. Without realising this, one cannot explain how someone with two young children and a fascinatingly designed house in a notionally salubrious district could have left home after three years of the move. (She had known Pat Edwards the original owner, and had shared in the excitement of watching Friar's Ash being built, albeit two or three hundred miles away, through all the bits and bobs that Kenneth Bayes the architect sent by post to Hampton Manor for the client's approval or other comments.) The crucial question was: Was the domestic ambience a fulfilling domain in which one could thrive, or was it experienced as hampering one's creativity? —A burning question for many a 60s

---

[19]   The name was very important to Jean—indeed, to us both—who savoured language at all levels and in every nook and crevice of life's landscape.

feminist. However, the severance is not as simply explained as that.

Which leads to a still more painful episode in the narrative. I was now less than five minutes walk away from school. I was able to take part in many aspects of school life from which I was hitherto prevented: more evening meetings, playing for the three Sunday services (I gave up the prestigious Eastbourne position at St Mary's which I had taken on), Christmas plays with all the many rehearsals (I played for all three, for several years), I got involved in life at Emerson College which had moved to Forest Row from Clent Grove in the Midlands, and no doubt there was more. We didn't have 'normal' family holidays—a new house, not a handsome salary and a heavy mortgage—though home life during holiday time was full of festivity with daily singing and visitors who participated in various aspects of music making.

Even so, and in spite of the above, the importance of which I by no means wish to overplay, the joy of boiling bottles, nappy changing and the like soon wore extremely thin, especially as Jean had gone through it all once before in the Cotswolds and the novelty (hardly an adequate or worthy enough expression) had worn off, deteriorating into an irksome chore. Not only a frequently absent husband (even if he was only two hundred yards across the garden fence at a teachers' meeting), but the grind of housewifery, became intolerable. Karl Nunhofer, the school's anthroposophical doctor, later once asked me if I had "neglected her" and of course I realised that this must have been the case, though being swept up with class teaching and anthroposophical work had contributed towards making me blind to the fact. The difficulties intensified until one day Jean faced me with a *fait accompli*: "I'm returning the wedding ring and leaving the anthroposophical books, but I'm keeping the engagement ring [a large sapphire encircled with diamonds] as it is valuable,"—or words to that effect. Oh, the joy and anguish of that two-sided coin: *value*!

Mercifully from one point of view, she did not contest my custody of the children—on the contrary, though her love for them always remained unquestionable and steadfast. So with my mother being the angel that she was, we got through a hard grind and stormy passage until at length Jean found her life's partner and sailed to Africa for her new professional life.

At first we corresponded only very occasionally. Since Henryk's death (her Polish husband)—though beginning somewhat before—more frequently. And I was able to visit Port Alfred, at her gentle but persistent persuasion, once I started travelling to South Africa in the 90s. I therefore believe that something of the thread of that twin-spirit which initially brought us together was never fully snapped, despite the tensions that it had had to sustain. I have safely kept all her letters and their multifarious enclosures so that at least that chapter of the 'story' may be investigated and so that my interpretation can be objectively viewed.

During my visits to Port Alfred there was never any hint of recrimination either in word or atmosphere. No 'regrets'. We had no difficulty in immediately finding a focal point from which we could begin 'where we had left off'—essentially in our mutual interest in the family ('interest' sounds *far, far* too inadequate), in music, and in anthroposophy which she had avidly taken up reading and on which she spent every Rand she could spare in order to acquire Steiner's printed works.[20] I met and was warmly introduced to her closest friends and neighbours whom she most affectionately appreciated. I dare say, if it had not been so expensive to travel from the various Waldorf centres where I worked to Port Alfred, I would have been a more regular guest. I know that she would have appreciated that. But perhaps the two visits were enough to witness and experience the unbroken thread—for which I give thanks and which, I trust, will stand the test of future karma.

One last impression—abiding for me. She continuously made quite lengthy lists of things she wanted to mention to me in her

---

[20] She enjoyed a postal link with Martin Wiegand, bookseller at the anthroposophical centre in Bryanston, Johannesburg.

letters. Her correspondence, as well as linking richly with the past, was often like opening a jack-in-the-box of the latest intriguing details of events, mostly parochial but not entirely, that had skipped and danced across her path of life. The last two letters she wrote were only aerogrammes and something of an exception to this.

When I last visited her, the lists were impressively long. But they were of things she wanted to show me, tell me about and play to me. And she made a special point of playing several of her Chopin pieces to me. This took place at an arranged time and was like a formal though completely unpretentious performance.[21] She played by heart—and there was wonderful heart in it—and complete absorption. She was living lovingly in her world. Chopin was Henryk's musical hero, they being both Polish. Though the love I had hoped to help her experience, now fifty years ago, had not taken on the 'traditional' family garment that I had envisaged—indeed, earnestly hoped for, en-visioned—there it was, I believe, in the quality of her playing. In that last impression, so much had 'come full circle'.

---

[21] It even seemed that she had given thought to how she should dress for the occasion.

1959-1966

Two huge changes took place in these years, one geographical and one, for want of a better word, vocational. After a wide-ranging search, the colleagues from Hampton Manor were able to track down a suitable and affordable property for a 'curative home' where every aspect of life could reflect an anthroposophical impulse—the stumbling block which had been the cause of the rift with the 'Three Roses' management team at Hampton Manor and our subsequent resignations. After the summer months of preparation, the first resident was welcomed in time for Christmas 1959. Inwardly I was over the moon: it meant a much closer fulfilling of all our ideals and, looking ahead to when Alison would enter Class 1 (which was in September 1965), at last we were within commutable distance of a Rudolf Steiner School, as Michael Hall presented itself to the public at that time. Outwardly it meant leaving one's roots. From Northumbrian and Warwickshire connections to living in Sussex where, it seemed, affluence had stealthily built a semi-hidden suburbia down every country lane you cared to investigate. How was one going to survive without the great-heartedness of the Midlanders, or the spirit-astir atmosphere of the Scottish border country?

Fortunately the curative work—especially establishing a new 'institution' from absolute scratch—kept one busy 364 days in the year (what *did* you do with the free time given you on your birthday?). Not just busy. There was the élan of freshness, the buoyancy of full and unstinting collegiality, the bringing of spiritual science into the minutiae of all aspects of life, the wonder and shared joy of our first child (with Richard arriving in February 1964), endless opportunities to be creative, the vigour engendered through hard, manual work and the threefold balance it gave to each day, the making of new friends (many, it transpired, such as Moana Bowron, Jesse Darrell, Diana Girdwood and Jim Byford—to mention only a handful—to become lifelong), and the feeling that, at last, one was making a significant contribution to the Age of Michaël.

And there came the rub. As one became aware of the world beyond the essentially cloistered life of a curative home—especially was this the case, as a result of the demanding task of building it up in its pioneer days—the question arose: Was this enough? Listening to destiny is not necessarily comfortable. Nutley Hall gave everything, but was *I* giving what those who were incarnating in a Michaël Age (1879-c.4000 according to the ancient Babylonian calendar) might need of me? And if not, how would I extricate myself in order to do so?

The life-changing move happened, not by any means without pain, fairly swiftly—which seemed to be an affirmative nod that one had heard the voice of destiny aright. I joined the Michael Hall Teacher Training Course—just in the nick of time, since it was the last one that Cecil Harwood was to direct. Halfway through, with René Querido on his way to North America, I was invited to cover his class teaching (Class 6), at the end of the year being confirmed as the teacher who would take them through to Class 8. I still hear some of his words from the conversation we had at the point when 'deputising' changed to permanency: "We hope you will make a major contribution, Brien, to Waldorf education."

Then came the U-turns and transformations. I gave up my prestigious organ and choirmaster post in Eastbourne in order to play for the Sunday services at school: the Offering Service at 10 o'clock, the Youth Service at 1030 and the Children's service at 1100 (which later had to be held twice since the room was not large enough to hold the numbers attending). I found a new rhythm in the day which, by taking a short nap after school of 20 minutes or so, enabled me (a) still to teach the 5pm lesson at Nutley Hall, so that the wrench was lessened; and (b) to fit in the considerable amount of research, marking and preparation necessary to teach the Waldorf Curriculum, as Dr Caroline von Heydebrand had outlined it in accordance with what was being practised in the 'mother school' in Stuttgart, guided from the outset by Rudolf Steiner. Finally there was the bricks and mortar component of the move from Morning Watch Cottage (a converted outbuilding at Nutley Hall, which had the cosy feeling of having been a harness room downstairs and haylofts up above) to Friar's Ash. It was five months after Richard's birth, and seemed to me to be destiny's clearest confirmation that the step I was taking was the right one. Such a fundamental change in one's domiciled arrangements will, perhaps, benefit from receiving a closer look, which clearly suggests karmic relationships.

In the late 50s Miss P. de L. Edwards (Pat to her friends) came to stay for several months at Hampton Manor, where I was teaching a variety of subjects to people who were then referred to as mentally handicapped. Her half sister had died just at the point when they were planning to move into retirement, though the unexpected death was not the reason for Pat's sojourn at Hampton. She came to stay because she had sold her house in Dorset (Swanage) and was still building the next one in Forest Row. Both architects had been inspired by Rudolf Steiner's organic approach to architecture. Harbour St Bride (the Dorset house) had been designed by Montague Wheeler, the architect of Rudolf Steiner House in London; Friar's Ash (the house being built in Forest Row) was being designed by Kenneth Bayes.

I say 'was being designed'. When she came to Hampton Manor there wasn't much left to do to the ground plan. But apart from the basic structure, a great deal of the 'finishes' were still under discussion. We would gather round the study coffee table most evenings and hear what Bayes had to say in his latest correspondence about colours of rooms (walls, radiators and other paint work), Venetian blinds (all windows were fitted with them), access to boiler house and so on. Being a female client meant a considerable emphasis on practicality when it came to capacity and positioning of fitted cupboards and wardrobes etc., though he did not go over the top with these as Pat had lots of beautiful furniture made by Betula, an anthroposophical firm operating 'before the war'. There was also the surround of the fireplace, but more of that presently.

As soon as Friar's Ash was complete, and Pat had moved in, we co-workers at Hampton were invited to stay there, one by one. I visited twice: once hospiteering in Michael Hall and once when going for an interview for a music adviser's post in Sussex. The interview was a failure, in that the panel offered me a job which was not identical with the one advertised, which I refused—far too arrogantly I suspect, my self-esteem being dented. But the week's hospiteering sowed seeds that I was unaware of at the time, seeds which germinated some five years later when I took up the training to become a class teacher.

It was during the training that I met Stephen and Libby Sheen, newly wed at that time. While preparing some songs for a concert we were to give, Libby looked out of the window of the room where we were rehearsing and nodded in the direction of Friar's Ash (it was just two doors away from the school), casually mentioning that it was being put on the market. There was no 'for sale' sign up, but I was round there like a shot after the rehearsal, ringing the doorbell (— yes it *was* the one that Pat had chosen with its ear-friendly ding-dong tone) and was invited in by the owner. On being shown round, I noticed that no colour scheme had been changed, so when we came to look at the last room of all, before the vendor opened the door I said, 'And is this room still blue?' *Still* blue. His surprise led to curiosity, the curiosity led to the story of my connection with the building of the house, and the connection (coupled with the fact that I was 'working in anthroposophy'—though the couple were not anthroposophists by a long chalk) led to my being offered a considerable reduction on the asking price—unsolicited.

There were two snags. The Wilmots had given first refusal to another interested purchaser; and I had no savings *at all* (a fact which I somehow managed to conceal). But to cut this part of the story short: the first refusal person refused; and I borrowed money for the deposit and arranged a mortgage.

It was two years later in mid-August that I made a detour on my way to Tintagel to see if I could get a glimpse of Pat's first house in Dorset. Only knowing roughly where it was, some sixth needle-in-the-haystack sense helped me to find it and I boldly knocked on the door (or was it another of her door bells?) and explained my interest. Over tea I heard the occupant's strange story. He had been in the British navy, finishing up with a post in the United States of America. I don't recall the exact level, but he was certainly high ranking. On retirement he and his wife wanted to return to England and had given the estate agents certain conditions, three of which were fairly eliminative: the site had to be free of street lights; the design had to be open plan; and the place had to have central heating. Given the likelihood of a prolonged and possibly messy transitional period, the third condition could have been managed anywhere, but the other two? Open plan houses are by no means common—or they weren't then. And where was one going to get guaranteed dark nights?—these, it turned out, were required by the naval officer's abiding interest in the heavens, an interest that lingered on from his life on the high seas, and resulted in his building a small observatory in the garden. The coast was the answer. But I am racing ahead.

They were sent a few prospectuses which appeared to match the conditions—properties are often all very well on paper!—but, as they did the rounds, when they came to Harbour St Bride and were viewing the property, a text on the top landing clinched it for them. It was of an Indian prayer, beginning, *Look well to this day, for it is life...* Astounded to see it there, there surged up within the husband a feeling of homecoming. Sailing from continent to continent had brought him into contact with other cultures and the philosophies that informed them. This text from India had become close to both their hearts—and I think he negotiated with Pat that she include it in the sale! And to add to the 'coincidence', it was a text we often used for Morning Song at Hampton Manor!

So back to Friar's Ash which was built by the best firm in the district, James Waters. There seemed to be nothing of the 'you can get away with it' attitude of some builders, that even my architect friends had had to wrestle with when they were building *their own houses!*—less than top quality door and window furniture, the plaster towards the middle of the walls pared away to its thinnest, and suchlike. So as we walked down the drive on that summer's day in 1964, with Alison aged 5 years and Richard aged 5 months, we stepped into *integrity,* embodied in bricks and mortar, woodwork and door handles.

Oh yes! And mosaic. One of our most delightful sessions round the Hampton manor study coffee table had been opening a package that contained three or four match boxes. Something inside each one rattled. They were Italian mosaics for the sculpturally designed fireplace. The client's prerogative was to choose which combination of colours she preferred—something that she had very definite ideas about. She could easily have kept the choice to herself, spreading the contents of each matchbox out in her own room upstairs, but it was characteristic of her warm social feeling that she shared the selection of even this feature, so central in what was essential the only downstairs room. (In fact, *en famille,* we've always simply called it 'the room'.) But, for some reason which the Wilmot's didn't divulge, they had whitewashed the whole of the mosaic surround. It wasn't a priority, of course, on moving into a new house, but I couldn't wait to get my hands on some wire wool to restore the centre piece to its original Italian glory.

The handsome Michael Hall salary—anything is handsome when you have virtually been working for no remunerative return—and the next-to-none maintenance bills, eventually enabled all the debts to be cleared and the mortgage paid off, at the same time permitting Nutley Hall to acquire Morning Watch Cottage, since it adjoined their land. It therefore seems appropriate that I should sing the praises of Nutley Hall—which I do in the following description of the early days, since it is about to celebrate its half century.

Nutley Hall
Acquiring the Property and Early Days

The camellias were smothered in blossom when Mary Bridger and Brien Masters were first shown round Nutley Hall on a sunny winter's day in 1959. It was Brian Place, the Peredur Trust accountant, who had alerted us to the fact that the house was up for sale. We went from room to room, from cellar to attic, with heart in mouth lest it should prove unsatisfactory, as had several other properties we had seen in the district. The most memorable of these no-go viewings stick in the memory: Saint Hill (now a centre for Scientology) and Dunnings Mill (now one of the buildings in a complex that offers sports facilities on the edge of East Grinstead). The memory of the former—with its cream-enamelled, tide-marked bath standing centrally in an otherwise denuded cellar for (as we were informed) the 'black servants', and its billiard room with an enormous fresco of primates bizarrely dolled up in boaters and bikinis, as I vaguely recall, having a good time—sends shivers down the spine and confused messages to the mind. While the memory of the latter, with its dark rooms and its low, forehead-bruising beams, lingers on as one of disappointment—hopes raised and dashed, for the estate agent had made an excellent job of singing its praises in the brochure, a song that already began to sound as you first caught sight of its considerable external charm.

Nutley Hall was neither unmanageably grandiose nor too pinching and dingy for our purposes. As the two clients descended the main staircase, pausing by the landing window to take a last glance over the shoulder so that the impression they had acquired could be conveyed to the third colleague back in Worthing (Margery Buckeridge) they exchanged looks for the first time, with eyebrows questioningly raised and very slight nods—so as not to give the vendor the idea that the asking price was too low!—and said almost simultaneously and with some relief at the hint of a feeling of 'Land ahoy!': "Adequate?!" Back at base—the bungalow to which the two ladies had retired from Hampton Manor, together with Margery's elder sister Kate Anderson, there was a frenzy of phone calls to the accountant, to anthroposophical friends in the area and eventually to the estate agent ... and within a short time contracts had been signed and Nutley Hall (or Perevale as it was to be called for its first few years) was ours.

During the summer of that year, a work party of colleagues—a fourth member, Martha Keller, from Switzerland, had joined the trio —with friends and relatives rolled up sleeves, donned overalls and decorator's headgear, scraped Edwardian wallpaper from the walls of rooms and corridors and transformed the smell of the kitchen, with the help of soap and water, scrubbing brushes and gloss paint, into something related to savoury. From soon after dawn till nearly dusk the buckets steamed and splashed, the brooms swept, the squeegees squeeged, and the open windows drank in the summer air as elbows, well lubricated with elbow grease, bobbed up and down as if they had been merry fiddlers', jerked to and fro and wafted elegantly in harmony with paintbrush bristles as the daunting task of preparing for the arrival of the first resident was attacked. Thus we nibbled our way, hourly, daily, and with joyful anticipation, through the calendar.

It was Mary Bridger and Margery Buckeridge who brought experience, warmth and wisdom to the project. They had met through Whitelands College (now part of the campus of the University of Roehampton), training to become teachers. Or rather, Mary was the trainee at the time, marginally younger than Margery, with the latter being in her first year teaching job and chosen by Mary's tutor as a good person to host/mentor her first teaching practice. The tutor was the formidable, kindly and insight-full 'old Noakes' (as they endearingly referred to her), who had introduced them—several other students at Whitelands, too—to the work of Rudolf Steiner. However, their path led them not into Waldorf education—which it could well have done since they were excellent teachers—but to curative education.

The first curative home in Britain had been opened in the suburbs of Birmingham in the Midlands, in the early 30s. As *Sunfield Children's Home* it moved to Clent Grove where Mary and Margery joined co-workers, and where they experienced all the rigours of leading a communal life in social therapy in support of the anthroposophically based curative education to which all were awesomely dedicated. In this, their main source of inspiration flamed through Dr Ita Wegman, Rudolf Steiner's medical collaborator, who visited Clent Grove frequently. Mary and Margery had carried the pioneer torch of this work to Hampton Manor in the early 50s and it still continued to burn vigorously at Nutley Hall.

When everyone was up and dressed, the day began with morning song: candles, an air of joyful ritual, the verse from Rudolf Steiner's Soul Calendar and other words, concluding with a festive (seasonal or religious) song accompanied by harmony provided by a full consort of recorders. This first 'deed of the day' took place centrally. The music rang through the whole house. When entering the hall through the front door, one walked into the atmosphere it created, seven days a week, the whole year round.

After breakfast, which concluded with the day's announcements and arrangements, everyone worked for a couple of hours. Mary, in particular, had cultivated an attitude toward housework through her deep, meditative life, which enabled her to assign every task to each resident—whether sweeping crumbs from the dining room floor, drying dishes, polishing wooden surfaces or whatever—which fitted each one's therapeutic needs and in addition, of course, to the social therapy of performing a task for all the others in the community. She had consummated this skill, I gathered, from working with Dr Walther at the Sunfield Children's Home where, over a long period of some twenty years, she had gained the insight to penetrate the complex nature of each resident's handicap—even bordering on the karmic—to whatever extent it was possible, resolving or at least addressing the problem while at the same time providing some life fulfilment by their being a member of a therapeutic community. Margery went straight to the weavery on these occasions and prepared warps, shuttles and pattern charts for the lucky ones who came under her supervision.

After coffee, we had main-lesson. All the residents attended: whatever their condition, whatever their soul disposition, whatever their mental capacity, whatever their age. Even in this last respect, there was a considerably wide spectrum during the first years at Nutley Hall. Nina, the youngest was entering her teens. As lively as a cricket, when she laughed she often put so much energy into it that she would literally fall off her chair. As the teacher, you felt like a test match fielder, being ready to catch! Betty, at the other end of the scale, had reached a stage of life which manifested in a sort of matronly condescension towards anyone purportedly teaching; her expression, especially when she was in a good mood, would often be wreathed in little private smiles—was it something that had happened thirty years ago, one wondered?

The main-lesson topic lasted a third of a year. We thought it should have the character of an adult's extended study. The residents' gift to the world (through manually-orientated workshops, such as weaving and basketry) was vitally important for the incarnation of each one concerned, but shouldn't they *receive* something too? The main-lessons aimed to do this: put them in touch with towering individualities who had changed the world (biographically orientated lessons), put them in touch, albeit second hand, with the modern environment and contemporary conditions, put them in touch with cultural streams (to which they might have belonged or would possibly veer towards at some distant point in the future).

Lunch was followed by rest hour and gardening. In pretty well all weathers we climbed into our wellingtons, five days a week, and cared for the grounds, collected material for building compost heaps (a wonderful activity for festival days, we discovered), and began very gingerly to cultivate bio-dynamically. Though not very 'professional' at it, we did what we could to encourage the two great vines to yield their juicy autumn bunches. We had bumper crops of lettuce, broad beans, tomatoes and other produce, though my memory of it all, fifty years on, is that it was more of beginner's luck than anything approaching horticultural-show pride!

After thirstily-gulped mugs of tea we gathered in the south room for artistic activities: literature, poetry, orchestra, singing and country dancing. Margery was ringmaster of the last, since she had been connected with the Cecil Sharp folk dance movement from an early age. Meanwhile, I pounded the keyboard with neither modesty nor delicacy in order to 'get things moving'. Home-made concerts were usually on Sundays, unless there was a birthday to mark. Once a week, too, we did eurhythmy—this entailed two round trips to the nearest railway station to pick up the eurhythmist from London, our only regular visitor, who provided us with news of the big wide world and always brought the spiritual breath that comes with eurythmy itself.

After supper and the quiet time that followed, the day closed with evensong—simpler and shorter than morning-song but still a dignified preparation for the 'journey' through sleep ahead. Following evensong for an hour or two on week days, the staff studied. The main contents were always something from a lecture or book by Steiner and ongoing case-studies of the residents, combined with reflections of the day, so that we could be sure that, to the best of our ability, the therapeutic aspect of our work and life together burgeoned.

I doubt if we would have got off the ground without benefactors. Some had made the financial side of the enterprise possible, not least the team themselves who had arranged their lives so that they needed no remuneration during the first year's 'trading'. Strange to say, I am unaware of the capital gifts ever being made public— perhaps the friends who helped in this way wished to remain anonymous, but their generosity must be recorded somewhere in the archives.

Rather is it the gifts in kind that stick in the memory. There was the three-gallon-a-day gift of Jersey milk from a neighbouring bio-dynamic farmer. There was the mini upright piano that came from the flat of a very elderly anthroposophist who sought us out within days of our arrival and happened to live within five minutes walk on the other side of the village. She is still in my mind when I play her favourite Schubert impromptu. There were the occasional treats to the theatre or a concert from another local friend, while the rest of us would 'hold the fort' (or *fire-watch* as tradition would have it); these were highlights indeed. And—in some ways the most astonishing—there was the gift of a boiler from a well-to-do friend in Cavendish Square, London who was upgrading her central heating system and thought her cast-off boiler might come in handy one day. It did. One nail-biting morning we discovered that the pipe next to the fire chamber of the boiler that had come with the house was leaking. And when the heating engineer who had been called in to see if something could be done 'pronounced the worst'—we would have to replace it—I led him into the stable where, behind the door, the monster from Cavendish Square had been put on ice and asked him, "Will this one do the trick?" I can still see him recoiling in astonishment before gasping, "Well ... er ... yes." And so that month's books were saved the ignominy of blushing (in the red)!

Let me conclude on a musical note. Every Tuesday evening during our first winter and spring we held a choir practice. Everyone in the house was there, their ranks being swelled by friends in the district: students—from the Michael Hall teacher training course, a car load of co-workers from Peredur Home School in East Grinstead, Diana Girdwood from Hindleap who was one of the most loyal friends for decades, later teaching art therapy and a regular attender at the Offering Service (her ashes were laid to rest midst birdsong in the south facing garden) and others. The choir practices went on until Whitsuntide when a resident string quartet which was invited for the week, rehearsing and giving concerts, was expanded into a small chamber orchestra for a gala concert. The only place for the audience, I seem to remember, was on the great staircase that fills the lantern of the main house.

One item was by Vaughan Williams. The eldest musician present —a viola player who went on to live to be over a hundred—always recalled the occasion when I saw him in the following years. His eyes—eyes that had seen a century come and go—would sparkle as the music of Vaughan Williams went through his mind. In his professional life—his first profession (and he had had more than one) had been as a hospital almoner. I learnt that he had introduced curtains between beds into the wards of British hospitals! So Mercury, the Spirit of Healing, or Raphael as he is called in the Apocrypha's 'Book of Tobit', had lived in him too, as it has lived— profoundly and blessedly so—in Nutley Hall, now for half a century.

1966-1973

The last third of my Sun-Michaelic planetary phase. The geographical and cultural wanderings of the journeyman years culminated in the horse-in-mid-stream change to Sussex; the awakening to the tasks of the 'Present Age' had culminated in the move from curative education to becoming a class teacher at Michael Hall; and these years constituted the trial by fire—not a raging fire—of educating children in the modern world. With the disabled it was as if one needed to call on all one's youthful forces to reach them. Some of Fried Geuter's sessions at the Sunfield Children's Home in the 30s were several times described to me as a 'circus'. This, I gathered, was due to his insight as a curative educator into the unique nature of each individual handicap (as Rudolf Steiner characterises it in the curative education course) and his creative genius in devising specific therapeutic 'exercises', for want of a better expression. Thus, his sessions came across as having a similar character to those of Dr Karl Schubert at the Waldorf School in Stuttgart whose class was known as the 'helping class' (*Hilfsklasse*), a felicitous term where, so often, we fumble to find something that is tactful and non-discriminative—e.g. remedial, extra art, therapeutic, learning support and so on. (Might we even import *Hilfsklasse* into the language one day to take its place beside other honourable imports, such as restaurant, fjord, kangaroo, alphabet, siesta, blitz, Caesar, rickshaw and a hundred and one others?)

So-called normal children certainly don't need this kind of circus approach. Insight, yes: youthfulness, yes; but not expressed in an outwardly (as well as inwardly) stimulating way. This I had to quickly learn, especially when I embarked on teaching the younger ages (6-9 years), and it was fortunate that the learning curve fell on the Mars-Jupiter-Saturn side of 'mid-life'.

Not that one is in a position to personally claim much insight.

However, those who become class teachers need to bring life experience to their calling. This is not likely to occur if—though I cannot think of a case where this happens in Steiner schools—the person concerned goes straight from school to teacher training and thence into class teaching without any 'world' experience, the increasingly popular 'gap year' notwithstanding. There are plenty of ingredients that constitute life experience: these may include travel, life-shattering events, experience in other (non-educational) walks of life or professions, among others. In my case, not laying much emphasis on either music or the Royal Artillery(!), it was curative education—with the reservation concerning the necessary transformation of approach mentioned. That that has been a continuous part of the signature of life is reflected in the essay which follows, in which I place a recurrent theme in education (the senses) into the perspective of the so-called pedagogical law, vital to all curative educators, and ultimately, I would urge, to all educators.

The Senses and the Modern Child
A way towards re-enlivening the teacher and of identifying and eradicating antagonisms that are clouding the Waldorf impulse[1]

Two worlds

A five-year-old was commenting on his little cousin's recent birth: "I saw S's rainbow bringing her to J from the angels." (J was his aunt, the mother of the new-born, S.) And a few moments later: "Has J still got a big tummy?"

Here we have a child who still retains perceptions of both worlds (spiritual and earthly), though I realise that I am somewhat assuming that his connection with the spiritual world had something of a *perceptual* quality about it. Certainly in the realm of *ideation* the worlds appeared to be of equal reality in the five-year-old's mind.

Preparatory reading

The preparatory reading material recommended for the conference, which includes the study of the senses by Willi Aeppli, as it does, relieves me from including here much of *what* should be brought as part of the experience of children during the second septennial phase.[2] Aeppli also weaves a rich tapestry of background for the teacher, referring the reader to Steiner's oeuvre. The origin of the senses—that they exist in the physical body—that they are connected to the will—that they have deteriorated during evolution from being life-endowed to their present condition of 'etheric

---

[1]   This article is based on a lecture given at Ringwood during the Easter Conference 2008, the conference being entitled *The Twelve Senses and the Modern Child*. The author's assignment was to address the situation in the Lower School (ages 6+-14) after the 'birth' of the etheric.

[2]   Willi Aeppli, *The Care and Development of the Human Senses;* Alfred Soesman, *Our Twelve Senses.*

holes'—that this dying process is what we witness as recapitulated in childhood—that one of the turning points in this recapitulation is at the time of the Rubicon—that there are topics in the so-called Waldorf curriculum which can be an invigorating experience for the senses—that much in modern life calls for such reinvigoration due to the harm that present-day conditions cause the senses of children, particularly in their formative years—that, given the educational principles and the in-depth study of the human being during childhood investigated by Rudolf Steiner, Waldorf schools have an unparalleled opportunity for protecting the senses and possibly even putting right some of the damage caused—and so on. All this is touched on to some degree or other by Aeppli and others, and can all be—or if the listener has done his homework in preparation for the conference, *has been*—absorbed.

With this background, the line that I shall follow here is to look at the education of the senses of the 'modern child' from the perspective of what Steiner refers to as the *educational law*, and see what conclusions can be drawn from that.

The educational law

This term appears in the lecture Rudolf Steiner gave on 26/6/1924 to a very small group of people at Dornach who had been invited for the course of lectures on Curative Education. One envisages that there were a couple of rows of seats in the Schreinerei, the building in Dornach in which lectures took place after the burning of the first Goetheanum, with a fairly tight limit regarding who was invited (mainly young medical doctors and curative educationists connected to the first anthroposophical 'home' at Lauenstein). Steiner's instructions that there should be no stenographer present also suggest very unusual circumstances. The participants were clearly aware of this and made extensive notes which resulted in the present publication of the lectures bearing the English title of *Education for Special Needs*. Was his reason for departing from normal practice, one wonders, because he included extensive comments about actual 'cases' of mental and other illnesses that were brought before him, and he wished to respect the identity of their individualities—what we now have embodied in law regarding data protection?

Be that as it may, we have the enriching indication that, for the curative educator, it is that member of her sevenfold 'constitution', which is one degree higher than that of her pupil's, which can bring about a therapeutic effect. Thus the teacher's etheric influences the pupil's physical; the teacher's astral influences the pupil's etheric; the teacher's ego influences the pupil's astral and so on. The example given by Steiner refers to the astral. The special soul-needs children that were brought before him were mostly referred to as having some malformation or dysfunction in their etheric makeup which prevented their soul-spirit nature from incarnating normally into the earthly 'vessel'. And Steiner gives examples of how the teacher can educate her own astral so that it has a beneficial effect on the pupil's etheric.[3] What perspective does this law suggest for pedagogical work on the senses?

The senses in today's world

In that the situation vis-à-vis the senses in our modern world is dire, one can argue that whatever education can do to help must therefore be therapeutic. However, the sense organs are embedded in the physical body—the *whole* of the physical body in the case of some of the senses (both lower and upper). At the same time, we learn from Steiner's spiritual scientific research that the senses came into being already during the Ancient Saturn stage of earth evolution (beginning with the sense of smell!).

Later in evolution came further developments. There is the occasion when Steiner describes how the senses existed (still purely in their etheric state) out of the astral desire-nature of the human

---

[3]   For examples, see R. Steiner *Education for Special Needs* pp.41-43 in the 1998 edition

being to perceive something. (Eve's awakening comes to mind, as recounted in Hebrew mythology.[4])

In his lecture of 13/10/1906 we hear of the 'chaste' equivalent of the senses coming into existence in the mineral world: in the case of hearing the chaste equivalent was the onyx, whereas the "carnelian developed with the sense of touch, topaz with the sense of taste, jasper with the sense of smell, [and *most significant for the 'making sense of it' aspect of life*] the carbuncle stone [developed] when man grew able to form ideas based on images." (This was the stone which, according to legend, Lucifer lost from his diadem when cast down from the heavens; the point at which Steiner advises the class teacher to start in the telling of the stories of the Old Testament *as world literature* in Class 3!). A little earlier in the lecture Steiner puts it this way: "[the] desire-free counter-image [of the organ of the sense of sight—the eye] is the olivine." One of my subsidiary aims in this article is to air topics which could well form the substance for future research. These indications give ample food for thought as well as research material for several disciplines.

Apropos the term 'etheric hole', it was coined by Steiner during his remarkable Hanover lectures[5] in which the senses—'opened' as a result of the Fall—are described as the effect of the predominance of the physical over the etheric, one of four results of the Fall, each a maladjustment occurring as a kind of Fall-knock-on effect, so to speak, between the four lower members of the constitution, physical, etheric, astral and ego. One is reminded of the red hangings with which Rudolf Steiner draped the congress hall, for the occasion in

---

[4]   The Roman Catholic church's attitude towards the woman has surely been bedevilled by taking the Genesis account of Creation as literal, and not realising that is has the quality of profound myth, i.e. that we have in the image of Eve taking the forbidden fruit, not the everlastingly guilty woman but the desire nature of the human astral. The driving force of modern technological investigation can be seen in this sense as the Eve-curiosity in the scientist pursuing an incessant trail of 'what ifs?'

[5]   R. Steiner *The World of the Senses and the World of the Spirit,* lecture of 29 December 1911.

Munich in 1907 in which the first Mystery Drama was to be performed, as a way of reversing the negative effect of the lost *life* quality in the sense of sight—a move which astonished the theosophists arriving for the congress, especially those who saw theosophy essentially as a body of knowledge rather than something which could lead to a path of inner experience! The red of the school service room might also be researched with this in mind, a facet of Waldorf that appears drastically to have fallen by the wayside.

The present status of the senses

So much for Lucifer's connection with the development of the senses. We are, of course, also under the influence of the other great opposing power, Ahriman, who would have us believe—and how frequently successful he is!—that the perception of the sense-world is all there is to it. For many a person, this Ahrimanic inspired view is now the *given*, and it becomes a particularly captivating perspective for the child who has passed across the Rubicon. Not only that: what sense experience there is is battered and deceived, attacked and atrophied, distorted and bombarded by modern life with all the inventions that the commercial world has spawned, as outlined above, splurging them on every corner of the High Street and insinuating them into every nook and cranny of the home. It was of course necessary in the long term for this package-deal of materialism, so to speak, to be taken on board in the interests of human freedom. But the next step is to find a way forward that overcomes the limitations of the senses, a way that is not the way of false asceticism, or the way of forced spiritual experience through substance abuse—or other enticements that have their origin in those powers that are opposed to the progress of humanity and human culture.

It is in the gift of the teacher to intervene in this train of evolutionary events, of course with the fullest possible feeling of responsibility (*Schärfe dein Gefühl für Seelische Verantwortlichkeit*), in a way that will prevent, counteract, divert or reduce the effect of the diabolical aspirations of the opposing powers to which I have just referred. As well as the teacher intervening with the 'what' (the content of the lessons to which Aeppli alludes) she may do so in other ways. It is these other ways to which I wish to draw attention, which brings me back once more to the pedagogical law, my main focus, and gives rise to the question: 'What can the teacher do to educate her etheric so that it has a benign influence on the sense-endowed physical body but at the same time sense-beleaguered body, soul and spirit of the modern child? In addressing the question I would like to commend four out of several possible means.

Teach in pictures
I have not researched how many times Steiner gave the advice, teach in pictures, but if one did research it the findings would surely amount to an exhortation. What does this suggest?
Pictures relate to a form of thinking with which we are familiar from the consciousness of earlier peoples, but more especially, since we are professional educators, with the consciousness of children of the age of 6/7+ until that mode of thinking which we associate with rationality has more or less totally superseded it.

If the rationality mode of thinking is pressed upon children prematurely it suppresses the pictorial thinking which is their natural mode of consciousness. Doubly unfortunately, because not only does this mode transform, in the ripeness of time, into that very quality of rationality which the adult needs to be able to exercise in the modern world, but it also hastens the child away from its natural childhood—a form of robbery, one could say. The widespread practice of forcing rational thinking onto child consciousness during those years, which research shows that it is detrimental to the very thing it is wishing to engender, beggars belief. It comes across, if unconscious, as one of the great ironies of the day—and, if conscious, one of the great evils, and in either case one of the great disservices perpetrated against the human spirit. Way back in 1981, the well-known example of the research sponsored by the then Bonn government bears this out:[6] children who had attended Waldorf schools in Germany who had been raised through the second septennial phase so that their pictorial mode of consciousness was preserved and nurtured proceeded to gain higher Abitur results than those children who had been subjected to a pedagogy which cultivated the rational mode of consciousness already well before puberty. Thus if the teacher sustains this aspect of childhood through teaching in pictures, it has a beneficial effect on the whole of life.

In this respect the traditional Waldorf curriculum for the first years of the Lower School (ages 6-11) is rich in material that stems from the older 'folk consciousness' which was alive on the imaginative plane. The fairy story in Class 1, the saint associated with his or her iconographic product of imaginative medieval consciousness in Class 2, the Hebrew, Nordic and Greek mythologies of Classes 3, 4 and 5 are amongst the most well-known examples.

To have to clothe these images in pictorially vivid language is already a boon for the self-education of the story-telling teacher's etheric body. However, there is a further step that the teacher can take: to *penetrate the imagery with understanding*. In the Gospels we have the example of Christ, having told the parable of the sower to the multitudes, turning to his disciples and explaining to them what the fertile soil represented—also the weeds, the rocky, thin depth of soil and so on.[7]

To penetrate the true images from the etheric world as they have survived in myth and folk tale means that the teacher begins to

---

6   Published in *Der Spiegel* 14 December 1981.
7   Luke 8, Matthew 13.

regain a form of thinking that complements her everyday causal consciousness derived from and attached particularly strongly to the sense world. The extent to which she has been successful in doing this is frequently made clear during the recall of the main-lesson on the co-called 'second day'. She experiences that where her verbal pictures have been vivid on 'day one' the children's recall is rich and ample, but not where she has cut corners—'the beautiful princess' is an expression that relies on the listener supplying what comprises the princess's beauty instead of allowing the listener to simply drink in the pictures that the storyteller verbalises. The latter registers in the listener's consciousness and impresses itself on the memory whereas the former does not have the same impact. Without laming her everyday bricks-and-mortar consciousness the teacher adds a dimension to it through a transformation process, one could say. She uses this to gain the higher imaginative mode in which, once gained, she is able to dispense with the consciousness of her starting point until she wishes to consciously return to it.

Nor does the possibility of educating the teacher's etheric nature stop with such well-known narrative. There is what Steiner referred to as the 'spiritual geography' of peoples across the globe, which can form an imaginatively enlivening introduction to the geography main-lessons in the 6th, 7th and 8th classes. The cave paintings at Lascaux, the fascinating Australian aboriginal patterns, the images on Aztec temples, somewhat gruesome to much European consciousness but nevertheless an image of the spiritual life of those indigenous peoples, the lace-carvings on ancient Celtic crosses ... all give the teacher the possibility of engendering insights into the past via activating her imaginative consciousness as part of the education of her etheric body.

History, too, is a cornucopia of opportunity in this respect. So often the facts are either well known or easily down-loadable: the Portuguese having first conquered the port of Ceuta from the Moors, built caravels and explored the west coast of Africa; through the strategy of Simon de Montfort at the Battle of Lewes in 1264 the first parliament came about; one of the leading figures of the reformation (Martin Luther) was mentally infuriated by the Roman church's acquisition of wealth through indulgences; Garibaldi, the Italian republican, buccaneered along the east coast of South America in the 1850s before returning to take up the cudgel of the unification of Italy; and so on. But such references are usually meagre, often skeletal, snippets of knowledge. And in any case, what teacher of history in the Lower School has the time (or available resources) to read all the epic poetry, historic novels and meticulous research that provide *visual* details of these events? It is manifestly impossible. Instead she has to rely on a few factually firm hooks on which to hang the garments which are the products of her informed imagination, which will bring colour into the events, impregnating them with visual memorability for the still important strand of pictorial consciousness possessed by her 12/14-year-olds.[8]

Thus, this material from the past already offers the teacher two steps in the conscious acquisition of imaginative consciousness. The third step—as a contribution towards educating her etheric body— would be where the teacher follows Steiner's advice in the actual *creation* of narrative material which lives on the imaginative plane. "Create your own fairy stories." "Tell nature stories which have the quality of 'parables'." "Invent pedagogical stories for individual children in which some element of the child's nature, which appears to be impervious to normal good pedagogy, is worryingly persistent, so that, through the story taking the (image of the) problem to its logical, grit-in-the-wound conclusion, the child's ego is sufficiently awakened to enter and be more involved in the process of eradicating the obstacle to its own development." "Introduce the letters of the alphabet through images derived from letter stories so that the harmful effects of premature literacy are combated."[9]

---

[8]   see B. Masters *Steiner Education and Social Issues* Chapter 2 for an instance of how this can work out in practice.

[9]   The quotation marks round these widely familiar references are not intended to indicate that the quotes are verbatim but rather 'words to that effect'.

Comments follow on these opportunities that the teacher is given to develop her own imaginative consciousness by using the etheric brain rather than the purely physical.

Create your own fairy stories

It is natural for a teacher—whether new to the job, or an old hand—to shrink from the seeming impertinence of this indication when there is the wealth of Grimm's fairy stories to hand as well as many other folk sources from other lands. Nevertheless, the different degrees of imaginative consciousness called for when recounting a Grimm's tale or when making up one's own (as you speak) are considerable, manifestly in significantly different strata. The latter implies that the storyteller has, at a certain level, been competently able to access an imaginative realm of consciousness. Easier said than done! But Rome wasn't built in a day, as the (pictorial!) *idiom* has it. A few bricks from the building of that Rome have more powerful—homeopathic, if you like—effect on the child than a whole edifice built by someone else, however skilled that someone else has succeeded in describing it.

Creating one's own fairy stories is, of course, greatly assisted by first immersing oneself in the genre of the genuine fairy tale, and then by beginning to interpret the imagery found there. There are many widely known publications on the interpretation of fairy tales. For the Waldorf storyteller, the *locus classicus* is, perhaps, Steiner's own lecture on the subject.[10] The telling of this interpretation and the creating of one's own tales offer the teacher a particularly valuable gift for the development of her own imaginative consciousness.

Nature stories

In referring to these as parables, Steiner clearly intended the teacher (storyteller, once more) to exercise two faculties. The first is the

---

[10]   R. Steiner *The Interpretation of Fairy Tales*, lecture given on 6 February 1913.

discernment of what is a particularly significant detail amongst the plethora of natural phenomena that surround her—significant from the point of view of revealing something of the spiritually creative force behind what actually gives rise to the natural object. The second, closely related to it, is the ability to extract from the quality of fantasy (*Durchdringe dich mit Fantasiefähigkeit*)[11] what that spiritual force actually is. According to the degree to which the teacher has developed her fantasy, of course, this will vary in accuracy. However, as the parable is in image form, one could say that the degree of accuracy is protected, compensated for.

Just as in the case of the teacher creating her own fairy tales, she can have soaked herself in the genre on the one hand and in spiritual scientifically revealed reality on the other, so too in the case of the nature story the teacher can practise raising her consciousness to the relevant imaginative level through studying spiritual science and the descriptions of the non-sensory-perceptible nature of plants as found amongst old herbalists, such as Culpepper, and the like. A couple of examples that spring to mind are the Mars forces in the oak, and the Ancient Moon quality of mistletoe.

There is a further degree of 'protection' against an interpretation that is too much off the mark. In the case of the fairy tale the teacher's fantasy expresses itself in image form—and, with images being open to a whole spectrum of interpretation, the child's own imaginative consciousness is given space to step into the process and has the opportunity of making adjustments, or finding the right angle of approach, i.e. of making the right interpretation, albeit in the realm of the sub-conscious. In the case of the nature story, the teacher's fantasy is expressed less through the image than through the dialogue between the object of the story and some other object which the storyteller introduces as a foil, so to say, to the thing

---

11   This, and the two German phrases which follow later in the text, are taken from the verse by Rudolf Steiner which is frequently used in teachers' meetings: *Imbue thyself with the power of fantasy, / Have courage for the truth, / Sharpen thy feeling for responsibility of soul.*

itself. This leaves the child with still more freedom to bring down from the higher, inspirational realm the spiritual reality and connect it with the precisely detailed phenomenon to which the teacher wishes to draw the child's attention.

Pedagogical stories

With this genre, there can be no escaping the exercising of the teacher's imaginative faculty. She observes impartially the child's behaviour, movement, idiosyncrasies, poise of the head, way of holding a crayon or paint brush, details of the physiognomy, shape of the shoulders, gait and a dozen and one other details. From this daily contemplative-observational pursuit there emerges, at first often hazily, what it is that is causing an 'obstacle' in the child's development which appears not to be removable by the everyday pedagogical means that she and her colleagues are implementing. And from whatever insight she can gain through taking all the relevant observations into her inner life and higher levels of consciousness, she then has to clothe her insight in a secure enough disguise (*teach in pictures*) and 'carry the child's incarnation problem in this disguise to its logical (bitter taste in the mouth) conclusion' so that the higher ego of the child can exert a greater— and therapeutical—force upon the lower ego (albeit, still only in its second septennial phase of incarnation) in order that, from within, something of the 'obstacle' can begin to be dislodged, expunged, whittled away or whatever.[12]

Introducing the letters

Perhaps even more urgent, imperative even, than the foregoing is the indication that Steiner elaborates on on so many occasions as to how to introduce the letters of the alphabet. We get an inkling of what it

---

[12]   For further rationale on the efficacy of the pedagogical story see B. Masters *Adventures in Steiner Education,* pp.106ff.

must have meant to Steiner that the Waldorf School was required by the local authorities to introduce literacy at an early stage. This was long before what transpired from his research, during the long series of lectures given in 1924, on the karmic consequences of being prematurely subject to literacy. The subsequent 'blocking' of spiritual attainment in earlier incarnations that is the outcome of being exposed to literacy in these early years of childhood, virtually means that, through this being the case with generation after generation in the materialistic age, the 'modern child' was born with Gutenberg and Caxton!

So how can we understand the remedy—or at least the prophylactic—of introducing letters via pictures? In order to do this, without simply replicating Steiner's oft-repeated examples, the teacher has to go to the spiritually creative source of the sound. Phonetics, that is, and only consonants. This necessitates keying into a still higher faculty than imagination: inspiration. From gleaning what the sound quality is in its spiritually creative dimension, she then needs to let this filter through into her imaginative life where the sound, combined with other sounds (as heard in words), produces the names of objects in the world. The 'W' is there, for instance in water, waves, whisper, way, wayward, wheat... The creative quality of 'B' is there in boat, baby, baker, boulder, bastion, bubbles, cob and so on. Combine the two and we arrive at 'web' or 'bow'—the inner meaning of which (I submit) we can begin to derive from the creative sound quality of the W and the B, however wobbly we may feel spiritually about the tightrope of our inner development upon which we are travelling! (*Habe den Mut zur Wahrheit.*) Even the whole pedagogical process following the telling of the letter story on days two and three, with which each Waldorf teacher is familiar, dwells lingeringly in the realm of the picture. Indeed, it is the lingering process which enables a bridge to be built between the realm of the spiritual origin of 'the word' (the spoken word) and the dreg-like relics of sound-creativity which we have in literacy. Although, *en passant*, the child is learning the letters of the alphabet, that is merely the vehicle for building the bridge between the two realms. (Hence a 'handful' of consonants is all that is necessary to be introduced in this way.) And one is inclined to think that the more the teacher steeps herself in the inspirational and imaginative realms the more secure and serviceable will be the bridge to and from the spirit for the incarnating child. Without this bridge, the spiritual attainment of the past fails to percolate through to the present incarnation.

Gesture among the elements

Here, with one exception, I am leaving out of detailed consideration, and only making passing reference to, the teacher's privilege and task of directing the children's attention to the wonder of form in the natural world (that of the animal in the 4th class, the plant in the 5th class, crystals and the topographical forms of the landscape in the 6th class, followed by cloud formations, the forms that are created by the flow of water and so on). And the exception? While most class teachers are aware of the indication from Steiner's *Discussions with Teachers* to draw parallels between the various stages of plant evolution and child development, numerous enquiries show that the importance also for Class 5 of the parallel between eagle, lion and bull and the three soul forces (thinking, feeling and willing) is not equally clear. It is one of those cases of where a curriculum topic offers the opportunity to both accompany a step in child development and, at the same time, ensure that the step take place in as mature and firm a way as possible.

As if in the Class 4 mode of animal main-lesson, the eagle—its form, habitat, movements and so on—is first described by the teacher. Similarly with lion and bull. Then, *from the children*, she elicits what she sees as parallels with human thinking. The eagle's talons become a metaphor for the way that thinking can take hold of (a thread of, or a weighty, evasive or challenging) thought. And the metaphor could be reversed. (Might there be room here, one wonders, in Class 6, for future research into the inner connection between the onyx and the sense organ for hearing?) All the while, the teacher, of course, is conducting (guiding) the conversation—the pupils' communal thread of thought. She will, where opportunity arises, also insert touches of her own—sometimes humorous. How bizarre it would be to see the webbed foot of a waddling duck pounce on, and grasp a tasty morsel of waterweed! It all amounts to *understanding the sense phenomenon* (the eagle) not simply through ordinarily responsive ideation (the talons are for grasping its prey) but through a potentised ideation which is not entirely confined to the causal plane. This vital step in the development of sense experience and the correspondingly conscious ideation bears further fruit in the teaching of Goethean science in succeeding classes.

Goethean science

After what I hope has been perceived not as a diversion but as a contribution to our theme like an eagle soaring spirally upward to gain an additionally advantageous standpoint, I shall now proceed to concentrate on an indication of Rudolf Steiner's given in the so-called Supplementary Course[13] with regard to the teaching of science—on this occasion at the top end of the Lower School. Although without claiming to be comprehensive, Aeppli, despite covering so much in his work on the senses, for some reason does not reveal or comment on this particular indication. It is: that after an experiment has been demonstrated in front of the children, the teacher should either stand aside or clear away the apparatus of the experiment and then briefly recap what they have just perceived—*but not in the form of a precise description.* Rather should she, when concentrating on the surprising part of the experiment—what happened after the apparatus has been described and the procedure explained—*exercise her fantasy.*

Each experiment is chosen by the teacher in order to make

---

[13]   R. Steiner *Education for Adolescence*, lecture 3, 14 June 1921.

manifest a phenomenological law. But the Goethean method of teaching which Steiner recommends is not that of stating the so-called law and then proceeding to 'prove' by experiment that it is true. Rather should the children first witness the experiment, take it in with all alertness—with the teacher having ensured that they exercise their senses to the full—and then on a subsequent day try to access through their stimulated thinking what the phenomenon reveals. This pedagogical procedure begins in Class 6, the age and stage of child development in which the power of ideation is ready to make causal sense of what the senses present. When Goethe arrived at the notion of the archetypal plant (*Urpflanze*) he realised that, compared with most prevalent scientific approaches of his day, this could lead to a 'new way of seeing'. Perhaps for children who have experienced 'the way of a child' as followed in a Waldorf school, it might be more accurate to call the activity a new way of reacting to the phenomenon than a new way of seeing.

With the nature stories and the emphasis on animal and plant form that has been a major part of the curriculum in the preceding years, and with the regular artistic work (form drawing, painting, modelling, eurythmy etc.) that has been a continually activating experience for the senses, one would hope that the sense perception of children would be vibrant and ready to question with their growing day-wake consciousness how it is that all the wonders perceived in nature come about. This reading in the book of nature must begin, of course, on the lowest rung of the ladder, with looking at the elementary phenomena of nature—elementary, meaning in the realm of the physical, inorganic elements of colour, sound, heat and so on.

That is where the 'fantasy'-description of the teacher plays in. In Class 6, depending on their chronological age and personal development, children will be enjoying various stages of causal thinking. The teacher's aim will be to facilitate that particular Eureka-moment of meeting the phenomenon observed with the penetrating force of ideation that arrives at the phenomenological law, not just in those children who are naturally inclined towards the subject but in every member of the class. The teacher's 'fantasy' explanation travels through the night between days one and together with what the children's senses witnessed in the experiment. It reaches back, so to speak, to the imaginative world, whence the children are travelling, so that they may continue to look at the phenomenon—now in the mind's eye—with both modes of consciousness: the imaginative consciousness (moving towards its dusk) and the causal form of consciousness (dawning by degrees). The one supplements the other. The teacher, in showing the experiment and in then 'fantasising' brings together the two worlds in a form that acts as a fertilising impulse to the new mode of thinking. Another metaphor would be that of the midwife.[14]

In order to be successful in this, the teacher must herself rise above the pedestrian outer reality of the sense-phenomena towards those spiritual realities which stand behind them. A further education for her etheric.[15]

The implications of the Bern lecture

During the summer of 1924, Steiner gave the short course of lectures we know as *The Roots of Education* to teachers in Canton Bern who had expressed an interest in Waldorf pedagogy. As several of them were already practitioners, he gave the invaluable indication that teacher development could be achieved (either during initial training or through ongoing teacher education)[16] by practising the three arts of modelling, music and speech.

---

[14] Via a phenomenological 'happening' the picture-thinking, characteristic of the 6/7+-year-old, is transformed into the rational mode of thought, which on the one hand is exact, but on the other leaves open the door, so to speak, for further scientific enquiry—ultimately, the birth of a form of science, one could say, which does not *only* take into account the purely physical (quantitative) facts.

[15] One recalls that Jesse Darrell, widely regarded as one of the doyens of class teaching, saw this indication of Steiner's as one of the most important ingredients in the pedagogy of Classes 6, 7 and 8.

The reasons he gave were connected to the teacher's powers of perception. Modelling helps to develop her perception of the child's etheric (formative) forces. Music works on the organ for perceiving the astral nature of the child. Speech awakens the teacher's awareness of the ego. The indication is brief. There are no riders: study music in this or that way; if done through singing, the voice should be produced in this or that manner; the amount of time spent on music during initial training should be such and such; certain styles of musical composition, and the connection with the development of human consciousness, should be anthroposophically understood; the following intervals will engender certain experiences as an important development in human consciousness as related to the future of evolution; it is imperative that all class teachers be able to play the recorder *and* be proficient in teaching it;[17] I could go on. But there was none of that—a hair-tearing nightmare for those who are paranoiac about accreditation, and looking for boxes to tick, whether driven by fear born of a creative vacuum or by the lust for power... In the 1980s when the teacher trainers in the UK met to ensure the quality of anthroposophical teacher training, criteria were set up in which modelling, music and speech were a vitally central element. Courses were permitted to begin when the teacher trainers from all existing courses were unanimous that the proposed new training (not merely a new 'institution' but also a new course being proposed by an existing institution—and the unanimity extended even as far as agreeing who should or should not be tutors!) fulfilled all the criteria. There is currently a move to return to this level of integrity.

Here, to begin with, I wish only to confine myself to modelling.

---

[16] See 'Teacher Training and Teacher Quality in Steiner Education—an interview dialogue with Drs Brien Masters and Richard House' in *New View*, Summer 2007 for an extended discussion on the essential difference between teacher training and teacher education.

[17] Without going into detail, insights which Steiner unveils in other places suggest that such facets of music education would be of benefit to teachers.

Although the reason that Rudolf Steiner gives for the inclusion of this in teacher development is so that the teacher can advance her powers of perception of the etheric nature of the child, it surely implies that the organs by which she does this are in her own etheric. Hence its inclusion here as a prime example of how the teacher can educate her etheric body—in connection with the benefit which passes on (the pedagogical law) to the child's physical body in which the twelve senses are implanted.

Bern and beyond

There is a further implication in this indication of Steiner's, however. The sculptor practises an art that has its origin in that realm of the spiritual world to which the angelic hierarchy primarily belong.[18] Of the seven members of which the human being consists —physical, etheric, astral, ego, spirit-self, life-spirit and spirit-man —the angel has six in common, i.e. all but the physical body. Steiner points out that the angel's seventh member—spiritual beings also have seven members in their constitution—is one degree higher than the human's spirit-man. He simply refers to this as an 8th member without going into detail. The constitution of spirit beings higher than the angelic world (archangels, archai...) leaves off, so to speak, yet another lower member, but gains a further higher member—the archangels' constitution 'begins' at the astral and adds a 9th member.[19]

Thus the arts which Steiner recommends as study, enable us, so to say, to resonate our higher members—etheric, astral etc.—with those higher realms and thus also gain something of those higher influences as inspiration for our work, to whatever degree of consciousness may be the case, this being a matter of destiny.

---

[18]   see R. Steiner *The Influence of Spiritual Beings upon Man,* lecture of 11 June 1908.
[19]   Ibid. lecture of 27 January 1908.

The hierarchies playing into decision making

When we conduct a College Meeting with knowledge of the so-called College Imagination we rely upon the education of our higher members to connect with the angeloi, archangeloi and archai. In the process of discussion, one College member's consciousness—who that is, of course, varies from time to time, as you would expect from a group of colleagues who are all taking seriously the professionally meditative aspect of Waldorf praxis which Rudolf Steiner went into in such depth—accesses the realm of the archai from which the 'drop of light' is then revealed as a hierarchical response to that spiritual striving of all concerned which has taken place at the angelic and archangelic levels. And it is in this that all can recognise the rightness of the 'drop-of-light' illuminated decision.

The tragedy of the mandate system is clearly not that it relieves College of hours of decision-making toil—Steiner makes the importance of *"delegation"* very clear indeed—it needs to be an integral and crucial part of the organisation of a Waldorf school;[20] and to what extent it contributes towards the education of our etheric (our present main focus) we need not dwell on here. No! The tragedy of the mandate system is where it has been sold (and *bought*, sometimes at a considerable financial cost) on the premise of 'groups don't make decisions: it's individuals that make decisions'. If this seemingly heinous misunderstanding or ignoring of what takes place as indicated by the College Imagination essentially eclipses real College working in harmony with the third Hierarchy, then (apart from anything else, fundamental to the spiritually scientific impulse at the heart of a Waldorf or Rudolf Steiner school), the opportunity to educate the teacher's etheric body (astral and ego, too) through this very potent means is undermined.

---

[20] see R. Steiner *Conferences with the Teachers of the Waldorf School,* 24 November 1922 & 31 January 1923.

The battle for humanity has been raging for a long time.[21] I don't know exactly what Churchill had in mind with his "blood, sweat, toil and tears". But three components of that snippet from a war-cry are connected with our fluid organisation, which points us to the etheric body, whose education becomes essential in as many ways as possible, if we intend to take seriously what Rudolf Steiner explained as the pedagogical law.

Conclusion

Of course there is more—much more—to the pedagogical law than what we have confined ourselves to here. It needs continuous research and work. Inset days devoted to it and so on. But however we go about it, it is vital that we include the teacher—that is, the education of the 'higher' members of the teacher—when looking for ways of addressing the increasing barrage of attack that is being launched on our children. The well-known Jesuit adage: 'Get hold of them while they're young' is currently driven by mega-commerce, in league with those powers that would prevent evolution from taking its next progressive step. That is, away from the materialism that is the inexorable and immediate effect of the onset of the Consciousness (Spiritual) Soul.

That, as we are aware, does not mean turning one's back on matter. On the contrary, it means delving into the material (sense-) world with an increasing understanding of it, i.e. with a consciousness that can access the spirit that works in matter. Sense phenomena and advanced ideation once more. This is the urgent need of our time—that which is abundantly addressed in the spiritual science that Rudolf Steiner indefatigably researched and gave out to his fellow Michaelic pupils in a modern, conceptual

---

21 Compare: '[Waldorf education] seems to me to be deeply bound up with the success or failure of Western civilisation, if not of humanity itself as an institution.' in O. Barfield 'Recollections and Observations' in *Owen Barfield, A Waldorf Tribute,* p.45.

form—free of mysticism and free of any organised religion. If we are not rallying under the banners of Lucifer and Ahriman, then we may count ourselves amongst those pupils, and there will be a chance that we have something to offer the next generation of Michaelic pupils who are incarnating into ever more drastically assailed earth conditions.

It is not likely to be an easy ride. We are not likely to avoid many a Via Dolorosa—as I write we are still in the aura of Easter. There will be times when we need to pro-actively overthrow the money tables of those who are desecrating the temple. The opposite too: times when we will need the utmost tolerance, the attitude of 'Father forgive them for they know not what they do'. Something in between too—I do not say in the middle—'Render unto Caesar that which is Caesar's'. But let us be clear: this can never apply to the human spirit in each child. As Waldorf teachers we need to fight energetically against moves which would make children pawns on Caesar's chess board.

So long as there are individuals incarnating—alongside the money grabbers and power seekers—whose spiritual senses are able to read a rainbow as the bridge over which the angel brings the newly-born child to earth, and *at the same time*, notice with the senses that are embedded in the physical body that the newly-become mother has lost her big tummy, there is surely hope that the bridge between spirit and sense-world can be rebuilt.

1973-1980

The occasion when my third class graduated coincided with the end of this seventh septennial phase, in July 1980. It is the phase which falls under the auspices of Mars, a fact which coloured several aspects of life, three of which I share here: the first parochial, the second global, and the third, as I perceive it (though I say it in all modesty) having some evolutionary significance.

My first class graduated in 1966. To celebrate we set off on a long walk on the South Downs. Larks sang overhead; the scent of thyme and marjoram brushed past; bees buzzed with summer-frenzied delight as the sun shone; and the presence of the blue ocean —as one might romantically refer to the English Channel on such a day—added calm to the joy we all felt. No-one commented, and as far as I am aware no-one felt, that this was an unworthy outing to mark—alongside the class leaving play and party—the transition from Lower to Upper School.

By the time it came to 1980, classleaving summer outings had become 'trips', many of enormous proportions, often involving flights abroad. The second-lieutenant in me questioned the pedagogical validity of this, right down to the seeming perfunctoriness of fund-raising through sponsored cycle rides and the like, which seemed to me to have no worthwhile reality—were certainly not an example proudly to present to the emerging ideals of adolescence. From this, with more consultations at all levels than I can remember, was born the Oriana project, a six-week tour of England and Scotland with its main purpose being to show the public and others what 14-year-olds from a Rudolf Steiner school could achieve. The programme included a eurythmy performance of Grimm's *The Seven Ravens*, a class orchestra performance of Mendelssohn's *Trauermarsch* and Chopin's opus 49 *Fantasie* (both arranged for the musically talented class of 32 children) and Shakespeare's *Henry V*. In the present context, let the bare bones suffice: adequate descriptive 'flesh' can be found elsewhere.

It was at the beginning of this phase that my colleagues sent me to visit two weeks of a Class 11 music main-lesson in Stuttgart, with a view to my teaching such main-lessons in the Upper School. The circumstances in Michael Hall which prompted this do not need to be rehearsed here, and there was someone to step in and take main-lesson with my own class while I set off every morning and revelled (if I'm honest) in my pet subject. As it happens, the main-lesson took me to other places—Kings Langley, Edinburgh, Harduf in Israel, Cape Town in South Africa and a host of others.

It also got transposed into a block of teacher training (addressing Steiner's indication in the summer of 1924 that music can give the teacher an insight into the child's astral forces). And the third application was in workshops/lectures/courses given in various settings ranging from Music Academy to laymen who had no musical knowledge and no acquaintance with spiritual science. But why do I attribute global significance to this? From the challenge of getting adolescents to listen with objectivity and interest to Baroque, Viennese Classical, Romantic and other styles of music, and having to find a successful approach when time was of the essence, I discovered that I had been mistaken in what I thought was enemy no.1—the music of the adolescent's favourite pop group! The discovery was in Kings Langley, where I taught several such main-lessons. With one class, who were polite and tolerant, I was reaching the end of the four weeks main-lesson, and felt from the mood in the class and from certain feedback, that they were champing at the bit, wanting to play some of *their* music. I made a space—it was considerable—for each to bring in a tape (yes, tape: that long ago!). To my surprise (musically speaking, though I don't know why I had been so naive) and absolute horror (pedagogically and culturally speaking) *not one* of the class said anything about the music—which was part of the deal: just as I had introduced the snippets of Monteverdi or Carl Philip Emanuel Bach so they were asked to introduce their Beetles choice or whatever. They spoke of the group 'stars', the date of the piece's release and the words, and they expressed what attracted them and why they'd chosen to play it to the class … but not a squeak about the music. My conclusion: what they took to be *their music* (a) was creating a barrier between them and their open-mindedness towards other genres; (b) was not even music in the first place; but (c) worst of all, perhaps, was taken to *be* music—all resulting in an appalling dearth of cultural experience.

Conflict no. 3 was something, well documented, that Rudolf Steiner had himself encountered. Not from the public, with its vehement critics of spiritual science, but from the members of the (then) Theosophical Society: his avowed life task of teaching about concrete karma and giving examples, and sharing his insights into a Western understanding of the phenomenon as well as meditative exercises connected with it. True, there was the unprecedentedly rich year of lectures in 1924, when the problem, encountered at first, was receding. But this wealth was cut off by Steiner's enforced withdrawal from lecturing, due to ill health.

Knowing all this, it was with joy that, in the early 70s, I responded positively to an invitation to join a group to study karmic relationships. We were small in number: William and Liselotte Mann, Joan and Siegfried Rudel, Edith Biermann (recently turned 100) and myself being the regulars. Others—Ursula Koepf and Adam Bittlestone among them—came and went. We occasionally presented the fruit of our corporate research to the branch of the local Anthroposophical Society and once went into print (in the *Golden Blade* of 1977), always in the hope that our efforts would inspire others to pursue karmic studies, either alone or in groups, and at least draw attention to Rudolf Steiner's research, if not further it.

The following essay is an example of precisely that, undertaken finally for a historiography conference in July 2006 organised by the Humanities Section in Britain, though based on a longstanding interest in the Roman poet Ovid. Compared with the article in the Golden Blade (on Ralph Waldo Emerson), which had to be succinct,

I have allowed myself in this one on Ovid/Oliphant to sprawl somewhat. In my mind, I felt justified firstly because of the extraordinarily unparalleled importance Steiner makes about the individuality and secondly because of the puzzlingly few biographical facts extant regarding the Ovid incarnation.

Two Crowns with but a Single Trunk:
Enigmas in the life and karmic background of
Laurence Oliphant
1829-1888

In referring to the fact that history is created by people, Rudolf Steiner went to some lengths to demonstrate that a true understanding of history is therefore only possible by including a consideration of the fruits of people's past lives. During his 10th visit to England in 1924, after the summer school held in Torquay, he returned to Switzerland via London. There in a lecture on karmic relationships (24th August),[1] he suggests that some of the enigmas of history are only explicable by "taking the ideas of karma and putting them to history." One of the outstanding examples of this is to be found in the unification of Italy. Steiner had just referred to the karma of Giuseppe Garibaldi (1807-1882) in this connection when speaking to the members in Arnhem during the previous July—an example he had cited on previous occasions during the year in which he discloses so much of his research into karmic connections.

In the lecture of 24th August Steiner is not concerned with historical events that stand as much in the limelight as does the Risorgimento. Not, at any rate, on first hearing. Time will tell, perhaps, what impact on history individualities he is there referring to will have. Certainly if one delves into the biography of Laurence Oliphant (1829-1888)[2] his connections lead one into the hot spots of history at the tail end of the Gabriel Age (1510-1879). In the case of Ignatius Loyola (1491-1556), too, the founder of Jesuitism, whom Steiner describes in the same lecture as reincarnating as Swedenborg (1688-1772), one can certainly see how his karmic background

---

[1]   Steiner. R., *Cosmic Christianity and the Impulse of Michael*, London 1953, lecture V.

[2]   See Villaneuve, C. (compiler), *Rudolf Steiner in England: a documentation of his ten visits,* Forest Row 2004, for references to Oliphant.

throws light on much that has happened in history—even though as Steiner explains Loyola himself, after death, did not remain united with the Jesuitic stream.

From Loyola-Swedenborg, Steiner goes on to describing how his research led him to spiritual beings ("genii") whose task is the elaboration of karma in the life between death and rebirth. He appears to strike a personal note[3]—though in an objective way— when describing how his investigations brought him before a Mercury genius. At this point in the lecture, he suddenly recalled two books that he had borrowed from London's Theosophical Society's library, written by Oliphant. It emerges that what followed his reading Oliphant's writings was "a figure who stood before me" "very often then". It is not altogether clear whether this figure was the Mercury Genius or that of the individuality Oliphant—probably the former, though there is obviously an intricate connection, one seemingly prompted by Steiner's reading. Perhaps the significance of this research becomes apparent when, en passant, Steiner refers to the initiate knowledge of nature, derived through the Mercury Genius,[4] which was obviously something that surfaced in the medical work that he and Dr Ita Wegman were collaborating over, resulting not only in the lectures to medical doctors and the praxis at Wegman's clinic, but also in the co-authored *Fundamentals of Therapy*.[5]

I am dwelling somewhat on this context a) because Steiner says so little (as far as wordage goes) about Oliphant; and b) because of the two other periods of history that he connects with the Oliphant individuality—the Middle Ages and Rome at the time of Augustus (63 BC-AD 14). Through these references we have a few clues to lead us into an understanding of the individuality with whom we are

---

[3]   Steiner is not often to be found using such extreme expressions as we find in this connection, where he describes how genii began to "interest [him] intensely".

[4]   Steiner,R., op cit. p.71.

[5]   First published in English translation in London, 1938.

concerned: that he had lived as the Roman poet Ovid (43 BC-AD 17) in the previous "significant" incarnation, in whose *Metamorphoses* we have such "wonderful *visions* of the Old Greek Age" (my emphasis); that Oliphant owes his "inspiration to deep cosmic instincts"; and that the being of Ovid was a "guide" to initiates in the Middle Ages(!), the example given by Steiner (to which he had also alluded in Arnhem, though not the connection with Oliphant) being Brunetto Latini (1210-1295), the teacher of Dante (1265-1321).

Admittedly, these are substantial references—amazingly revelatory. Nevertheless, what Steiner says—and possibly, even more, what he does *not* say, presents several enigmas.[6]

a) The first of these which I want to raise here is that Oliphant is a largely forgotten individuality now. If, in his post-Ovid journey in the spiritual world, he had been a leader of initiates, might one not expect to find some greater evidence of his incursion into the recent course of history?

b) A corollary to that: of those who reviewed the biographies that appeared since his death—not counting the biography by Margaret Oliphant, a distant relative by marriage—there is hardly any mention of Oliphant's *spiritual development*.[7]

c) Why does Steiner, who clearly regarded Ovid-Oliphant as a remarkably outstanding figure (of "most far-reaching import"),

---

[6] The review of Henderson's biography (see below), which appeared in the *Daily Telegraph* on 26 Oct 1956, encapsulates some of the enigmas well. And two weeks later on November 11th in the Sunday *Observer*, the reviewer of the same biography (Harold Nicholson, whose father knew Oliphant personally in the late 1880s, and from whom he gained important 'first-hand' impressions), closes with the same sentiment: "a fascinating [life] which leaves us very perplexed".

[7] The Oliphant scholar coming closest to appreciating this faculty is Anne Taylor in her biography, *Laurence Oliphant*, Oxford 1982. On the whole, she presents the faculty as one of prophecy; see, for example, p.161: "Once again [Oliphant] foresaw events lying in the future."

not even refer to him on his return to Dornach, as he did in the case of other individualities of whom he had spoken during his summer travels?[8]

d) In view of the seemingly profound influence that Thomas Lake Harris (1823-1906) had on Oliphant—at the very least on his outer circumstances—why is there no hint of this in what Steiner has to say in London (knowledge of his connection had, after all, been in the public domain for over 50 years)?[9] Nor of what could be regarded as something of a parallel event (karmically parallel) in the biography of Ovid: his banishment (or 'relegation' to be more legally precise) from Rome?

e) Is there any significance in the fact that Steiner refers to Swedenborg as the reincarnated Loyola in the same lecture? That is to say, apart from the fact that it is well known that both Harris and Oliphant had a high regard for certain aspects of Swedenborg's philosophy? The description Steiner gives of the importance of the spiritual genii in his research, and the part they play in the karmic development of Loyola-Swedenborg etc., would suggest that there is some connected significance in the case of Ovid-Oliphant. How far can we go with this assumption without straying into misleading speculative byways?

f) Finally, seeing that the case of Ovid-Oliphant is summed up by

---

[8] Not that no-one in Dornach would have been aware of Oliphant. It is more than likely, for instance, that Marie Steiner von Sievers would have been present at the esoteric lesson given by Steiner on 1 December 1906 in Cologne, in which he cites Oliphant—his upbringing in a household in which the parents were loving towards one another as well as towards him, his (and his wife Alice's) giving over their inheritance 'to the poor' as Steiner puts it (presumably tactfully, in view of the known facts concerning Harris), their vision in Palestine, and the subsequent writing of *Scientific Religion* at his deceased wife's dictation—as an example of the effectiveness of the second line (of four) of the mantram he is using as a basis for the lesson.

[9] See Taylor, op cit. especially Chapter 6.

Steiner as "one of the most illuminating you could find",[10] the question naturally arises: illuminating what?

Ovid

Let us approach these enigmas first by entering into the known biographical facts of the individuality concerned, proceeding chronologically.

A great deal of our knowledge of Ovid's biography has arisen through interrogating his extensive oeuvre, generally acknowledged to be greater than any other Classical author. There are not all that many obvious biographical references, however, not judged by the trendy standards of present-day chunky-paper-back biographies, memoirs, and the like—nor, indeed, by the increase in biographical literature in Rome seen beside that of Ancient Greece. So, on the one hand, the various references smack of author after author trawling incessantly through the same biographical waters; while on the other, because the facts are embedded extensively in verse, it allows different perspectives to open up; and that is what is being attempted in the present study.

Publius Ovidius Naso—his full name—though born in the countryside east of Rome (20 March 43 BC), essentially he throve in the atmosphere of the big city. The father was wealthy enough to set both of his sons, educationally, on a senatorial career. It would seem that Ovid went handsomely through all the paces—and, indeed, was technically able enough, but that the prospect of a career that would enable him to rise to the top of the senatorial ladder did not concur with his inner nature. After two minor magistracies he renounced his career. Looked at through hindsight, perhaps one could say that what he gained through rhetoric, a central component of Roman education—and in his case, learnt from a distinguished tutor—was ultimately transformed into his poetic writing. His stepping out naturally disappointed the father initially, but, seeing that the latter

---

[10]   Steiner, op cit.

lived until the age of 90, he came to recognise the fame that was accorded his only heir—Ovid's brother, Lucius, having died young. The death of the brother had positive implications for Ovid, obviating the necessity for him to become harnessed to a career which carried remuneration. It would seem Ovid was well aware of this good fortune, stating (in *Amores* I.15) that his art was more important than wealth, and that his one aim was to be a poet and thereby fulfil himself and satisfy his public. This he certainly achieved, launching himself between the ages 20-25 in the congenial company of other young poets and socialising with the 'idle rich'— the idleness clearly being a breeding ground for the relaxation of morals and a concomitant increase in divorces. A heartening fact in all this, however, which, later in life, he clearly had taken to be a nod of destiny, was that his peers encouraged and admired him as a poet (*utque ego maiores, sic me coluere minores—Tristia* IV.10).[11]

On the domestic front, we know that he had three marriages and was twice a grandfather. However, when his exile from Rome struck (in AD 8), he did not compel his wife to suffer the same fate. Based on a passage in one of the works (*Amores*), despite the fact that in its totality it irritated the emperor Augustus (in that Ovid appears to address lovers rather than wives), we can deduce that there was a fair degree of conjugal happiness in the home—in a nutshell, words to the effect: honour your lady with devotion. However, though he does not speak of excess, he also admits that in him was a streak of the unreformed flirt (*Amores* II.4). Indeed, he seems to revel in playing to the gallery in this respect: there are passages in his *Ars Amatoria* III that read like the blurb of a modern beauty parlour, with recipes for various cosmetics—rouge, face powder, eye-brow pencils etc. with explicit reference to improving the complexion. *However,* the gold dust in all this welter of society-matrix is clearly there when he exhorts the young ladies, whom he is largely

---

[11]   Poetry seems to have oozed out of his very being—it was even said that his everyday speech was like poetry put into prose.

addressing, to see to their moral character first and foremost (*at primum vobis morum tutela petatis*). Augustus, on the other hand, clearly felt unequivocally that his crusade (if that is not too strong a term) for moral reform was being undermined by Ovid's all-too-popular pot-boilers, his advocating that good taste must go hand in hand with beauty, notwithstanding. And although Ovid himself was showing signs of superficiality-fatigue (already in *Amores* II) where he expressed how he feels called to more serious (*graviore*) writing —and it would seem, moreover, that the new style and content is what he wanted to be remembered for (*post mea mansuram fata superstes opus*)—when it came to the crunch and the fatal incident occurred, Ovid's part in which Augustus never forgave, neither the *Fasti* (the calendar of the Roman year written prior to AD 8) nor the *Metamorphoses* (on the way to completion by AD 7) had any significant effect—works, of course, that were to form the substance of scholarly discipline and thought for centuries in the shaping of European culture. An indictment of imperial judgment? Hardly, if one takes into account that an emperor who had banished both daughter and granddaughter, no less, from Rome on account of their blatant sexual indiscretions, thereby making a notoriously public example of his own flesh and blood, was hardly likely to be mollified by lines of poetry, never mind what they might come to mean for posterity.[12] Ovid pleaded for pardon—many critics would say ad nauseam. He grovelled more intensely even than Horace (d.8 BC) the poet laureate had done—extolling Augustus in the years following the title given to him in 2 BC of 'Sancta Pater Patriae' (*Fasti* II) as the earthly manifestation of Jupiter (*hoc tu per terras,*

---

[12] In view of the scandal at the very time he was making efforts to bring about reform, he asked the Senate for the legal penalty. Of the two main lovers, Tullus Anthony committed suicide and young Graechus was banished, while Julia was to suffer an exile in Pandateria that, like Ovid's, was never rescinded, off the coast near Naples. Like mother, like daughter, the younger Julia, also discovered in adultery, was banished to the isle of Trimerus off the Apulian coast, where she died after some twenty years.

quod in aethere Juppiter alto). But Augustus remained obdurate: Tomis, the place of Ovid's exile, was also the place where he was to die—in AD 17.

To what extent does the life of Ovid shed light on the above enigmas? Comparatively little, perhaps, at first sight, though we shall find several obvious correspondences between the two lives. In fact, the veil which history has largely drawn over the Ovid banishment is an enigma in its own right, let alone as a background to one who becomes a force in the Middle Ages (guiding initiates)— something that sounds as if it is tantamount to a spiritual influence emanating from the ranks of the hierarchies themselves.

Oliphant

In the case of Oliphant, the sand-smoothing tides of time have had infinitely less opportunity to allow the document-based facts to evade the biographer's search. So much so, in fact, that it will be necessary to be highly selective if we are going to get a satisfying overview of the karmic wood amongst the plethora of biographical trees.

Oliphant was born in Cape Town in 1829. He was descended from the Oliphants of Gask, a Scottish family whose main claim to fame is the family link with Robert the Bruce. Thus Oliphant had Scots blood—with all the firm social connections that that implied in the 19th century—while at the same time living when the British Empire sprawled across the world.[13] The father, Sir Anthony, was among those in the highest of diplomatic circles—he was Attorney-General in the Cape at the time of Oliphant's birth, and afterwards Chief-Justice in Ceylon—and had an interest in the occult, but to

---

[13]   As far as his inner character is concerned, the crystalline and granite-like certainty of Scottish thinking would seem to have been ideally mingled with the *sang froid* of the British diplomat. "However fuming," he once remarked, having observed his seniors under the extreme stress of the negotiating table, "they never showed it by impulsive action." This ability, of course, has considerable bearing on the inner life, albeit transformed.

what degree this affected Laurence appears unknown. Lady Oliphant, his mother, devoted her whole life after her husband's death, seemingly without reservation, to the brand of spirituality cultivated by Harris in America. She was instrumental in introducing Lawrie (the parents' familiar name for their son) to Harris and, long before that, maintained a keen interest in Oliphant's inner life, a fact substantiated in their copious correspondence.[14] Though the deeper connection appears to have been between mother and son, the family were an intimate trio, whose relationships were of the finest quality, verging on piety.[15]

It was partly due to this strong family (clannish?) bond that Oliphant 'escaped' a rigidly formal education (i.e. British public school followed by Oxbridge), though this appears to have been a distinctive quality in Oliphant that was discernible not so much in his character but only on paper.[16] His inability to secure a high diplomatic position, despite weighty efforts on his part,[17] string-pulling presumably, and fiery ambition, has been attributed to that.[18] Again we may read into this fact of destiny, an element that saved him from the danger of getting 'stuck' in the rut of the Civil Service

---

[14] This could be partly attributed to the self-examination which her evangelical background encouraged even in childhood, but it went much further than that. See Taylor op cit. p.2.

[15] It is, perhaps, a measure of family closeness that Oliphant, being on the high seas when his father died, related how he "saw" Papa on board in the night and realised when the news came through that it had been the night of his death. This seems to be too isolated an occurrence in his life simply to be brushed aside as a relic of the Celts' 'second-sight'. At the same time, to incarnate into two hereditary Scottish streams might indicate a predisposition for some degree of spiritual awareness. Taylor (op cit. p23) recounts how, after his wife's death on 2 January 1886, their spiritual relationship manifested in a remarkable way: one night, when he was still deeply mourning "the light seemed to burst through and she came to me so radiant ... that my own grief seemed to be lifted..."

[16] There was, in fact, a brief time (8-12 years of age) when he attended a boarding school in Salisbury.

[17] Taylor (op cit. p.68) depicts him as agonising over how to "persuade the panjandrums of the Foreign Office to recognise him".

or the War Office and thus butterfly-pinned onto the cork board of
political conformity.[19] Even when the possibility of a change—
through Cambridge and studying English law—came his way in his
late teens, he slipped through the net, and, instead of taking the
conventional academic bull by the horns, dallied with a Scottish
legal training (because it was quicker!), and thence embarked on his
colourful life.

Adventurousness was in any case already a strong trait in his
make-up—witness the well-documented elephant hunt in which he
participated![20] In what appear as his wild-oat days this went to
extremes in the lawless exploit from New Orleans to Nicaragua.
When captured, it was his family connection that saved his skin,
whereas his confederate was hanged as a filibustering pirate.[21] Even
professional adventure features in his early life, where he is known
to have taken part in 23 cases of murder trials, practising as an
unqualified barrister in Ceylon, where his father was posted! But
apart from this, four outstanding qualities in his character deserve
mention here in relation to these early years and in view of our
present study.

a) He was extremely *popular* in high society[22]—wherever he
    went, life brought him into connection with those who were

---

[18] In 1865 he was elected as MP for Stirling, but a) Westminster must have
    seemed intellectually as well as geographically claustrophobic in the extreme
    compared with his adventurous sallies of the recent past into countries across
    the globe; and b) his future destiny—the meeting with Harris etc.—and the
    huge change of direction that this was to bring about in his life, was immanent.

[19] He refused the offer of Lieutenant Governor in the West Indies, on this score.

[20] See Oliphant, Margaret, *Laurence Oliphant*, Edinburgh 1891 (7th edition) I.45f.

[21] See Taylor op cit. pp.42-45.

[22] Oliphant, for example, was a member of both the St James Club and the
    Athenaeum. He was welcome both at Osborne and Marlborough House while
    already in his early twenties he made close friends with Jung Bahadur Rana, the
    de facto ruler of Nepal.

leaders in their several spheres.[23] This, in turn, led to his being sent many times by Palmerston, the Prime Minster, Russell (of the Foreign Office) and others on special-agent-type missions to various hot spots across the world.

b) He was a gifted *author* and always on the lookout for something to write, his travel and adventure books receiving popular acclaim.[24]

c) He had an *inner life* that was remarkable for the times—we become aware of this through his correspondence with his mother which was profuse. In it, he shares his 'know-thyself' perceptions and makes clear his moral standpoint even on apparently perfunctory matters, these being unavoidable in the society in which he found himself.[25]

d) Particularly bold features are his interest in and leaning towards the *supernatural and mystical*. Notwithstanding his

---

[23] Famously, there is the incident to which his cousin Margaret Oliphant refers in her two-volume biography (I.244f) when he found himself booked into the same railway carriage as Garibaldi on the eve of the latter's sailing to Sicily with 'the thousand', and witnessed the revolutionary hero tearing pieces of paper into shreds—the names of volunteers—thus covering the floor of the compartment 'ankle deep' with them until it resembled 'a giant waste paper basket' (and this is not the end of the story)! Then there was the occasion, shortly after in 1862, when he 'bumped into' the Prince of Wales in Vienna! These are two examples. In the case of Garibaldi, we read in Steiner's lectures that he underwent an initiation in the Hibernian mysteries in a previous incarnation. In view of his post-Ovidian role in the Middle Ages as 'guide' to initiates, one wonders which of the other world leaders he met in the Oliphant incarnation might have had similar karmic backgrounds. At all events, the young Oliphant's bafflement—"Why I should take such an interest in affairs that don't concern me, I don't know" (I.249)—strongly suggests that it must be connected with the karma of those leaders which he, if he has had a 'guiding influence' in the past, is only *indirectly* party to.

[24] Another outcome of these two traits—thirst for adventure and highly gifted writer—is his gift for languages. For instance, despite the typically British superficiality which prevailed, resulting in the linguistically lazy brush with which its people have so frequently been tarred, Oliphant had no hesitation in launching into Turkish or other languages as the need arose in his life.

detestation of what he called 'popular Christendom', against which he launched a "perpetual assault",[26] he experienced deeply religious feeling together with what he terms his "intuitions and revelations" though it is difficult to assess fully what these might have been before the appearance of his books *Scientific Religion* and *Sympneumata* began to lift the veil.[27]

It was in 1867 that he followed Harris to America and began his mendicant-like life in the community at Brocton.[28] Could it have been a further ramification of the family's evangelical leanings? Sir

---

[25] Margaret Oliphant, op cit. I.208 and I.261 in which it becomes transparent that Oliphant's inner life gives him a clear perception of his own divine nature—"in God's hands" as he puts it on one of the occasions when he had cause to feel his life was endangered. There can be little doubt that he based his inner life on the purification of his own 'lower forces', desires etc., a fact strongly affirmed by Steiner in a lecture given 15 Oct 1916 in which he emphasises that Oliphant purified this 'polarity' in his being. But there is the other side to the story, where the strength won through strenuous inner discipline bursts out— reminiscent, in some ways, of the inner forces that build up before a volcanic eruption. His first biographer alludes to this (I.135) when conveying his views on many of his fellow parliamentarians and their pursuit of an "unendurable [life] which he ... could support no longer; ... that no-one, except a few powerless individuals, cared for the country or the real benefit of people, but each party for the real benefit it could win over the other...' This sudden burst of indignant disgust with the realities of life, so fiery and lofty in tone, so unexpected from those easy yet eloquent lips, to which banter and jest seemed more familiar than denunciation..."

[26] Ibid. I.239.

[27] To be in his publisher's shoes must have been distinctly uncomfortable at times in this respect. On the one hand there were the successful sales; on the other, how were they (Blackwood of Edinburgh) to appear to be party to such apparently extreme views concerning the 'establishment'? This tight-rope-walking situation is well exemplified in correspondence in which the publisher suggests that it might be tactful to 'let sleeping dogs lie' where the popular church is concerned, to which Oliphant replies: "It is just the sleeping dogs that I am determined to poke up. They have no business to be asleep..."

[28] He remained there for three years, that is, until embarking on the Spirit-Self phase of his life.

Anthony is known to have been a follower of Edward Irving, a revivalist preacher with the same genuine streak that Oliphant initially saw in Harris. The puzzling extent to which he leashed himself to Harris's ideas is compounded by his persuading his young wife Alice Strange to share in the communal life there where, though newly wed—a wedding held at the fashionable St George's, Hannover Square, London, albeit with a bare minimum of guests— they were deprived of living together. Also by the fact that he and Alice, as well as Lady Oliphant, made over most of their wealth to Harris—in good faith, presumably, despite the fact that when the shadow side of Harris's character became painfully evident, Oliphant took him to court, 'for robbery' as one commentator put it, and was able to regain some of his losses. Despite this, he was unusually discreet when referring to Harris, a sense of loyalty which expressed itself freely also regarding other acquaintances.[29]

After the break with Harris, he and Alice were reunited, left America for ever,[30] and were immediately welcomed back into those ranks of society which Oliphant had enjoyed in earlier years. But they did not stay long in Europe, travelling until eventually making their home in Palestine on Mount Carmel near Haifa in the proximity of a biblical site connected with Elijah.[31] When Alice died, the Druses and others in the neighbourhood mourned her as a saint and treasured her memory, such was the impression she had made in a comparatively short time. Oliphant remained on Carmel

---

[29] Harris is a compound character. The 13th edition of the *Encyclopaedia Britannica* singles out certain traits, among which are the following. He had the gift of improvisation in a very high degree. He purchased land on which he set up a wine industry claiming that his vintage was "filled with divine breath". [D.N. Dunlop, who had visited Harris in America, retailed some of these wines in Dublin for a short time!] He held the view that God is bi-sexual. He was originally honest. He withdrew from the public in 1876. His followers [certainly not Oliphant by this time] clung for three months to the belief that his death on 23 March 1913 was only a sleep. Oliphant presented what is generally acknowledged to be a picture of him in his novel *Masollam*.

[30] ... except at the time his mother died.

and wrote 'at her dictation'[32] his final work, published, as had been his other books, by William Blackwood and Sons of Edinburgh. The froth and entertainment of his earlier writings were totally absent in his last works, causing the society that had been enchanted by his writing hitherto to be completely dumbfounded. As referred to earlier,[33] the perplexity caused by the two tiers of Oliphant's existence had in no way diminished in most quarters, even after three-quarters of a century. It could hardly have been otherwise unless one followed Steiner's lead, deeper into the vault of karma.

This ensuing silence and disbelief could be taken as symptomatic of what it was like for humanity to wrench itself from a way of life and thought that had become inextricably bound up with materialism, and in doing so find a new approach to, or re-connection with the spiritual world. There are historical 'symptoms' which substantiate this: the greed which grew rather than abated with the expanding empires of Europe; the generations-long struggle that the abolition of slavery—after the Enlightenment—took to bring into effect the removal of any of the residual racism that lurks in the emerging cosmopolitanism of our time; the unshakeable stance of positivistic scientific thought despite many sincere doubts 'at the top' as to its validity, in persistently ruling out, as knowledge,

---

[31] Biographically it may be of minor interest that many of the colonising Jews at the time came from Romania, from the district to which Ovid had been exiled. This was partly the result of the Russian pogroms. Oliphant made it clear that, while he was not 'pro-Semitic', he supported the Zionist movement as it was then expressing itself.

[32] This remarkable fact is communicated in the postscript to the Preface of *Scientific Religion*. "Her thoughts entered mine as if they were my own." Her input into the previous book had taken place, probably also in the summer house on Mount Carmel, before she died. In the esoteric lesson given by Steiner on 1 December 1906 (referred to above), he attaches some importance to the *place* where this 'dictation' had occurred, it also being the room in which Alice had died. What Oliphant himself does not say is that (and this is according to Steiner) the spiritual thread which linked them snapped after a short time—presumably, his writing of *Scientific Religion* then stopped.

[33] Nicholson, H., op cit.

anything that cannot be (physically) weighed and measured; the yawning gap that existed between biblical Christianity, for want of a better term, and the lip-service paid to it 'at home' amongst the affluent and, if one looked behind appearances, amongst so-called missionaries in the colonies abroad.

Being born and raised on the cushion of colonial glitter, so to speak, Oliphant met all of this head on, and ostensibly went with the flow of the superficiality that resulted from a society morally blinkered by its own materialistic success. It is clear from his correspondence with his mother, however, and by the unmistakable gesture of his life as a whole, that the revolt seething in his inner nature was never far beneath the surface in the earlier part of his life, while standing nakedly revealed in the last years. The enormous effort that he and Alice put into rehabilitating Jews into their land of origin (with strangely karmic overtones that the effort was successful with Jews from the western shores of the Black Sea, the place of his Ovidian exile, because they were technically citizens of the Ottoman empire)[34] could be seen as a metaphor for his/their anxious drive to *restore humanity as a whole to a spiritual state*, at least the equivalent of its pristine (androgynous) beginning. Somewhere, too, the enigmatic years in which he seemed to be bowing to some—*bizarre* it appeared to the outside world and probably in some measure still to most of us today—spiritual supremacy he apparently saw in the person of Harris, cannot simply be overlooked or altogether effaced as if those years had never been. Inescapably, they have somehow to be dovetailed neatly into the total biographical picture.

Correspondences

Looking at the biographies side by side, resonances between the two (Oliphant and Ovid) certainly become immediately apparent.

---

[34] The first colonists arrived in Palestine in autumn 1882 (Taylor, op cit. p.212).

1. Both Ovid and Oliphant were born into families whose life-
    styles were the outcome of national wealth. The Roman
    Empire in Augustus' day was at its height. The British Empire
    reached its zenith in Queen Victoria's reign. Ovid was 12 years
    old when the Pax Augustus settled over the conquered world
    and the last convulsions of a dying republic were spent. At the
    end of his life, Oliphant poignantly and pointedly reflects
    (*Sympneumata* 268): "The slow degradation that corrupts the
    pleasure-seekers, results, as malady, from the hyper-
    development to which they urge a limited set of faculties, and
    the absolute atrophy to which they leave the larger wealth of
    those with which as human beings they are necessarily
    endowed." Phrases like: the world is a gigantic lunatic
    asylum,[35] a perception which ran parallel with Oliphant's
    decreasing appetite for gaiety, resonate powerfully with Ovid's
    distasteful summing up of Roman Society, as consisting of
    three careers—money-making, gaining power, and the avid
    desire to exercise authority—compounded with the bitter
    observation that all else was pleasure-seeking (*otium*). And this
    was despite the fame of Virgil and Horace, the company of
    whose followers he eagerly sought. His whole being recoiled
    from the sordid greed which he was surrounded by, if not
    embroiled in, and the brutality of war, a somewhat out-of-focus
    prelude to the fact that Oliphant, as a war correspondent, was
    frequently in the thick of it—be it in the Polish insurrection in
    January 1863, the Crimean, the Franco-Prussian War or
    elsewhere. Yet one must bear in mind that despite the military
    genius that others recognised in his potential (cf. the advice he
    gave over the Crimean, and the mistaken identity of him as
    'top brass')[36] and despite his eagerness to procure a 'position'

---

[35]   See Henderson, P., *The Life of Laurence Oliphant*, London 1956, p.130.

[36]   As an ancillary to his duties as War Correspondent, so to speak, he would
       conceive an entire plan of campaign for a forthcoming engagement—as in the
       case of Balaclava.

for himself that would attract status in the fashionable society to which he was attached, he remained adamant about not being "a soldier".[37]

2. Perhaps, as a brief aside, some may see significance in the fact that Oliphant's first book led to his being viewed as a source of extremely valuable information regarding the very part of the world (the western shore of the Black Sea) in which, as Ovid, he had lived so many years in banishment—not that he could complain of overbearing Roman control there.

3. It was nevertheless a fact that Ovid's father was ranked next below the Senate (and who therefore had the means to launch sons on senatorial careers), a fact that perhaps resulted in his punishment being no worse than it was for whatever discretion he was deemed to have committed. Not that Augustus jibbed at meting out severity where he considered it was due—witness his treatment of the two Julias—but he was also a ruler with principles, and Ovid could not have been seen as a threat to the State's political security. Might there also have been an element of his popularity among the nobles that tempered Augustus' sentencing? His writings were well received, especially as, to begin with, they chimed in with the free and easy manner of Roman society at the time. Be that as it may, there is no doubt whatsoever that Oliphant connected hand-in-glove with the upper classes wherever he went—from meeting

---

[37] C.N. Scott, in his *Memoirs*, describes the presence which all and sundry obviously experienced in Oliphant (from Generals to guardsmen) as "something uncanny". It appears even to have come across in print, judging by the reaction of the War Office when his book on the Crimea appeared and a mounted orderly rode to his house in Half Moon Street, summoning him to report and elaborate on what he knew of the Sebastopol environment! Nicholson (op cit.) comments that if the authorities had attached greater credence to his account of the Sebastopol defences the war would have been curtailed. Taylor (op cit. p.165) comments that although he was often abroad as a journalist, his reception seemed more appropriate for an ambassador. We shall further examine this aspect of his character later.

Queen Victoria at Balmoral, or her sister Princess Alice in London, to being genuinely mistaken for a Turkish officer, to his salmon-leap as attaché to the Governor of Canada, to hobnobbing with the Prince of Wales, to ... to ... Even at the eleventh hour, when he and Alice, belatedly on honeymoon, were in Spain they "ran across King Amadeo" who invited them to join him on his royally decked-out frigate for a sailing trip. A coincidence? So Oliphant said, "but it was of the special Oliphant kind which habitually delivered him to the source of potential trouble or upheaval.[38]

4. It was through such society strata that he was invited to accompany Lord Elgin[39] on his North American mission where Oliphant, still in his early twenties, proved to be a remarkably suave negotiator.[40] Again the parallel is there when Ovid, appreciated as an orator, accompanies Aemilius Macer of Verona on his tour of Asia.

5. In both incarnations travel featured prominently. In 'real' terms these may have been similar. In actual terms, however, the means of global travel having increased enormously during the intervening centuries, Oliphant covered infinitely more ground —from Japan in the Far East, to California in the far West. Not only that, he considered travel, for him, to be equivalent to education. A modern tourist can, of course, cover the same ground in a fraction of the time, but apart from a rich album of snapshots, and no doubt some intriguing anecdotes, he is

---

[38] Taylor, op cit. p.173, who comments that Oliphant's part in the dilemma in which Amadeo found himself was "maddeningly unclear". Again, one is reminded of Steiner's 'take the ideas of karma and put them to history'.

[39] James Bruce, 8th Earl of Elgin.

[40] He acquired several feathers in his cap in this respect throughout his life, stepping in to play a central role in the Paris peace talks in 1870 after they looked like breaking down; he was at the negotiating table at the Treaty of Tientsin regarding navigation on the Yang Tze, he negotiated the sale of land that 'belonged' to the American Indians, on behalf of the Government, and so on.

unlikely to have anything remotely approaching the output of Oliphant's travel books (for want of a better word) to show for it.

6. This brings us to education itself—not as close a parallel in the two lives as are other aspects listed here, but nevertheless, having a similar nuance. Ovid's education differed little from that of other Roman lads, at least to begin with. From that point of view, one could count him as embedded in the culture of his day. However, as his birth coincided with a new age in Roman literature, coincident with the Pax Romana, his leaning towards poetry was easily fuelled by connection with his like-minded contemporaries such as Bassus, Ponticus and Propertius.[41] A career in literature was not exactly what his politically eminent father had in mind, though, and despite or perhaps *because of* being aware of how poetry came to his son with "fatal ease"[42]—with Oliphant it was prose—he expressed his disapproval in no uncertain terms. Ovid's well known reply speaks for itself!

> *O father dear, make it no worse*
> *I vow I'll never more write verse...*

With Oliphant his 'escaping' the traditional education for boys of his class—packed off back to England for gruelling years in boarding school and then to read at university (probably Classics: *Ovid* and co!!)—is more life shaping. His wide reputation was the result of his 'pen' rather than any high ranking position in parliament or the Civil Service.[43] Indeed, his failure to secure such a position has been attributed to his out-of-line academic background, a fact which most commentators communicate with a hint of 'poor old Oliphant',

---

[41] Two stylistic influences deserve mention here: the flamboyant style of Marcus Porcius Latro from the west and that of the Asiatic virtuoso Arellius Fuscus.

[42] See Rand, E.K., *Ovid and his Influence.*

rather than the connotation I am attaching to it as a *saving grace* which released instead of confined his energies and prodigious talents. I am further emboldened in taking this stance by Steiner's emphasising[44] that a person's education is not likely to give the investigator karmic clues. Nor was it wealth that endeared him to his wide circle of high-society friends. When first returning from Brocton in 1879, his depleted financial state was abundantly evident: when being met at rural railway stations for country house parties, where he was invited as before by the 'great and good', he had to wait for the train to move forward so that 3rd class passengers could alight.[45] But he came through such embarrassments, and through the curiosity and ridicule of what people surmised his life with Harris must have been, basically unscathed.

7. It would be unfair if, at this point (regarding education), a word were not put in for the connection that the individuality with whom we are concerned had—in both incarnations—with law. This is not particularly surprising in Ancient Rome, where law held as integral a place in the educated classes' education as the multiplication tables held in latter days.[46] In Oliphant's case, too, it was commonplace for sons to follow in their father's footsteps, at least with the first born—and in his case

---

[43] This lack of formal education did not appear to limit the esteem in which others held him. He met other war correspondents, of course, and one of them, whom he met in Paris, refers directly to the impression he made, of one who was a "highly cultured, very intellectual and greatly gifted Englishman" (see Lord Dunraven's *Memoirs* Vol.1). However, the fact that his only Government 'employment' in June 1862—1st Secretary of Legation in Japan—lasted only 10 days(!), due to the life-threatening danger to which he had been subjected and the resultant concern for his mother's peace of mind, needs no further comment.

[44] op cit. p.57.

[45] See Taylor, op cit. p.148.

[46] Ovid, of course, did take his law studies as far as *laticlave* before abandoning them; and it has been noted that his knowledge of law has filtered through in the form of legal terms sprinkled throughout his poetry.

there were no siblings. No-one would have batted an eyelid if Lawrie had gone through the mill of being called to the bar and eventually securing some exalted, possibly enviable, diplomatic post. But in both incarnations, life took a different turn. I have said enough about Ovid. In Oliphant's case there were three stages in his somewhat truncated legal career: firstly practising unofficially *but for real* in Ceylon, secondly spending time at Lincoln's Inn embarking officially on his legal training, while thirdly abandoning this and swanning off to the less arduous training required to qualify in Scotland— which, in turn, soon apparently palled so that it was good-bye for ever to anything resembling an official legal career. However, there is an aspect of law that was supremely concordant with Oliphant's inner nature, to which we shall return when considering what Steiner refers to as the Mercury genius.

8. Thus we see Ovid and Oliphant, despite their self-groomed and highly regarded family backgrounds, set adrift essentially as freelance writers: Ovid principally as poet, Oliphant initially as journalist, novelist and travel writer—watersheds in their lives, one might say, where the hereditary stream fully gave way to that of the incarnating ego. In this, we find them both hard working—witness their output—and exercising a degree of self-control a cut above those around them, where Ovid could easily have gone the way of drink and dissipation; and where the young Oliphant likewise could have easily reflected in his inner life what appeared on the surface as being ensconced in endless partying (he "sugar-doodles the ladies", as Edward VII vividly yet off-handedly put it!). We know from his opening his heart in his letters home to Lady Oliphant, his mother, that that was far from the truth of what was unfolding in his inner life. An extract from one of his letters touching on this

follows.[47]

> "My experience has always been very slow indeed, and
> while I recognise that an important change has been going
> on in my sentiments upon many things, still I feel as much
> embarrassed and perplexed as I ever did. Not that I am
> rendered in any way so miserable as I used to be, nor that
> I ever experience those violent revulsions of feeling; but
> wherever there is a struggle there must be times of
> depression. It is a merciful thing that I take little pleasure
> in that gaiety in which I am obliged to mix, and by which
> formerly I should have been intoxicated. And perhaps the
> pleasure of life seems much diminished by the reflection
> that one must be in a dangerous condition if one is not
> sacrificing some favourite passion, however much it may
> be changed by the progress of time etc. etc... My
> difficulty is to realise divine things sufficiently to
> encourage me. The strongest incentive I have to follow
> my convictions upon such subjects is the inward peace
> and comfort which doing so has always brought to me,
> and the opposite effect of indulging myself. Therefore
> upon the lowest grounds I am disposed to practise self-
> denial."

9. Surely his sojourn in Brocton and his way of life there has a lot
    to do with this. When Ovid was sent to Tomis to life-exile in
    AD 8, the fact that whatever it was that he witnessed was
    classified as 'relegation' rather than the more culpable
    banishment, a sentence for which neither Augustus nor his
    successor, Tiberius, granted him reprieve, did not alter the
    radical change that the exile brought about in his way of life.[48]
    Although Tomis had no library to which Ovid could refer, he

---

[47]   See Margaret Oliphant, op cit. I.116.

completed what is often considered his magnum opus there, the *Metamorphoses*, the amazingly comprehensive account of the Greek myths, from which posterity has derived so much of its knowledge of this aspect of Greek culture. Commentators, in pointing to this have attempted to explain the phenomenon as the result of Ovid's prodigious memory—and of course he may have had just that. Steiner refers to the *Metamorphoses* as Ovid's 'visions'. In the likelihood that he was not merely using the term 'vision' as a sort of metaphorical cliché—it just doesn't sound like Steiner—it would be fair to conclude that the *Metamorphoses* arose, not (or not only) through any prodigious memory but through some unusual mental access to the Imaginative realm from which derive those truths of human evolution which are encapsulated in mythology—in this case influencing (guiding?) generation after successive generation.[49] In turn, this would imply some level of initiate consciousness either directly at work or at least filtering through. Might the breakthrough to that consciousness have been occasioned by the drastic life-change from Rome to the hostile bleakness of the western shore of the Black Sea? —Whether it was residual from a past initiation or not? And might one not view in parallel fashion the move of Oliphant—as self-exiled, so to say —whether authoritatively forced by Harris or not, to Brocton? Not just the move, of course: the life-style of humility,

---

[48]   The climate compared with that of Rome unfavourably, the landscape appeared bleak to him, and people carried weapons. Poetry, he said, kept him singing, like a slave chained to the oars!

[49]   In a lecture in which he refers to Oliphant, of 15 Oct 1916, Steiner points out that it is through the life ether that free spiritual imaginations arise within the soul. Had Ovid's incarnation been earlier (and in Greek culture) his gift of imagination might not have appeared so head and shoulders above his contemporaries. Even so, it would have indicated his exceptional connection with the etheric world. It is worth noting in this context that his poetry contains *dozens* of references to nature spirits, those spiritual beings closest to the etheric life of earth itself.

harshness, deprivation and denouncement that Oliphant underwent during the three years, or so, while remaining there? And the eventual rehabilitation (albeit temporary) into the open arms of 'London' society in 1870, notwithstanding the climacteric change that had evidently come about as a result of the (self-)purging at Brocton as manifest in the move to the Carmel and what was written there in *Sympneumata* and *Scientific Religion* by Oliphant's hand but with input from Alice (of which more later)? An initiate quality once more shining through? This comes to the surface in passages such as: "If a divine power is necessary to overcome the depravity of one's human nature, [then] a divine revelation is necessary to enable one to discover wherein that depravity precisely exists."[50] And as a result of that discerning he came to pinpoint how people's behaviour affected the etheric forces as the cause of so much ill in the world—a theme which we shall follow further.

10. Then there is the obvious resonance of the gift of widely read authorship of Ovid and Oliphant *influencing* their contemporaries. Augustus had to resort to the almost unheard of measure of burning Ovid's books in order to destroy, or at least dent, his popularity, as a sign of imperial disapproval. In Oliphant's case, from the first he was a best seller,[51] his first book *A Journey to Kathmandu* is not only reputed to have been written in ten days, it sold 2000 copies in the same short period.

11. Ovid's visionary capacity could be seen as transformed into Oliphant's "I have long since taken refuge in my intuitions".[52] These are legion and gained him a many-faceted reputation for what Queen Victoria called a "remarkable talent and

---

[50] Margaret Oliphant, op cit. I.244.
[51] He was deemed to be amongst the 'best' writers of his day.
[52] Margaret Oliphant, op cit. I.239f.

understanding of foreign countries and their conditions".[53] Of many examples the following can be cited. His part in the Reciprocity Treaty between Canada and the USA (1854) preserved Canada's sovereignty and saved it from being engulfed by the USA. His shrewd assessment of the situations in China and Japan took him into the trades treaties which were being negotiated in the late 1850s. The Prince of Wales, when he was denied access to affairs of State frequently relied on Oliphant's knowledge to put him in the picture regarding the 'balance of power in Europe' and kindred matters. In the Franco-Prussian war of 1879, Delane of *The Times* sent Oliphant to France as reporter, where he reported in the newspaper's leader articles what he saw as signs of civil war that would raise its head in the aftermath of the conflict. When the Canadian Government was confronted with the problem of the trans-Atlantic cable monopoly, Oliphant devised a Bill, passed in the Senate in 1875, which enabled competition to be brought in and the Anglo-American Cable Company's high tariffs to be brought down.

12. In both life-times, too, the backlash comes. Augustus' stern measure seems to have resulted in a desertion of Ovid's friends. While the stunned and silent reception of Oliphant's last works has already been referred to.[54]

13. An affinity with Oriental beliefs is also evident in the spirituality of the (two) authors. Rome was attracted by these, as religious life had become more institutional than emotional;[55] at the same time, lipservice had to be paid to the gods of Rome. For all his *incarnation* in Anglo-Saxon culture and his first big breakthrough in life beginning when Oliphant accompanied Lord Elgin to the West, he was surrounded by,

---

[53]   See Taylor, op cit. p.110.

[54]   This must have been despite the echoes of past conversations in which he had edged towards mystical and spiritual matters in the early years of his social popularity. See Margaret Oliphant, op cit. I.196.

steeped in and influenced by the East. At the same time, he developed his own brand of Christianity, permeated by Cabalistic qualities, something which reached its peak when he ended his days in proximity to the Druse community in Palestine.

14. And one final correspondence—entailing a considerable degree of speculation on my part. *If* the 'relation' to Tomis had a positive outcome, as suggested above, it certainly did not have a positive origin. Julia, Augustus' grand-daughter, was the dark shadow which all the light, intended by Augustus to bring about a renewal in the moral fibre of Roman culture, could not dispel. Indeed, John Buchan in his biography of Augustus (London 1937) strongly suggests that Ovid was an "accomplice" to Julia's adultery—and he points the finger at Silanus.[56] We need not deeply enter this debate, certainly not try and solve this aspect of the problem for our present purposes. Suffice it to say that Julia comes across as a Queen of Night-like figure. In Oliphant's case, regarding any possible shadow side in his life, the focus of suspicion falls on Harris— and I accept that this may be partly due to the unknown: Harris's behaviour being often behind closed doors, and Oliphant's loyalty and discreteness which have helped to preserve the closed-door secrecy. Undoubtedly some great good for the inner development of Alice and her husband came out of their immersion in the Harris communities (if that is a true description of what they really were) at Brocton and

---

[55] Having said that, it would be unfair to Augustus if one overlooked the fact that he had statues of himself destroyed, counteracting the megalomaniac impression that some of his predecessors had created; but he strengthened the religious observance of Numen—the spiritual reality behind the world of the elements. Looked at from this perspective, there is a definite and little acknowledged connection between him and Ovid (Buchan p.103f—see below).

[56] There have been many waters of scholarship which have flowed under the bridge since Buchan's time, but the perception coming from a later Governor of Canada is worth passing on.

elsewhere. But the overriding impression left after reading all accounts of what took place is one of some sort of demon presiding—albeit, for those who would give Harris the benefit of the doubt, one of misplaced, or mistimed forces of good.[57]

A karmic pattern

To overlook any of the above cross-incarnation resonances—and there may be more than I have set out—would be short-sighted in any karmic study. Still more short-sighted, however, would be to take these as the most fundamental. To plumb the depths further, we will have to look at the biographies more closely in certain respects. This implies less of the *what*—the gifts, events and circumstances that the two incarnations lend to being correlated—and more of the *how* those gifts were used. There is universal agreement on Ovid's position (laureate in nature if not by appointment) amongst those who formed the vanguard of the new age of Roman literature into which he was born; but it is what he did with his gift that comes into question in a karmic study. Even his use of imagery is regarded as unparalleled in Augustinian poetry, but we will need to go farther than this.

To gain this more farsighted karmic view, therefore, it will perhaps be best if we return to the two materialistic civilisations in question: Rome at the height of its power and Britain at the height of its imperial supremacy. Leaving on one side what it might be that these cultures had to offer the rest of the world (as a sequel to Alexander the Great's having taken the treasures of Greek life and thought to the earlier centres of Post-Atlantean epochs), let us look at how Ovid-Oliphant related to the two respective civilisations, both of which, in his view, lacked sufficient *moral advance*, this quality lagging far behind Rome's military prowess, and in the case

---

[57] Robert Hale, a reviewer of Henderson's biography, voices his no-benefit-of-the-doubt view of Harris in searing tones: "... as obviously crooked a charlatan as can be found in the chronicles of religious mania."

of the West, lagging behind its intellectual development.

a) Their family backgrounds allowed them (—I shall use the pleural frequently for clarity's sake, as if I referred to two different people, rather than one individuality in two of its incarnations) in principle the *freedom to follow the course of their karma* without any material impediment.[58]

b) They nevertheless got the best of both worlds, accepting the means which made them free, while at the same time—at least to begin with—*connecting strongly with the entire layer of society into which they were born.*

c) Yet while seeming to 'go with the flow', they became acutely aware of the downside: affluence in a large majority of cases did *not breed life styles that supported self-respect and other kindred moral qualities.*

d) While at first keeping these perceptions to themselves, *they cultivated* not only a wide circle of personal friends but, through their writing, still *wider circles of appreciative readers.*

e) Initially they liberally *fed their readers with the addictively tasty morsels that, to the verge of psychological obesity, they wanted to hear:* Ovid the Roman equivalent, albeit in elegant verse, of the gossip columns; while Oliphant, as journalist pandered to the excitement of war, as travel writer to the hunger for vivid, racy descriptions of seldom heard-of, far-off lands,[59] and as novelist (especially in his *Piccadilly*) to the penchant that the young consciousness-soul had for tickling its fancy through indulging in satirical sorties into its own superficiality, indulgence, aimlessness and snobbery.

---

[58] The Oliphant family motto—*I seek for higher things*—at least expressing this in some outwardly visible form.

[59] Lord Russell, Foreign Secretary, told Mowbray Morris who was Manager of *The Times* that Oliphant was a writer of "immense power" (see Taylor, op cit. p.158).

f) Meanwhile they supposedly translated their perceptions of the ills of society into what might be of *healing* value—healing reaching beyond the generation which gave rise to the symptoms of the prevailing malady.[60]

g) At the same time, the forces needed for their (writing) skills to be harnessed in this way were engendered through a deep *spiritual experience*. (Did this experience connect them particularly with what Steiner describes as the Mercury genius? 'Healing' would certainly suggest that.) As mentioned above, this occurred *at similar phases (not ages) in their lives* through Ovid being exiled in Tomis, and through Oliphant subjecting his will to Harris. (In the same lecture Steiner points out that strong forces are to be derived from unreserved obedience. Thus, if Loyola gathered such forces by regarding the Pope as an infallible authority, Olpihant may well have gained similar inner strength through his carrying out Harris's dictates, seemingly to the letter.)

h) Perhaps it is worth noting that Ovid's *break with society* was inaugurated by Augustus, though the *cause* of it was what Ovid directed his attention to, compelling Augustus to exceed his threshold of tolerance. In Oliphant's case it was he himself who, finally, made the break with Harris—though it is difficult to believe he had not seen through him earlier as he strayed more and more outlandishly away from practising in his personal life what he preached to his ever-increasingly benighted followers. We could therefore summarise this aspect of their lives as a cheerful immersion in society from which

---

[60] Oliphant was clearly aware that the U-turn in his life which he was about to release on an unsuspecting public through the publication of his two main books—those to which Steiner refers after he had borrowed them from the Theosophical Library in London—would create a possible barrier for his publisher. "If I go astray, it is through faulty perception, not through any desire to exchange the treasure I have found for the dross which I hope I have left behind for ever," he reassures.

perceptions were gained, and then a decided break with society during which a diagnosis was arrived at, followed by *writing* which contained seeds for future healing.

i) Finally, and deserving some emphasis, what is common to both was a whole nexus of issues around the problem of how contemporary society related to *love* and of how that fell short —certainly in Oliphant's case, far short—of their ideals. In order to gain some perspective on this problem, it will be helpful to look at the three (known) historic periods connected with the individuality Ovid-Oliphant and the attitudes towards love that prevailed in each.

Rome

In the Roman society in which Ovid lived, male dominance manifested itself, inter alia, in the very different attitudes towards sexuality, the husband (as very distinct from the wife) being broadly accepted as at liberty to 'shop around' for his sexual pleasure. Though Augustus was at pains to counter this and reinstate family values, and despite his rank as emperor, the tide of sexual freedom for the male had clearly hardly begun to recede, the irony, though with a different nuance, of his daughter and grand-daughter (the Julias) being made scape-goats for his beleaguered policy notwithstanding. (An uncannily similar irony is depicted in the Medieval Coventry Cycle of Mystery Plays in the scene where some women come before Herod bearing the body of his own son who has tragically not escaped the slaughter instigated by none other than his own father. The so-called Coventry Carol mournfully comments on this.) Ovid owed his initial popularity as a writer to his reflecting his contemporaries' attitudes toward love. Though it clearly repelled him, he plunged (up to a point) into the gunge of social life enough to gauge popular taste, and pander to it in his writings. Even if his exile was the result of ingenuousness—he was less privy to some affair, and merely happened to be a stander-by whose misfortune was to be in the wrong place at the wrong time, and he failed to get out of the way quickly enough, for example—the burning of his works, considered by Augustus to be enflaming the very quality that he sought to douse and reform, is indication, if not proof, enough of the direction in which the problem lay.

Middle Ages

In the Middle Ages, the precise time to which Steiner refers in connection with Ovid's guidance (from spirit realms) of Brunetto Latini points to the 13th century.[61] This is the time, too, of the troubadours, trouvères, mastersingers and minnesingers. Wagner's inner affinity with the essence of what lived in that culture is evident in his *Tannhäuser, Die Meistersinger* and, because of the origin of the 'story', *Parzifal*—the Grail texts being gradually popularised through Chrétien de Troyes "the Provençal" and through Wolfram von Eschenbach "which [brought] the story / To German lands..." (Book XVI lines 672f). In Dante's *Divine Comedy* his guide is Beatrice, for whom he expressed the highly refined love which blossomed in such a widespread way in the troubadour tradition (*fin' amour*).[62] Echoes of Ovid exiled from Rome's decadent society and of Oliphant distancing himself (both physically and metaphorically) at the end of his life from the society of the West, which caused him inwardly so much anguish, come across strongly in Dante's explanation of what prompted Beatrice to 'go down' and

---

[61] Brunetto Latini returned to Florence from exile in France in 1266 after the Guelph defeat at Montaperti. In Canto XV.85 of *Inferno*, Dante acknowledges his teacher as having taught him how man can make himself eternal (*m'insegnarate come l'uom s'eterna;*).

[62] Dante and Beatrice Portinari (1266-1290) were both 9 years old, Beatrice a little younger, that is around the time of the so-called Rubicon of child development, when Dante fell in love with her. We learn this from his *Vita Nuova*, written a year after her death. In Canto II.70-72 of *Inferno*, appearing to him in spirit, Beatrice urges him to go forward with his journey through all the spheres of the *Divina Comedia* saying that it was love that moved her to come to him and to speak (*amor me mosse, che mi fa parlare*).

urge him to undertake his (initiation-like) journey, namely when she realised that he had also retreated from society's vulgarity on account of his love for her (*non soccorri quei che t'amo tanto / che uscio per te della volgare schiera?*)

In the thousands of troubadour poems (including, of course, those of kindred 12th and 13th century genres), the central theme is usually one aspect of love or another.[63] Parzifal's (the Wolfram spelling, rather than Wagner's) own long journey to the Grail is intricately entwined in love themes: his own naive mishandling of the meeting with Jeschute and her subsequent unjustified suffering at the hand of her understandably outraged husband Orilus who, until Parzifal swears innocence, suspects her of infidelity; his three meetings with Sigune; the first with her slain Schionatulander on her lap in a gesture redolent of what we know later as a Pietà, and so on; the little discussed counterpart of that, witnessed by Gawain in Klingsor's domain[64] of a knight in a woman's lap, from whose wounds blood issues forth—"full-blooded to excess" as Stein puts it[65]—all of the incident leading up to Gawain's affair (might one call it) with Orgeluse; the enigmatically changing relationship between Parzifal and his own wife Kondwiramur, the intimacy of which is poetically hinted at in Eschenbach's "a woman's sleep is holy"; "throughout the night so courteous he bore him"; "each found their life in the other and each was the other's love"; "I ne'er might see [her] / For well nigh five years," 'five years' signifying that his connection with Kondwiramur had to be "renewed out of the conscious will".[66] Act II of Wagner's *Parzifal* presents his interpretation of love in the domain of Klingsor, first being

---

[63] In his article on the Troubadours in *The New Grove Dictionary of Music and Musicians* (London 1980), John Stevens lists "love and courtesy, love and the hostile spies, the 'service' of love and the idolatry of the lady, resistance to sensual desires, the deception and despair of love, love-sickness and death, the joy of love, the lady's power [and so on]."

[64] Eschenbach Book X.52f.

[65] See Stein, W.H., *The Ninth Century and the Holy Grail*, London 1988, p.168f.

[66] Ibid.

represented by the seductive side of Kundry's unredeemed, sensuous nature, which gives rise to Parzifal's inner awakening through his being able to resist her enticements. This central motif in the opera has to serve for the whole transformation that Christian love can bring about: the healing of Amfortas, the destruction of Klingsor's realm, the redemption of Kundry, and, in the final analysis, Parzifal's attainment of the Grail.[67] We thus find the human being in a welter of change regarding attitudes of love at the time when Ovid is a "guide" to the initiated in the Middle Ages.

Victorian 'England'

With Oliphant the topic is raised to an altogether different level of consciousness, one that requires many intricate strands to be taken into account. By 'raise' I do not mean that Olpihant is only concerned with the loftier aspects of love as set out in his thoughts about the Divine Feminine.[68] His life—a karmic echo of his Ovidian experiences if the correspondences outlined above ring true—in the early years, or rather when he had flown the nest and was working alongside Lord Elgin on his North American mission, brought him as near to the seamier side of human relationships as he could have wished.[69] Not only night after night did the Americans lay on parties at which Lord Elgin (and of course Oliphant) were guests of honour: through this exposure he became acutely aware of the life-style of the majority of those present. What on one occasion he calls the 'American sex-stream' is something that he connects with life forces

---

[67] See Naylor, N., 'Wagner, Wolfram and Waldorf' in *Child and Man*, Jan 1995, pp33-36, for a discussion of the Eternal Feminine, to which, significantly in the present context, Oliphant alludes *in German*, and quoted from Goethe's *Faust*, as a kind of motto/dedication at the beginning of his *Scientific Religion* (*Die Ewig-Weibliche zieht uns hinan*).

[68] These thoughts reach something of a climax in Chapter XXI of *Scientific Religion*, the title of which was originally *The Divine Feminine* until the publisher prevailed on him to change it: "It would put people off." (See Taylor, op cit. p240.)

which had "degenerated into the filthy and obscene mysteries" (he is neither explicit nor specific as to date). Brunetto Latini's comment to Dante in Canto XV.114 of the *Inferno* inevitably comes to mind when, referring to the place where Andrea di Mozzi, guilty of sodomy, met his end, he pointedly says: "where his sinfully erected nerves were buried" (*dove lasino li mal protesi nervi*).[70]

During his time in America Oliphant visited the Shakers and also the Freelovers at Oneida Creek; but it would be too naive to deduce that his view was prompted by anything that he might have become aware of during these visits.[71] It seems far more likely that he is profoundly intent on drawing attention to the necessity "to counteract the invasive sex-current" and to raise consciousness so that those who were under the illusion "that their experiences are from celestial sources ... will find out the grievousness of their mistake [before] it is too late". And all this was a considerable time before the 'pure' animal nature (as Oliphant was to call it) was stirred up into brothel-lust through the use of jazz in New Orleans etc.[72] While remaining loyal, to a degree, to Harris—although it

---

[69]   A deep stream of love still lived in Oliphant even after Alice had died. On reading letters to James Murray Templeton, written by Rosamond Dale Owen, the grand-daughter of Robert Owen, who was to become his second wife, he exclaimed, "I must see that woman!" The tenderness he showed her was picked up by a porter on one of their train journeys, who was heard to remark, "Don't put anyone else in that carriage with the lovebirds!"

[70]   Musa, Mark, trans. Penguin edition 1986.

[71]   The long-term view implied by his "a more scientific approach to the spirit is needed" would appear to come from a higher perspective altogether. Steiner (1 December 1906), in referring to this aspect of Oliphant's work, states that it does proceed from a "pure occult perspective (*von rein okkulten Standpunkt*)".

[72]   See Lissau, R., 'Jazz' in Stebbing, L., *Music its Occult Basis and Healing Value,* East Grinstead (undated) pp.137-145. Lissau, being the disciplined scholar he was, must have been well aware of the various *musical* origins of jazz, especially in relation to the (slave-trade) social background to which its first adherents were, of course, connected. Essentially, he does not discuss this aspect: it is the *use* of the genre upon which he focuses.

seems clear that he had seen through him[73]—he singles out "spiritualistic circles" as those in whom the illusion was working most strongly. And despite the fact that the prudishness of Victorian society—at least at that level—was as thin and fragile as could be, such practices as those to which he is referring were "as a rule [kept] profoundly secret: they are constantly increasing however both in England and America, especially in the latter country, and statistics on the subject, would they be obtained, would astonish the sceptical and afford an extensive field of operations for the Psychical Research Society, who, nevertheless, would escape from the dilemma in which they would be placed, by the easy expedient of calling them 'subjective', a term which explains nothing."[74] Oliphant seems intent on tearing chunks of plaster of Paris off one of the most guarded of Victorian taboos.

He then goes on to view the stance of science and theology on the subject: science is "powerless to meet the evil"; theology while "denounc[ing] it as of the devil … probably does not believe in the devil, … or may mistake him for an angel of light"!

His solution to the "bane which can only be met by its antidote" is an inner one, which originates in the astonishing spiritual certainty with which he speaks. "[A]s it is the result of the direct operation of invisible beings from the nether region of our own world, it must be met by the direct operation of invisible beings from the upper one"—a battle ground, might one say, that is right at the heart of the human soul. Hence: "Persons must … be found who will brave the dangers, suspicions, ridicule, or obloquy with which they will be ascribed in their attempt to acquire the power that will not only

---

[73] It seems that it was at the point when Harris realised that the writing was on the wall, as far as his control over Oliphant and the wealth that he and his family had made over to him was concerned, that Harris made a last ditch attempt to have him incarcerated in a lunatic asylum.

[74] It seems clear that spiritualism dragged on in England, and was part of the motivation behind D.N Dunlop's inviting Steiner to give a course of lectures in Torquay in the summer of 1924 in which the title speaks for itself: *True and False Paths in Spiritual Investigation.*

enable these to beat back that invading influence, but to draw down
into the world such currents of divine purity as shall cleanse the foul
magnetisms which taint all social and domestic relations..."[75] And,
the final stroke: "[A]ll the miseries and woes of humanity are
primarily due [to this evil]." Small wonder that the champagne-
frothed society, amongst whom he had been such an outstandingly
popular figure, and from whom—as a *phenomenon* of contemporary
social life—he (and Alice) had gained their perceptions, stopped
dead in its tracks and reacted to the testament he was propounding in
Sympneumata and *Scientific Religion* (both of them formidable
volumes) with stunned silence. What else could it do? He was laying
the axe of his diagnosis of society's ills at the very root of their
pleasure, pleasure undoubtedly the 'fruit' of affluence acquired
through the empire-building avarice of the Old World, on the one
hand, and, on the other, the concomitant use of the untold, and
hitherto untapped natural resources of the New World—again an
Ovidian echo, where the shaky moral code of Roman behaviour
engendered the raffishness that Augustus was intent on eliminating
(the war *on his own lands* at home in an empire which had created
the stability of the Pax Romana!), and which Ovid surf-boarded in
gaining the popularity of a writer, a popular readership which he
was to address through the *Metamorphoses* and other mature works
in such a way that at least something of that realm from which
Oliphant saw flowing the "current of divine purity" must have

---

[75] See Blaxland de-Lange, S., *Owen Barfield: Romanticism Comes of Age*, Forest
Row 2006. One suspects that what attracted Owen Barfield to the form of the
novel, as distinct from the philosophical works which were responsible for his
rise to academic fame in America in the third quarter of the 20th century, was
the possibility it offered him to express in powerful and unveiled terms what his
perceptions were in this regard—as for example in *Night Operations*:
"Darwinism, directly and through Freudianism, has been responsible for the
artificial abstraction of 'sex' from gender or humanised sex. One's imagination
boggles at the convulsions that must accompany any struggle of anal and oral
eroticism to turn into something like romance or the marriage of true minds or
even something altogether new..."

entered into general public awareness and private, individual consciousness.

Man-woman Woman-man

The question of whether the initiates of tomorrow will be able to be permeated by the Ovid-Oliphant guidance when they are incarnating in the future, as Brunetto Latini (and the other initiates to which Steiner alludes) was in the "confusion" that the historical shock combined with sun-stroke brought about in Latini's consciousness— which we could reasonably take to be a pathological condition, even if passing—is one that must remain open, of course. But the wide-open speculativeness of it is surely narrowed at least a sliver by reading between the lines of Steiner's lecture of 24 Aug 1924, and juxtaposing that reading with what might be the inner essence of the individuality as manifest in 'their' lives. As well as the above observations and comments of Oliphant (and this includes the mystery of Laurence-Alice) which plunge us directly into the daily life of individuals and their relationship to their own etheric nature, there are further implications of Oliphant's significance. One wonders whether Steiner's "One must will to overcome the forces of Nature sacramentally" in his lecture of 15 October 1916—in which he points out that Oliphant is coming from the same direction (pole) as Freud but "purified"—is indicating as much. Certainly the subtitle of *Scientific Religion—Higher Possibilities of Life and Practice through Operation of Natural Forces*—would suggest as much. The following passage from *Sympneumata* reveals something of the vista in which Oliphant saw the significance of the life-forces.

> [T]he idea of virtue existing only by reason of an apparent relation to that of vice, as a sign of conditions superior only by comparison to inferior ones, will fall away from all who apprehend that every human being is endowed alike because of the organic contribution of the whole of

> humanity, with all the elements of purest and divinest
> humanness; and that man's errors arise from that
> organised mismanagement by the whole society of the
> world of the individual life-forces which are its joint
> capital for action...[76]

Again rooted in his experience of American society, it is significant
that Oliphant initially directs his concerns to the ladies—though it is
by no means evident that he has achieved the high vantage point as
evidenced in Sympneumata and Scientific Religion[77] at this point in
his remarkably varied and adventurous life. His connections with
'the fair sex' seem to be totally misunderstood by his biographer
Henderson, indeed grossly misinterpreted. In a talk by A.P. Ryan,
reported in The Listener 31 May 1956, despite the talk's coming
across to perhaps the most earnest anthoposophical student of
Oliphant at the time (Mildred Kirkcaldy, editor of the
Anthroposophical Quarterly), as "frivolous and superficial"—a view
gathered from undated typed notes of a lecture she gave some little
time after the publication of The Listener article—he emphasises
how critical Oliphant was of the trap into which the fear of being
seen as unfashionable had lured them: "I don't object to your riding
in the park: the abominable constitution of society makes it almost
the only opportunity of seeing and talking to those you like without
being talked about. But you need not rush off for a drive in the
carriage immediately after lunch... You are too restless to stay at
home: first the park and young men, then lunch, then Marshall and
Snelgrove, then tea and young men again, then dinner, drums and
balls, and young men till 3am ... that is the treadmill you have
chosen to turn without the smallest profit to yourself or anyone else.
If I seem to speak strongly, it is because my heart yearns over you."
Ryan describes the objects of this homily of Oliphant's as "girl

---

[76]   For this and further description of "life forces" see *Sympneumata* p.279.
[77]   The latter is teeming with concepts close to or identical with those found in
       anthroposophy.

friends"—not, of course the connotation in 1956 that would attach to the expression now. Yet one cringes at his possible misinterpretation of what was going on in the 'yearning heart'. To do the speaker justice, however, he does end with a hint of greater vision, quoting Oliphant: "The world with its bloody wars, its political intrigues,[78] its social evils [here he strikes the note that is to ring so resoundingly in Scientific Religion], its religious cant, its financial fraud and its glaring anomalies, assumed in my eyes more and more the aspect of a gigantic lunatic asylum."

In response to this, it must have been the universal *healing* of the world—rotten to the core in so many respects (for now, we'll leave today's picture on one side), if we accept his diagnosis as unexaggerated—that concerned him. A lifetime is too short, of course, to deal with such an overwhelming global sickness. But, via identifying the right symptoms, the devising of 'medicine' for the future, in whatever form, is clearly the course of action open. And so he starts with 'the ladies'. That they are more powerful than "the young men"—either in themselves, or through their more cosmically open constitutions which make them (looking on the negative side) more vulnerable to the "operation of invisible beings from the nether regions of our own world"—seems the inescapable conclusion (the 'behind every successful man is a powerful woman' syndrome of pre-feminist-liberation times?). In citing the 'macrocosm within the microcosm', on the whole we tend too glibly to rule out the shadow side of the macrocosm. However, this is not a matter of subsiding into what Oliphant refers to as the popular

---

[78]   His biographer tells of how perceptive he was in that he had figured out the US 'agenda' within a month. This could be replicated several times over—with many instances echoing on today, far from faintly: his advice on how best to capture Sebastopol, his grasp of Russia's politics in the East, the "customary prescience" (Taylor op cit. p.30) with which he saw the threat to the Union over the differing attitudes towards slavery of northern and southern States, his foresight in seeing the power that could be wielded by a united Muslim world, and so on.

church's interpretation of the 'Fall' which tends to lumber Eve with the guilt of plucking the forbidden fruit, through Adam's '*She* plucked it' exonerating him sufficiently for having eaten of it instead of sticking to his guns. Oliphant recognised the mote in the eye of society as that which had resulted in the enslavement of the woman in Western civilisation. Not that he gave the woman a clean bill of health in this respect, but at least he puts her and her partner on the same level: "To find the deepest and truest of their instincts and to be true to them, is the simple duty and necessity which men and women prove for the most part incapable of performing; and this incapacity lies behind all the most poignant and oppressive of the world's sufferings". And the long remedial road: "Freedom for development, and for application of pure moral impulse, is now the hunger of humanity; mutual coercion and suppression of this impulse is its crime."[79]

In the immortal saga of Odysseus, the male travels far and wide to find those 'deepest and truest instincts', while Penelope, his wife, weaves her constancy and purity into daily domestic life. In Tomis, in his *Tristia* (I.5), on one of those many occasions when Ovid is lamenting his fateful exile, he compares and contrasts his situation to that of Odysseus. The hero, tossed endlessly hither and thither on the surface of the waves, as if persecuted by Neptune, is at least in the end able to get back to his beloved home. Just in time, we are led to believe, as Penelope holds off her suitors who approach her, thinking—and hoping thereby to persuade her— that Odysseus is gone for ever.

Neptune was the Roman's Poseidon. Amongst the Greek gods he was the *macrocosmic equivalent of man's etheric nature*. How poignant it is that Ovid chooses precisely this comparison. For as Oliphant, he is to laud the sacredness of the life-forces as experienced in the weddedness of man and woman—a magnificent transformation of the image of Penelope, in her faithfulness (—the

---

[79]   *Sympneumata* p.251.

female being the representative of the human soul), constantly waiting for Odysseus' return (—the male being the representative of the ego) having endured and triumphed over his trials—his *Odyssey of initiation*—at the hand of an angry yet optimistically and persistently protective macrocosmic etheric (Poseidon).[80]

Oliphant, his heart increasingly urgent in its yearning, is once more led in those last years on the Carmel to cry out: "The slow degradation that corrupts the leisure-seekers results ... from the hyper-development to which they urge a limited set of faculties and the absolute atrophy to which they leave the larger wealth of that which as human beings they are necessarily endowed."[81] This would be enough to speak to the sensitive heart of any humanist—or simply any decent person. Oliphant spring-boards from there towards his conception of the divine: "Let loose the powers of actual nature in you—man-woman, woman-man—that God may be incarnated!"[82] The 'guide of initiates' could hardly comment more appositely on the pathological dilemma of the age.

Thus we see Ovid-Oliphant on two levels. In earthly incarnation he slithers into the dragon's skin of contemporary society, outwardly verging on the exultant, and certainly a 'hit' amongst the leading circles of his day, but inwardly recoiling—fist gradually and then, at his life-changing moment(s), incisively—from what becomes apparent to his (visionary) perception. Between incarnations, he acts as guide to those initiates who would bring the macrocosmic into the

---

[80]   It is also perhaps significant that in the *Metamorphoses*, although Ovid makes a few other references to Penelope, it is in the context of the myth Pomona and Vertumnus (Book XIV) that he brings out her most poignant characteristic—i.e. in the love story in which the female's virtue is pictured as a garden which she tends devotedly, a particularly moving image worth singling out as Ovid does, being the vine that entwines the branches of an elm (elm being a Mercury tree). This etheric constancy (female) is eventually wedded to Vertumnus' ardent love, outwardly resourceful in its changeability (his many guises) but equally constant—an image of utterly purified (astral) instinct.

[81]   *Sympneumata* p.268.

[82]   Ibid.

microcosmic in ways pertinent to their age, Dante ('inheriting' Brunetto Latini his teacher's initiation experience) expressing some of it in his immortal poetry, as indicated by Steiner in this regard. Might one detect a kindred process taking place in the poetry of the troubadours and thereby influencing the culture that derived from it? With the thread of Ovid's visionary insight contained in the *Metamorphoses* stretching unbroken through the twelve intervening centuries? Together with Virgil, he is, after all, the most quoted poet in Dante's epoch-influencing *Divine Comedy.*[83]

At this level, the Mercury genius could be seen to work powerfully. Steiner all but indicates his connection thereto. In not being more explicit, might he still have needed some confirmatory experience in the course of his research, or the right circumstances/conditions/constellation of audience in Dornach to take the matter that one further step foreword? And this is not even to broach the question of how that Mercury genius might have worked in the Ovid-Oliphant incarnations themselves—viz. the two incisive and utterly life-changing events: Ovid's exile and Oliphant's social hibernation (and simultaneously spiritual endowment) in the tantalisingly enigmatic Harris episode! But leaving this impenetrability aside for the moment, let us look at the Mercurial qualities in Oliphant's life. I shall briefly address four: the connection with empire-building, the flow between people in society, the forces of Mercury at work in the inner organs, and the sphere of Mercury through which the soul of the deceased passes after death.

1. In the word 'merchant' the quality of Mercury is encapsulated, and with it the essence of money. Money needs to flow

---

[83] Though it seems self-evident that Oliphant himself didn't need it, it is worth noting that throughout the 19th century and earlier the cultivation of the right brain must have been enormously supported by the study of Ovid's imaginative writing—both as regards content and style—as practised in public and grammar schools.

mercurially between giver and receiver, lender and borrower, vendor and purchaser. Of course, this has to be in the right relationship. Steiner referred to the economic sphere as being under the sign of 'brotherhood' (*fraternité*). The associative principle ideally is what should hold sway. Spendthrifts and misers have extreme relationships to money; and the problem with so-called developing countries is that they become a prey to financial tyrants. We have seen that Oliphant declared himself 'not a soldier', yet if one were to do the necessary maths, it seems likely that one would find that a large portion of his life is connected with the acquisitive greed of the powerful nations either vying with one another for more wealth (land, power, resources) or involved in conflict with what nowadays we might refer to as the 'dollar under-dog'. The leaders, both of his own country, as well as others , were frequently motivated to make use of his shrewdness (transformed 'cosmic instinct'?) for such purposes.

2. The Mercury force in the human soul is that which brings diversity into harmony. Oliphant wielded this quality seemingly with unparalleled skill. What other person, having been abroad, essentially incommunicado for some years as he was in Brocton, and in what his associates saw as *very* questionable company, could have made the instant come back that he made on his reappearance in society—*high society*—in 1869? Margaret Oliphant, who, as related to the family, met him on his return, noted his exuberant nature, as if nothing untoward had intervened, and the way he slotted back as 'heart and soul of the party'. "He was too piquant in his personality and amused society too much to fall out of its favour"[84]—and this is not even to mention the questions he constantly had to fend off, the concealed (or not) ridicule he had to circumnavigate about the New Life to which he had been

---

[84]   Margaret Oliphant, op cit. II.66.

subject: petticoat sewing, stable mucking out 'n all.

3. In the physical body Mercury's corresponding organ is the kidney. Enough has been said about a certain (large) sector of society's preoccupation with the renal system to necessitate repeating it here. But it is clear from the towering tidal wave of his observations in this sphere of life, which crashes with such force in *Sympneumata* and *Scientific Religion*, that his concern for humanity then and into the future could not have been more dire.

4. Finally, it is in the Mercury sphere that the soul in its post-mortal life experiences either hermetic loneliness or re-connection with those of its loved ones who have gone before, as well as the benediction of spiritual beings. Steiner speaks frequently of this when, particularly from 1912 onwards, he is elaborating the soul's journey through the planetary spheres after death. Moreover, spiritual isolation or connection depends on the degree of morality practised during the previous life on earth. Again, enough has been said already to demonstrate how deeply concerned Oliphant was for the moral tone of his contemporaries, from the highest political level, to the general conduct of everyday life (where the law finds its *raison d'être*); and from the everyday intimacy between man and wife to what he aspired to through Alice "to reform the world [and] restore woman her rightful place in it."[85]

While these Mercury qualities form the main colours in the mosaic of his life, it is perhaps the U-turn which is evident during and after the Brocton years to which we should look for the strongest indication. Other elements give us hints of what was pending: the looseness of his constitution made possible through the lack of formal education; what looked like a "prolonged adolescence" during his twenties when he was clearly not grounded in the

---

[85] See Taylor, op cit. p.170f.

physical world;[86] the sense of "responsibility for all mankind" which by contrast followed;[87] the permeability of his mind when Alice dictated her thoughts to him; and the silence that fell over his mystical experiences by contrast with the ebullience with which he spoke of spiritual things in his earlier conversation, and so on. For what it is worth, also, we have the account of Nicholson's father who described how Oliphant would interrupt some light-hearted conversation: "Suddenly the glow would fade from his features, a spasm would pass over his shoulders and arms, his eyes would become expressionless and he would burst into" what the incredulous observer referred to as "senseless prophecies"— senseless enough to Nicholson snr. for him to label Oliphant as "schizophrenic". (This reaction to a spiritual phenomenon is not surprising in the 1880s.) Whilst none of the above 'proves' the point, an embodiment by a Mercury genius to some degree is surely not out of the question.

Ovid's closing words in the *Metamorphoses* could be dismissed as poetic fantasy: "And now my work is done, which neither the wrath of Jove, nor fire, nor sword, nor the gnawing tooth of time shall even be able to undo. When it will, let that day come which has no power save over this mortal frame, and end the span of my uncertain years. Still in my better part I shall be borne immortal far beyond the lofty stars and I shall have an undying name ... and, if the prophecies of bards have any truth, through all ages shall I live in fame."[88] At the same time, something of a higher divine nature rings through them, which would certainly be compatible—seeing how true the 'prophecy' was to become—with the concept of an inspiration agency (embodiment) of exceptional magnitude.

Oliphant is self-evidently not in that same category—not as yet:

---

[86]   Ibid. p.47.

[87]   Ibid. p.123.

[88]   The Loeb Classic Library, Cambridge Massacusetts and London 1984, translated by Frank Justus Millar. *Iamque opus exegi, quod nec Iovis ira nec ignisnec poterit ferrum nec edax abolere vetustas.*etc.

there are still 10/11 centuries to go if one places the two lives
commensurably side by side—but might not his final work not only
escape the gnawing tooth of our spiritually turbulent times (and
Ahriman's fangs are surely infinitely more active than merely
gnawing!) but in prompting us to *wrench* ourselves away from
massive current trends (to use another Barfield notion)[89] be in line to
make a spiritually-scientific contribution, in whatever form, to the
progressive tread of human evolution? And might not that
contribution encompass a quality of Christian love that will prove to
be the antidote to the 'American sex-stream' in a way that reflects,
yet takes further, the antidote that Troubadour culture was injecting
into contemporary society in the wake of Roman decadence?

In his book on Moses,[90] Bock, a commentator on the Old
Testament, who took Jewish legends into account as well as the
findings of spiritual science, draws attention to the importance of
Moses' 40-year sojourn with Jethro. The two leaders can both trace
their origins back to Abraham, Moses as Israelite, Jethro as
Ishmaelite. It would seem that the union of the two streams has been
grossly and dangerously overlooked, particularly in modern times.
Could there have been something stirring in Oliphant's karmic past
that drew him to the cause of rehabilitating Jews on Palestinian soil?
Jew and Arab would thereby be in close geographical proximity
which, as history has all too tragically shown, also has its fragile
side. The fact that Alice and Oliphant left their first abode in Haifa
and found a place to live on the Carmel is surely significant, since it
was a place that brought them intimately into contact with the local
Druse population. Today the Druses (Arabs) speak Arabic as their
mother tongue but retain a closer bond with the State of Israel than
Arab Israelis. Add to this the fact that their closely-guarded religion
reputedly dates back to Jethro and you have a powerful image of the
possibility of uniting—and therefore of healing—the division that

---

[89]   See Blaxland de-Lange, op cit. for an extensive psychographic excursion into
       Barfield's thought.
[90]   See Bock, Emil, *Moses*, Edinburgh 1986, 2.5 'The Mystery Centre of Jethro'.

has been one of the major 'faults' in the anthropological crust of the earth. Add further to that the fact that *Sympneumata* and *Scientific Religion* were written precisely in that setting—where there was the possibility of opposites coming harmoniously together—and you have a remarkable instance of what Steiner referred to as Ovid-Oliphant's 'cosmic instinct'.

For all his detailed knowledge of and insight into Palestinian geography/geology, Bock doesn't appear to place importance on the existence of Druse villages on the Carmel. He does, however, go into considerable detail concerning the decadent effect on the life forces (etheric body) of the Moabite cults from eastern Jordan. Phinehas the grandson of Aaron triumphed with his "pure graill-lance ... over the plague of sensual intoxication" that had infected the Israelites.[91] Later, as Elijah, the same spiritual entelechy overcame the cult of Baal *at the very place where the Oliphants settled on the Carmel.*

Lime and oak crowns

On St John's eve, Latvian folk tradition draws virtually the whole population out into nature—to coastal plain, garden plot, the soft verge of roads, woodland, lakeside, 'waste' ground beside the old Soviet blocks... Everywhere, the St John's fires are ablaze throughout the night to welcome the birth of the Baptist as the one who heralded the increase of the inner sun as the outer sun stood close to, yet a minute step beyond its zenith, anticipating the decrease of its power as the year moves towards the 'Natus Est' turning point at the heart of the dark winter months.

Everywhere the flames rise into the midsummer night—hardly more than twilight, actually, in those northern latitudes—with the fires even set afloat on lakes; flickering flames slowly drifting in the sun-absent stillness of night. Many people, old and young, are decked in colourfully embroidered folk costume as they sing and

---

[91]   Ibid. p.131.

dance together in the fiery glow (like Ovidian elegiac couplets: hexameter and pentameter, dancing tirelessly, as it were, hand in hand). The dead wood, releasing warmth and 'imprisoned' sunlight, is the toughest element of the plant world—the earthly image of the etheric. As the flames rise, they symbolise how our etheric nature, if purged of lower impulses that live in the astral, can also aspire to the heights, loosened from the physical—the counter image of what we have in Salome's dance before Herod, at the instigation of Herodias.

The Baptist's message is, of course, heralding the incarnation of the Christos, the Sun Spirit, though it merely carries further what must have existed annually in so-called pagan times at this high summer season of the year. He proclaims his message at the 'turning point' of historic and evolutionary time. Ovid, who died just after this Baptist was witnessing the 'wedding' of the Zarathustran Ego with the Mother Lodge-Soul of the so-called Luke Jesus child (more or less on the same longitude, the same fault line in relation to the world cross), encapsulates the essence of what lives in the Latvian St John's fire in mythological form.[92]

His narrative appears in the *Metamorphoses* (VIII lines 618-724) telling how Jupiter came to earth with Mercury in human guise, to a district where they sought hospitality. All households turned them away save that of Philomen and Baucis, an elderly couple, who lived in the humblest of cottages. Generously they shared the best of what they had, while miraculously they became aware that they were entertaining gods. On being asked what they would like in return for their kindness, they replied that their most earnest wish was to serve the gods in eternity and not witness one another's death. Both wishes were granted to them by their divine visitors. They ascended a nearby hill and, looking back, saw that the valley in which their neighbours dwelt had been completely flooded with water; only their cottage was saved, though now it appeared as a

---

[92] I am not suggesting, of course, that these overtones are exclusive to the Latvian tradition.

temple. Beside it, they found themselves being transformed into two branches of one tree. They shared the trunk; Baucis became a lime and Philomen an oak.

Traditionally, each Latvian dancer on St John's eve wears a crown; the male's crown is entwined from oak twigs, the female's from linden or lime (*ozols* and *liepa*). In the *Dainas*, the remarkable collection of Latvian folklore which contains tens of thousands of verses, the references to oak and lime are so ubiquitous—there are over 150 in volume one (out of ten) alone!—that one gets the impression that the midsummer crowns, woven anew each year from the trees, are part of a tradition that is rooted deep down in the folk psyche, having environmental, social, moral, and vastly and incomparably pre-ecclesiastical, yet fundamentally Christian, religious significance.

May we interpret the myth of Philomen and Baucis to mean, perhaps, that Ovid-Oliphant will guide humanity, through the incarnated initiates of the future, towards that state which Oliphant expresses, in which humanity will aspire in an exemplary way towards the two fold Divinity of male-female? Not a reversion to the androgynous state of 'man' we find at the beginning of the biblical account of Genesis, but an evolutionary step forward to an era in which the life forces of present day humanity will have blossomed into those of a new race—what Oliphant refers to as the new race in which the 'American sex-stream' (the misdirected life forces, brothelised through jazz-lust, and thereby contaminating every nook and cranny of society as a whole) will be submerged in oblivion and the physical body (Steiner's reference to the "sublime physiology and pathology" of Oliphant) will have become a temple in which the *divinely-aspiring human spirit of the future* (man-woman woman-man—be it in singles or families) will find a *worthy dwelling place*. Whether we shall have to travel as far into the future for that worthy temple-dwelling-place to come about (be created), as we have travelled since Manu led the leaders of the then future from an Atlantis that subsided as the result of a former but different misuse

of etheric forces, history will eventually tell.[93] Perhaps, when we
have arrived there—hopefully even before!—we shall not only be
the beneficiaries of the historical events that will have been created
by those people permeated by the Ovid-Olphant impulse: an
enlightened understanding of karma will also be able to *illumine*
further the enigmas (Mercury mysteries?) I have here sought to
identify and address.

* * * * *

At this point 'intuition fails', as it did with Dante at the end of the
Divine Comedy when he experienced the fantasy-level at which his
mind had arrived, revolving like a perfectly balanced wheel (one of
the chakras?) and his "will and ... desire [was] impelled / by the
Love that moves the sun and the other stars"[94]

> *All'alta fantasia, qui manco possa;*
> *ma gia volgeva il mio disiro e il velle*
> *si come rota ch'egualmente e mossa*
> *l'amor che move il sole e l'altre stelle.*

---

[93] Steiner's research into Atlantean times (see 22 April 1909 and 9 November
1919) revealed that the subsidence of the continent was caused by the immoral
use of nature forces contained in seeds of the plant. Further light is shed on this
problem (22 March 1909) when Steiner refers to how the Ahrimanic forces
work in the Intellectual Soul "the transformed part of the ether body", while it
will be for the Asuric powers to work in the Consciousness Soul where they
will "generate evil with a far mightier force than was wielded by the Satanic
powers in the Atlantean epoch." This refers to the (near) future, but "the
prominent signs of this [evil] are *the dissolute, sensuous passions that are
becoming increasingly prevalent*" (my emphasis). It is, perhaps, sobering to
realise that the 'increasingly prevalent' (and therefore historical) march of these
powers to which Steiner alludes was nearly a century ago in 1909...!

[94] Musa, op cit. *Paradiso* XXXIII.143-145.

Bibliography

Blaxland d-Lange, S., *Owen Barfield*, Forest Row 2006

Bock, E., *Moses*, Edinburgh 1986

Buchan, J., *Augustus*, London 1937

Dante, *La Divina Commedia*, (Sansoni ed.) Firenze 1905

Dante, *The Divine Comedy*, translated by Mark Musa, Indiana 1971, 1981, 1984

Endzelius, J., (ed.) *Latvju Tautas Dainas*, Riga 1936

Filton Brown, F.D., 'The Unrealaity of Tomitan Exile', in *Liverpool Classical Monthly*, Feb 1985

Frankel, H., *Ovid: a poet between two worlds*, California 1945

Harrison, J.A., *Ovid on Himself*, London 1969

Henderson, P., *The Life of Laurence Oliphant*, London 1956

Heyer, K., *The Middle Ages*, Forest Row 1994

Kirkcaldy, M., Notes and correspondence from her literary estate (sent by executor Bill Milne) plus extracts from:

[Conan Doyle, Sir A., *History of Spiritualism*, 1926]

[Dunraven, Lord, *Past Times and Pastimes: Memoirs of Lord Dunraven.*]

[Hale, R., 'Illustrious Maniac' in *an Aberdeen newspaper*, 1956][95]

Lissau, R., 'Jazz' in Stebbing, L., *Music, its Occult Basis and Healing Value,* East Grinstead (undated)

Naylor, A., 'Wagner, Wolfram and Waldorf', in *Child and Man*, Jan 1995

Oliphant, L., *Piccadily*, Edinburgh 1870

Oliphant, L., *Sympneumata*, Edinburgh 1885

Oliphant, L., *Scientific Religion,* Edinburgh 1888

Oliphant, M., *Laurence Oliphant,* Edinburgh 1891

Ovid, *Amores*, translated by Frank Justus Millar, London 1914

Ovid, *Artis Amatoriae*, translated by Frank Justus Millar, London

---

[95]   [ ] denote that *full* reference details have not become available.

    1924

Ovid, *Metamorphoses*, translated by Frank Justus Millar, London 1916

[Rand, K., *Ovid and his Influence*, 1926]

Rees, G., *Music in the Middle Ages*, London 1941

Ryan, A.P., 'Laurence Oliphant: A Rich Victorian Eccentric', in *The Listener*, May 1956

Savitch, M., *Marie Steiner-von Sivers*, London 1967

Stein, W.J., *The Ninth Century and the Holy Grail*, London 1988

Stein, W.J., 'An Appreciation of D.N. Dunlop', in *The Present Age*, Dec 1935

Steiner, R., (Stenographic reports of lectures given:
    1.xii.1906 Cologne
    15.x.1916 Dornach
    18.vii.1924 Arnhem
    24.viii.1924 London
    10.ix.1924 Dornach

Stevens, J., 'Troubadours', in *The New Grove Dictionary of Music and Musiciains*, London 1980

[Syme, R., *History in Ovid*, 1978]

Taylor, Anne, *Laurence Oliphant*, Oxford 1982

Trevelyan, G.M., *Garibaldi and the Thousand*, Oxford 1909

Villaneuve, C., *Rudolf Steiner in England: a documentation of his ten visits*, Forest Row 2004

[Wainwright, *Ovid in Exile*, 1906]

Wegman, I., & Steiner, R., *Fundamentals of Therapy*, London 1938

Welburn, A., *Myth and the Nativity; the virgin birth re-examined*, Edinburgh 2006

Wilkinson, L.P., *Ovid Recalled*, Cambridge 1955

1980-1987

There's an old adage: Those who *can*, teach; those who *can't*, inspect. It's not difficult to see both the truth of it and its limitations —its ramifications, too, into the roles of head-teachers, advisors, Education Ministers and all the rest of us beyond the chalk face. But what about teacher training? Is the line of demarcation just as clear? I have often had cause to stare the question in the face when I've been asked as a guest abroad to teach a lesson—with "to demonstrate how it should be done" either made explicit or remaining implicit!

It is well known that Steiner was an exceptionally gifted teacher, the most common example cited being his pupil, Otto Specht, the boy suffering from a severe hydrocephalic condition who became a medical doctor. But the riddle of how Steiner, not as a teacher but as a teacher trainer, managed to launch the first Waldorf school (and through it a movement consisting of a thousand schools worldwide and about half as many again Kindergartens) with a 'crash course'— what else to call it?—of exactly fourteen consecutive days, has never fully been unravelled.

There was something infinitely more than osmosis going on, and that something was clearly the way in which he was able to conceptualise his insights into the nature of children and into the nature of pedagogy.

Consider a teacher of, say, 15-year-olds who is introducing trigonometry in a maths lesson. She will certainly need to have all her conceptual antennae on the alert. But if it is a Waldorf class, grouped chronologically and therefore non-streamed, she will also need all the pedagogical skills she has at her disposal. Now a teacher is in the classroom situation x hours a day, so by the time she has taught trigonometry for a decade or two, it is understandable if she tends to take the conceptualisation of the subject and the pedagogy involved in teaching it for granted. But if she does subside into taking the pedagogy for granted, she will surely come a cropper sooner or later. No wonder Steiner emphasised the importance of developing pedagogical *instinct*—yes, *developing* instinct!

One conclusion would therefore be: the teacher trainer's main challenge is how to conceptualise, how to develop pedagogical instinct in the student. And if we go back to 1919, and are hypothetically thinking of replicating the circumstances, we would have to *add* *in a fortnight, without a curriculum, with no classroom experience and without the teacher trainer observing the student teacher in harness!*

This is to light upon a mountain—which I do not claim to have climbed. Yet I don't think my way of teacher training has been to walk round the mountain's lowest contour and then rely on adviser's sitting in with graduates the moment they step into the classroom to paper over the cracks. However, without tracking the journey, I am particularly grateful to three factors:

(i) being called upon to take 'main-lesson' at Emerson College at a time when student revolts were rife;

(ii) being invited to teach in the Edinburgh Teacher Training Course in Summer 1980 which led to a long association with colleagues there (going there for three fortnights each year) and having to formulate what I had to bring for Scottish thinkers;

(iii) being inundated in the Michael Hall Education Seminar with Israeli students—in my twelve-year association with it, there were times when Israelis outnumbered all other nationalities put together—and the subsequent visits to Israel (over c.12 years) which required a further enhanced conceptualisation for Jewish thinkers of all components of so-called education theory: aims, nature of the child, curriculum, pedagogy and (the 5th component which I argue strongly in my doctoral thesis) *the teacher.*

The London Waldorf Teacher Training Seminar
Report to the AGM of the Anthroposophical Society 2008

The London Waldorf Teacher Training Seminar (LWTTS) began its life on the top of an Edinburgh no.10 bus. Or at least the sweet-hearting between those who had had the idea and me did. I put it that way because the top of a bus crammed with passengers in dripping wet raincoats lurching through the rush hour didn't seem like a very formal interview. The bus was going from Waverley, the main-line station in the centre of the city, to the Rudolf Steiner School of Edinburgh, taking members of an assembly of the Anthroposophical Society in Great Britain to one of its meetings.

The idea of a teacher training seminar centred in Rudolf Steiner House, London had germinated through people connected with the house management prompted, they said, by the part-time course at Michael Hall that I was leading at the time, which had commenced the previous year and which, while gaining momentum, had slowly become known. Edinburgh, too, was a significant factor, in that it was there, during the six-week tour I had made at the end of my previous Class 8 (summer 1980), the school being one of our ports of call, that the commitment, earnestness and punctuality(!) of non-full-time students had struck me one evening during a lecture I gave, as something that the healthy future of the Waldorf movement in the UK and Ireland sorely needed.

The year in which the seminar began 1982/83 was a year of reassessment for me personally. Travels during my sabbatical year had taken me far afield—the farthest was South Africa—and although I taught several Class 11 main-lessons, it was initial teacher training (*Ausbildung*) that seemed to be calling, rather than going back into a 'permanent' classroom situation. Bristol, Michael

Hall, Glencraig in Northern Ireland, Kings Langley and Aberdeen were the main teacher training centres with which I was engaged at the time. The call crescendoed with the London proposal, with the result that teacher training became the main focus of my life and has remained so for the last quarter of a century.

London seemed as though it would be a feasible place for such a training—which takes place essentially on one day per week, Saturday. Arterial routes all lead to London in this oligarchic country of ours and in the early years students commuted from geographically peripheral places such as Canterbury, Ringwood, Bangor in North Wales, Cornwall and Dumfries across the Scottish border, though strangely there were few Londoners, despite the Waldorf School of South West London having opened its doors at the same time as the seminar (September 1983). On such occasions we usually parade our most illustrious coup in this respect: a student who commuted from Munich, eventually making her home in this country. The characteristic of students commuting from outside London has essentially remained though with certain shifts. The distances have decreased and the proportion of Londoners has dramatically increased, and of those many only have English as a second language. The first hint that the training course was to become international in this way occurred when Olga arrived from Delrowe. Since then we have welcomed students from about forty countries across the world—though we are still waiting for a few outliers to arrive, such as Kuwait and Paraguay! About a third of each new intake brings this cultural richness into Rudolf Steiner House. It is of course undoubtedly the nature of the metropolis that is responsible for this, plus possibly that, unlike British universities, we make no discrimination in the fees which 'foreign' students are required to pay.

Tutors also commute into town, with one or two exceptions. The first exception arrived near the beginning and under rather colourful circumstances. I had been lecturing in South Africa and teaching a main-lesson in medieval history when, one evening a day or before I was due to return, out of the blue someone called and offered to take me to the airport. She was the wife of a Dutch diplomat who was anticipating her husband being posted to London. She offered her services if ever they were needed in the future. They were. Our first eurythmist handed on the work to Els who brought a breath of high society into the seminar—coloured not only by her Dutch (cum Afrikaans) accent but also by expressions that stimulated the phagocytes. The most priceless one—made in a fairly non-subdued voice in the long lunch queue, I may say—went something like this, "Oh, I have had such a marvellous experience last Wednesday at [such-and-such a] convention: I rubbed shoulders with Prince Charles ... *all day*! Knowing and relishing her joie de Dutch vivre, and that she lived near Kensington Palace, one could almost have taken it literally!

The constellation of tutors still has this diaspora-like character, despite efforts a few years ago to try and build a core of tutors from the London schools as a sort of syndicate with Amanda Bell being in the forefront. The idea is still there, though perhaps it came prematurely, since the students seem to enjoy the wider regional representation: Thea Kaesbach and Josie Alwyn from Michael Hall, Elaine Holt from Ringwood, Rudolf Kaesbach from Emerson, Anne Ayre from Kings Langley, Tom Towey from South Devon, Eileen Whitworth from Maidstone, Bodo Gottschalk from Wadhurst and others.

On the whole, the course has attracted mature students (aged 28-35) though some years there are remarkable exceptions—the new intake for 2006 contained a high proportion of students in their 20s, giving a welcome opportunity—necessity?—for fresh approaches. Most students have at least a first degree. One year it looked as though we were netting two PhDs but at the last minute the male PhD couldn't make it (*PhD = phizzled detrimentally?*). Enquirers often ask what qualifications are required to get onto the course. Academic qualifications are usually an advantage of course but life experience is a vital factor in teaching, parenthood being included amongst the most valuable.

Talking of parenthood, at the end of one interview, more or less as we were saying goodbye and the applicant had been offered and had accepted a place on the course, she came out with: "Perhaps I ought to say that I'm pregnant!" But hastened to reassure me by adding, "I expect I'll have to miss a Saturday or two." And that's how it panned out. Like those indomitable peasants in the past, she gave birth (behind a haystack so to speak) and then went on with the harvesting. It was very special to hear the little gurgles of delight from one corner of the classroom as feed time came round, Saturday by Saturday. Some ten years later I was at a barbecue and met the mother for the first time since her graduation *with the no-longer-babe-in-arms* standing beside her holding a sausage on a skewer! And—the saga continues—during a lecture I gave at a recent educational conference, there she was again (the mother) still a committed class teacher. It would be mind-blowing if the same thing happened again at the end of an interview, particularly if the applicant happened to be that same daughter.

The seminar can claim a little outreach, too, as there are always a handful of educationists among the students. This is welcome as it anchors discussion in experience. Not only those disillusioned with the State system (q.v. the Ofsted maths inspector!) who remain in mainstream, taking what they can of the Waldorf impulse into their own practice and making a mark here and there further afield. There was also the occasion in Rudolf Steiner House when I personally was interviewed by Dr Martin Ashley of the University of the West of England as part of the Government's enquiry into Waldorf, when it was considering State support for Steiner education in England. Another welcome feature has been the increase in ex-Waldorf pupils doing the training. This was very slow to start, but most years now attract one (or in a bumper year, two) old scholar(s)—nothing, fortunately, to make the movement appear incestuous. Some seven have entered the Waldorf movement.

The seminar has been more than fortunate with its Trustees.

Daniel Donahaye instigated a very simple Trust Deed way back in the year dot. We were three tutors, virtually rubber-stamps who complied with the law's requirements, meeting once a year. As Charities have come under increasing scrutiny and attack due to unscrupulous practices rearing their ugly heads, this simple format has no longer proved adequate. This side of the Trust's business is presently conducted by Josie Alwyn a valued tutor and an Upper School teacher with an adult education background, and Drs Richard House and Christopher Houghton-Budd, the former a senior lecturer at Roehampton University. With the increase in other training courses in the country following the demise of the Teacher Training group who regularised matters into the 80s and early 90s (John Thompson and Georg Locher from Emerson, Shirley Noakes and Karla Kinniger from Edinburgh, myself from London and colleagues from in-service courses run periodically by various schools), the Trustees decided to amalgamate with two other courses in Rudolf Steiner House. These were under the leadership of Lynne Oldfield and Dot Male, both involved in the early years movement. A new leaflet was produced, presenting these as the London Centre. The feeling of solidarity that this engendered has been furthered since the refurbishment of Rudolf Steiner House, which has meant that we can all meet under the same roof.

After various experiences in teacher training between 1962 and 1982, I personally became more and more convinced that good lecturers did not necessarily—I won't say did not ever—make good teachers. We have Steiner's *Discussions with Teachers* as more than a hint substantiating this. They took place daily alongside the no.1 study material *Menschenkunde* (August/September 1914). And similar to the intention of the part-time Edinburgh training course which had been established in the 70s because of the need for new teachers, so the London Waldorf Teacher Training Seminar's aim was to provide teachers for British schools. So, how to do this?

We based the seminar on the three arts that Steiner singles out in the Bern course as being the basis for the teacher's observation of the child's higher members: modelling, music and speech—John Wells taught modelling, John Nixon (and others over the years) taught speech and Anne Ayre and I taught music. Moana Bowron (succeeded by Chris Bennett) taught 'Study of Man'. I, for my part, wished to cultivate an adult education approach that was seminaristic, with student involvement from the beginning—not of the student council type which was increasing in popularity everywhere but of a *participative* nature within actual sessions. School life is about teachers engaging with students, parents, authorities, outside bodies (media, politicians) and colleagues; so similar guided sessions in which students participate through prepared assignments, through spontaneous minor presentations, through master-class type workshops and through interaction seemed (and still seems with increasing relevance) a practical and effective way of going about a training which needs to prepare for the classroom experience (a minimum of eight weeks on the LWTTS) so that the student-teacher's most acutely perspicacious judges, the pupils, are won over sooner rather than later. As a child in my third class quietly observed at supper one day when the class had been taught that morning by a student-teacher on practice: "You know, if you can't make it in the first two minutes you may as well give up!" She was ten years old ... I was relieved to hear that the student-teacher was not from the London Waldorf Teacher Training Seminar!

Having said all that, an unexpected situation developed. The anxiety-engendering difference between supply (trained teachers) and demand resulted in some schools making appointments when students were only half way through the course. Indeed, there have been subject teachers who were employed, who were sent onto the course, financed by the school itself, as a condition of employment. At first, we set our face against the former practice and refused to supply references, but life took over. Not all appointments of this emergency-type nature were successful, sadly but not altogether unexpectedly, but there were sufficient that *were* successful to convince us that filling a teaching situation in this way was preferable to (what otherwise not infrequently happened) head-hunting from the parent body and, albeit as supportively as the school could manage, hoping for the best.

By and large the seminar is meeting its aim. The figures are as follows. Intakes are typically 20-24 students p.a. Of those, two-thirds to three-quarters graduate after the two years (those taking longer usually being people whose life circumstances require teaching practice to be fitted into a third year). Of those, one third to a half enter Waldorf education. This means that 5-8 graduates become teachers each year. This does not include graduates who have taken a gap year before going on to teach. We do not have a data base, but that means that there have been between 125-200 graduates over the quarter century who have made/are making a professional contribution to the movement in one way or another. A very conservative estimate. This includes nearly all the schools in the UK and Ireland, many of the Kindergartens, and several over the years who have gone into curative education. Some abroad too. It should be added here that most of the students are parents, so that apart from the professional contribution mentioned, schools benefit enormously from having parents who are aware of Steiner's educational ideas and can really support what Waldorf education is doing to put these ideas into practice.

These reflections would not be complete without mentioning the unstinting support of the personnel in Rudolf Steiner House: juggling the room allocation with other bookings, the help in the library given to students baffled by 6000 Steiner lectures and bulging shelves of other literature, the friendliness in the bookshop, the consideration and flexibility of those providing refreshments (our coffee, lunch and tea breaks are hardly ever the same weeks running), not to mention always finding a suitable corner for the Course Director when he appears out of nowhere for interviewing, forty or fifty times a year. One seldom realises what a team-work is involved, although it became poignantly palpable last year at the funeral of Christine Muller. It is vital that, as well as students receiving the picture of a cosmic world order emanating from Rudolf Steiner's research, their (for most of them) first experience of anthroposophy in practice is positive.

Perhaps the most outstanding example was Ruth Goldie who presided over refreshments for many years and who quickly got to know all students by name. What a contrast it was to the tutor who persistently after years had not even got that far with his relationship with the students, sending out, of course, completely the wrong message to would-be teachers. Fortunately that unhappy episode in the life of the seminar has receded into history. Ruth also displayed a high degree of originality. One of her most sparkling creations (when the first ones in the coffee queue had used up all her small change and she served someone in trust that before they went back to class they would call at the counter and 'settle up' *and* that trust had failed) was when she would call out cheerily as they passed by, deep in conversation and oblivious of the debt: "Stefano, would you like to pay me now—or would you prefer to meet me in Kamaloka?"

A quick, back-of-the-envelope calculation will show that during 25 years, some 13,000 seminar hours teaching in Rudolf Steiner House will have taken place, and it may appear at first sight that the fruit of that work in the classroom is not so enormous. Those who have dedicated their lives to this work, however, are firmly of the belief that if a generation of children have benefited then it has all been worthwhile. After all, our children are the Michaelic touchstone for the future.

1987-1994

These were years which gave rise to questions regarding the gush of goodwill during the previous decade towards the low-incomed, who wanted Waldorf education for their children, which had resulted in difficult economic circumstances and therefore difficult life circumstances for teachers. Morwenna Bucknall is attributed with having had the fortitude to start the Bristol Waldorf School in this way—the last of the so-called 'contribution schools', incidentally, to give up the completely free approach to financing along these lines.

Tremendous energy went into solving the problem of under-funding, in conferences, in meetings and, of course, in the day-to-day running of the schools themselves, not to mention teachers seldom being seen dressed in anything other than charity-shop clothes and their children in hand-downs. The suffering from burn out was openly and frequently discussed. They were heroes for Waldorf—equal, at least, to the sacrifices made by many parents.

Not that this trend was universal. The Canterbury Steiner School trod an economic path that was more conventional. I don't know how they were seen by the other developing schools, and as far as I know those responsible (Moana Bowron was the founder teacher) did not iterate any principle other than wanting to make it work out for all concerned. There was no hint of fanaticism in her approach, though those who had the privilege to work alongside her well knew how much of a stickler she could be when it came to something that needed inner integrity. Again, as far as I am aware no searching analysis of what went on at that time was undertaken. It is perhaps also important to add here that Moana, herself, later devoted some of the last energetic years of her long working life to one of the London schools which ran a form of contribution scheme.

My suspicions that the problem was deeper seated than we realised clustered around the thought that it was not healthy to let the principle of freedom (in the context of Liberté, Egalité and

Fraternité) reign supreme in the economic sphere. But when I expressed the suspicion it was only the pianissimo of a bed-time lyre, and my conviction—seeing all the children receiving Waldorf education who would otherwise not have done so—was not strong enough to turn the pianissimo into a blaze of trumpets, trombones and clarions. In any case, I thought, surely all those so admirably fired with the Threefold Social Order—indeed, quoting it as the very basis for their embracing a contribution approach to funding—would have the insight and expertise to be able to diagnose clearly which way to go would be healthy. With hindsight, my then misgivings now convince me that the reasons that this wave washed upon the shores of the Waldorf movement in the British Isles lay elsewhere than in the Threefold Social Order.

Thirty years later it resounded—from a medical doctor! Michaela Glöckler was speaking to students of the London Waldorf Teacher Training Seminar and some teachers working in Waldorf schools in London. A question had been asked about the main-lesson in Class 7 frequently referred to as 'Health, Hygiene and Nutrition'. She took up the question with exceptional deliberation and energy, emphasising not surprisingly, the *health* aspect. Not only that, she broadened the horizon of the subject into present-day issues, relating them to the Threefold Social Order and highlighting two issues in particular.

The principles of (i) freedom (liberté) in the cultural-spiritual sphere, and (ii) association (fraternité) in the economic sphere have been skewed. 'The market' basically rests on the principle of freedom in the economic sphere, with its dog-eat-dog competition. (How often are prospective customers wheedled into considering the purchase of some article with the expression *a competitive price*?) The paranoia behind the desire for accreditation—and the whole regiment of validation, assessment, mentoring, advisory services, quality assurance etc. that marches in one guise or another behind that banner—is in conflict with, if not preventing, the individual's inner creative striving and freedom in the cultural sphere of education. Religious fundamentalism is essentially in the same category. These were among her main comments.

So there is an unhealthy crossing over reminiscent of the diagonal cross in which St Andrew was crucified (though the tradition seems only to date back to the 14th century). Dr Glöckler's talk was on 29 November, the day, we later discovered, on which the martyrdom of St Andrew is commemorated...

Distinctive Features of Waldorf Education and their Relevance For or Bearing On Assessment

Notes based on a paper prepared for and presented to the Israeli Government's Experimental Schools Committee[1] (Northern Region) 4 November 1997

1. Introduction: assessment—why bother?

In an educational context, assessment (as distinct from self-assessment or peer-assessment) is primarily thought of as something imposed on the pupils. Its aim could be described as getting the pupil to acquire self-knowledge in such a way that progress is prompted, spurred on by personal endeavour. At the same time, it has become customary to associate the concept of assessment with some sort of *measurement*—measurement that is presumed to be an indication of the extent to which the aim is being achieved.

This is not the occasion to get embroiled in the question of what are worthy aims; or to what extent aims stipulated by an examination board as worthy possess any intrinsic value. For the time being, they constitute the *status quo*, and it should be recognised as such—neither more nor less.

Yet if one asks how people such as Columbus, Michael Faraday, Martin Luther King, Nelson Mandela, Michelangelo, Florence Nightingale, Schubert, Tolkien, Wilberforce and a host of others achieved the aims for which they are acclaimed, one cannot but acknowledge that life presents mirrors for self-knowledge, golden opportunities, spurs for action, challenges, climacteric moments, vital turning points, significant meetings … i.e. almost everything *but assessment*, that on hindsight prove to have been the real stepping-stones of one's biography. Moreover, such examples could

---

[1]   This paper was written at a time when the author was appointed Senior Academic Consultant on Waldorf Education in Israel in 1997.

be multiplied a thousandfold, whether considering prominent personalities or the ordinary person in the street. In view of this, one might well ask why the whole of the Western world—including its academic outreach into developing countries—has not only become blinkered to this 'fact of life', but allowed the pendulum of assessment to swing education so far in a direction that seems opposite to that in which those stepping-stones lead, which life itself affords so abundantly? Is it that trust in 'life' has arrived at an all-time low, so that only external motivation inspires confidence? Or, to look at the reverse of the same coin, is it that society has lost all faith in inner motivation, in the value of introspection and in the power and effectiveness of inner resolve?

One might press further: are not such forms of self-knowledge more long-lasting than the 'carrot' of the sought after/ feared/anticipated assessment exam result? After all, while a carrot once eaten is gone, discovering the means of cultivating carrots will surely be more productive and the harvest of life be the better for it.

A well known example of such a harvest (from literature), provides the entire dramatic momentum for Shakespeare's last play. Prospero, in *The Tempest*, in an introspective moment near the beginning of the play, realises that as Duke of Milan—his status before we meet him on the island where the action is mostly set—he was too much taken up with studying his books and thus too little concerned with outer affairs of State. It is this flaw in Prospero's personality—seemingly rather innocent—which has opened the gates to his brother's duplicity. Not that in Prospero we are presented with a character racked with self-reproach. Nevertheless, his vision of the past has obviously become unclouded through the introspection that he has had the opportunity to pursue during his c.12 years' sojourn on the island. A melodrama could have been written, no doubt, about such realisation, with the usurper's malicious schemes culminating in the evil act of bundling Prospero into a "rotten carcass of a boat", with his distressing cry—all too late—of poignant self-censure as he tragically drowns together with his heir, his only daughter Miranda. Shakespeare takes a different line: he unfolds the action that Prospero takes, with the help of his 'other worldly' minions, after his moment of self-examination, self-knowledge, self-assessment, in order to rectify his error—and, by so doing, with the aid of 'magic', to bring restitution to the evil that has come streaming into the vacuum, created by his original sin of omission.

Inspired by this example, one might well argue that qualitative means of assessment are preferable to quantitative, since it would seem, by definition, that the qualitative depends on and therefore guarantees *inner* motivation, while the quantitative—a handy 'carrot', though not necessarily one to inspire industry from within —might, at its worst, prevent genuine motivation all together.

The aim here is to show how Waldorf does what it does do, in order to achieve, by another route, what quantitative assessment purports to achieve. Or, in other words: to show what Waldorf has at its disposal for nurturing inner motivation in the ordinary course of the school day, the school week, and the school year, to the end that the education arrives at its destination?

2. Does Waldorf's emphasis and reliance upon inner motivation work?

The few research papers on Waldorf education that do exist may not be enough to convince the sceptic that it should/does work. Nevertheless, it cannot be denied that a body of supportive research has been building up during the past two decades. (It might also be pointed out that those in power during the Nazi regime apparently did not need a large dossier of research for them to decide on the effectiveness of the Waldorf schools: they systematically closed them down as a threat, presumably, to the totalitarian State, seeing the education as one which cultivated independent thought and strong individuality.)

But regarding the effectiveness of Waldorf, as a matter of

common-sense it might first be well to glance briefly at possible external pointers indicating whether a Waldorf school is being seen to 'achieve' its aims. Amongst these are: its roll call (parents 'voting with their feet', in this case voting *in*), the flow of applications, 'early' school leavers, teacher turnover, external exam results (where applicable), the sheer willingness of children to attend school, old scholars' achievements at university, its performance in (e.g.) sporting events against other schools, its participation in national '6ᵗʰ form debates', the vigour of participants at youth conferences, its Upper School work experience at various levels, the interest/attainments of old scholars and so on. However, while these are important, they do not necessarily distinguish a Waldorf school from other types of school—unless one begins to look beneath the surface. (E.g. is the basketball score the result of a specially picked and coached 'school team' that practises fiendishly or is it a single, mixed-ability class who simply play regularly, say, once per week? And if so, *how do they do it?*)

That neither key-stage testing nor other forms of internal examinations are practised in Waldorf education is common knowledge. At the same time, it is self-evident that the achievements of Waldorf pupils in A levels, Scottish Highers, Matriculation, Abitur and similar school leaving exams across the world would not be possible without sustained *effort and achievement* throughout the child's school career. The truth of this is borne home all the more when one realises that only some half/three-quarters of the school day is given over to exam syllabi, the remainder being spent on various components of the actual Waldorf curriculum. It is, however, the intention here to take a deeper look, not so much at the 'effort and achievement' referred to above, but rather the pedagogy and cumulative psychology that it implies.

Three immediate and connected questions devolve from Waldorf's success in the field of school leaving examinations.

- How are the results that Waldorf achieves possible on such

a reduced schedule?
- What was Steiner's attitude towards exams?
- What motivation arising from self-knowledge does Waldorf contain that is the equivalent of and—judging by results—clearly serves the same purpose as the kind of quantitative assessment that grades and examination marks provide?

3. How are the results that Waldorf achieves possible on such a reduced schedule?

A full answer to this question could only be given if one explained Steiner's understanding of child development—with its threefold acquisition and assimilation of knowledge, as pursued in Kindergarten, Lower School and Upper School pedagogy. The considerations here (see 7 below) will confine themselves to those components in Waldorf education which have bearing on the process of learning normally thought of in conjunction with the precept of assessment.

4. What was Steiner's attitude towards exams?

This is a complex issue. Statements by Steiner made in teachers' meetings on the subject of exams have been collated and, for the sake of completeness, appear as an appendix to this paper. From these it can be seen how Steiner, discussing examinations with the teachers of the first Waldorf School in Stuttgart, made his expectations of Waldorf education clear: (see especially 10 May 1922). However, in that the *aims* of Waldorf could be achieved without the passing of exams—and possibly better achieved without the loss of time spent on exam preparation—it becomes abundantly clear that an alternative to exam-type assessment must have been for him an imperative.

5. Retaining traditional terminology

Notwithstanding the above, and even though Waldorf's approach to
motivation is to stimulate that which is inner rather than what has
been presented above as outer, for the sake of comparison,
traditional terminology has been retained in what follows in
connection with assessment. Also, although assessment is normally
understood to mean the assessment *of pupils*, for the sake of
completeness a brief consideration of teacher assessment will be
touched on. This is based on the manifest principle that learning
which produces 'results' is highly dependent upon effective
teaching. Teaching and learning form a partnership.

Pupil assessment as such will be considered under four main
headings: self assessment, peer assessment, teacher assessment (of
the pupil) and parent assessment. Assessment of the teacher will be
considered under three headings: self assessment, collegial
assessment and external assessment. In each case, however, we will
be looking into those distinctive features of Waldorf that have
bearing on the theme.

6. What motivation arising from self-knowledge does Waldorf contain, implicitly and explicitly, that is the equivalent of and—judging by results—clearly accomplishes and supersedes the purpose of the kind of assessment that grades and examination marks provide?

After the above introduction, and the perspective on assessment that
Waldorf education has to offer, we can now embark on the
interrogation of Waldorf's distinctive features, one by one—
sometimes under more than one heading—so that as fully
comprehensive an impression as possible can be gained of Waldorf
educational theory, to inspire confidence in its rigour, its
achievability and its practicality through clearly identifying the
sources of its effectiveness.

For facility of reference, the structure of the following sections of this paper is given under sub-headings which are listed here:

7. Pupil Assessment
7.1 Pupil Assessment—Self-Assessment
  7.1.1   *Year Opening and Year Closing*
  7.1.2   *"... that strength and grace and skill, for learning and work, in me may live and grow."*
  7.1.3   *Main-Lesson Books*
  7.1.4   *Public Occasions*
  7.1.5   *Reports*
  7.1.6   *Pupil Feedback*
  7.1.7   *Individual Projects*
  7.1.8   *Upper School Tutor/Counsellor*
  7.1.9   *School Leaving Profile*
7.2 Pupil Assessment—Peer Assessment
  7.2.1   *Class Ethos/Class Spirit/Class 'climate'*
  7.2.2   *Human Centred*
  7.2.3   *Whole Class Teaching*
  7.2.4   *Public Occasions*
7.3. Pupil Assessment—Teacher Assessment
  7.3.1   *Equal Responsibility and Transitions*
  7.3.2   *No Text Books*
  7.3.3   *Check List*
  7.3.4   *The Teacher's Preparation*
  7.3.5   *Child Study*
  7.3.6   *Public Occasions*
  7.3.7   *Reports*
  7.3.8   *Learning Support*
  7.3.9   *Report Verses*
  7.3.10 *Nurturing the Whole Child*
  7.3.11 *Arts and Crafts*
  7.3.12 *3-Day Rhythm*

7. Pupil Assessment

7.1 Pupil Assessment—Self-Assessment

7.1.1   *Year Opening and Year Closing*
At the beginning and end of each year it is commonplace
in Waldorf schools for the whole school to be assembled

and for each class, in the presence of the full assembly, to be addressed 'from the platform' by a teacher (the class teacher in the case of the Lower School and, often, the class guardian or main-lesson teacher in the case of the Upper School). About 3-5 minutes per class is the usual time allocation for this. At year opening, a preview of the year ahead is given; at year closing, the achievement of the class as a whole during the year is broadly evaluated. On both occasions a form and style are given to each mini-address, suited to the age and consciousness of the pupils, but in a manner that is suited to a 'public' occasion, while at the same time conveying a clear message to the class in question. Each pupil therefore has the opportunity to individualise what is being said in such a way that resolves for the future are stimulated by both preview and review. Such resolves, of course, only have value if they *are* individualised and they will need affirming in the months ahead. Nevertheless, they promote the health and stability and thus the progress of the individual within the totality of the class.

7.1.2   *"... that strength and grace and skill, for learning and work, in me may live and grow."*

These are words that occur in the so-called morning verse which Steiner composed to be spoken in speech chorus at the beginning of each day (though in the lower classes there are other words, albeit with a very similar concept lying behind them: "... that I with all my might may love to work and learn..."). In the fourth lecture of the *Practical Course for Teachers*, where Steiner is giving advice for the very first lesson in Class 1, he suggests that the children's attention be drawn to their hands as the media by which that which is learnt in school lessons is made manifest in the world. The morning verses may be

taken as indicators that the pupils' awareness of the reason
for being at school is raised on a regular, daily basis,
likewise the inner resolves referred to in 7.1.1 above. This
in turn presupposes that awareness in children is a
significantly operative factor in *self-motivation*—as
distinct from what traditional assessment aims to achieve
from without.

Through this, it could be said, Waldorf places confidence
on emphasising through reiteration, and in the context of
'school rituals', the *aims* of education at the beginning of
each day, rather than running the risk of the pupil gaining
no conception of any purpose in education outside the
exams that can so easily become the focal point of
traditional assessment.

7.1.3   *Main-Lesson Books*
The practice in Waldorf schools of the pupils making their
own text books day by day, containing summaries in
written and illustrated form of the content of all lessons,
means that each child is constantly aware of what it is
absorbing of the lessons as well as of the developing skills
needed to make such regular entries. Such main-lesson
books thus become a source of self-esteem, confidence
and motivation, all vital ingredients in pupil achievement
via self-assessment.

7.1.4   *Public Occasions*
An important maxim in Waldorf education is that of
teaching the whole group but at the same time ensuring
that each individual within that group has absorbed
whatever he or she is capable of. The opportunity for self-
assessment is obvious in the latter case. Steiner also
inaugurated so-called 'monthly festivals'—these are
festivals in which educational achievements are shared—

in which class after class comes before the whole school and 'performs' some item arising from the lessons (reciting a poem or a mathematics table, singing a song, moving an item of eurythmy or gymnastics, performing a play, displaying works of art etc.). Having to appear before the whole school has several virtues. Here it is a matter of looking at the assessment value. On such public occasions, the individual, albeit supported by the group, is placed in the position of representing the class. This strengthens the individualisation process, putting each pupil on his or her mettle. Not that the aim is to polish each presentation to the standard of what is customarily considered a 'public performance': the presentation should be *representative* of what the class is achieving with each month-long main-lesson, as well as in other branches of the work. It is an occasion when being on collective show helps the learning process become *consolidated more deeply* than would otherwise be the case.

7.1.5 *Reports*

Waldorf reports tend to be lengthy documents and are written once a year in the Lower School—more frequently in the Upper School. Steiner's advice with regard to the way the pupil receives the content of the report has been characterised as follows. While the parent reads the report aloud, it is as if the pupil listens 'over the parent's shoulder'. (The reading of the report might also take place, of course, in the extended family circle in some cases.) Hearing the report in this way has the effect of elevating the pupil's consciousness towards that of the parent's. And although the event occurs usually only once a year (though it is in the parent's gift to repeat the reading of the report once or twice, say, during the ensuing holidays, or at the outset of the new school year), the anticipation of such occasions lives throughout the preceding year, affecting motivation from within.

7.1.6   Pupil Feedback

The practice of asking pupils, say from age 11/12 upwards, on the last page of their main-lesson book, to express what the main-lesson has meant for them, enhances each pupil's self-awareness during the writing of such a piece. And, again, the anticipation of doing this during the main-lesson (sub-conscious though it may be), means that the student inwardly accompanies his or her own progress through the main-lesson more attentively and purposefully.

7.1.7   Individual Projects

Though there is a multitude of occasions when the individual work of the pupil is given space to come to expression, at a certain point during their development— say from age 12 onwards, the age, in this case, depending on the school rather than any indication deriving from Steiner—each pupil will be required to produce a personal project, usually related to the subject of the main-lesson. The culmination of this practice in many Waldorf schools across the world is the Class 12 project, prepared over the course of a whole academic year, and presented in written or some other visual form (where appropriate) as well as through a verbal presentation to some section of the wider school community. The latter will include the fielding of questions related to the project from the floor, requiring similar background and skill to that involved in a *viva voce* exam. However, the procedure is not one of examination but stems from real life interest—the interest of one human being in the work of another. Or, it might be said, the interest is concrete rather than theoretical.

7.1.8   *Upper School Tutor/Counsellor*
While the class teacher in a Waldorf school provides pastoral care during the years c.7-14, in the Upper School this role is taken on by someone else. The four years spent in the Upper School may embrace a series of Upper School teachers who assume this responsibility in turn. However, the nature of the adolescent being what it is, it is recognised that though the pastoral care of the class as a whole may be adequately covered collectively, it may not follow that each pupil's more personal educational needs will be met in this way. Therefore, it has become customary for each Upper School pupil (certainly, from Class 10 onwards) to choose a personal tutor. Conversations with the tutor may involve some counselling from time to time, though the main point of focus will be to assess verbally the student's progress. This most conscious of all means of assessment—a dialogue rather than a curt remark, or still curter mark at the end of a piece of work—is a vital factor in helping the pupil maintain a degree of progressive continuity in the natural 'ups and downs' of adolescence.

7.1.9   *School Leaving Profile*
At the end of Class 12 (or 13) the pupil's effort and achievement in relation to each subject taken is recorded in a document which also summarises the curriculum content, supplying what is in essence an open character reference. Through this document, the footprints of the pupil's journey through school—particularly the Upper School—becomes visible. Knowledge of that forthcoming visibility carries something of value for the one making the journey—the pupil. Notwithstanding that the designed value is future-oriented, the profile, as a formal document,

is part of the built-in assessment infrastructure of a
Waldorf school.

7.2 Pupil Assessment—Peer Assessment

7.2.1   Class Ethos/Class Spirit/Class 'climate'

Through chronological grouping, Steiner would maintain,
and through whole class teaching (see also 7.2.3) for most
of the day—the main exceptions being subjects where
space constrictions dictate small groups—an ideal basis is
provided for peer assessment, which will range from the
most subtle to the out and out direct. Such a class ethos
engenders an atmosphere not of competition (exam papers,
percentage scores and 'league' positions in class) but of
mutual concern. The positive aspect of attainment is
emphasised (—Where have you succeeded?) rather than
what can easily become a negative aspect (—Where did I
fail?).

7.2.2   Human Centred

One of the maxims of Waldorf is to relate as much subject
matter as practicable, within the context of the lesson, to
the human being. It follows that an atmosphere will
prevail that is permeated by human interest. What more
effective or more naturally provided starting point for
putting this into practice could there be than a group of
peers cultivating and being helped to cultivate interest in
one another? The formal ties with family and with
teachers do not hold sway over such relationships. The
child's natural disposition—something that peers are
notorious for 'rubbing corners off'—is something that
plays a part in the relationship *outside* of the learning
process. Within the learning process it is possible to
nurture, through the human-centred nature of Waldorf, an

appropriate peer assessment that will not need to bring into expression the rubbing off of corners but which will have in it something of the quality of 'in the same boat' together. This supports self-esteem without erring towards the egotistical.

7.2.3   *Whole Class Teaching*
The value of whole class teaching could be questioned if thereby the individual student were overlooked or neglected. Steiner was emphatic about avoiding this pitfall. But he also saw advantages. The enthusiasm of one pupil or a group of pupils (for example, all those with a choleric nature) can be contagious. More: the understanding of those more gifted in the subject being 'studied' can assist the others through the peer group dynamic that builds up over the years.

7.2.4   *Public Occasions*
These are mainly mentioned here (in addition to 7.1.4) for completeness' sake. Nevertheless, because each pupil is more in the public eye than normally vis-à-vis his or her school attainment, such appearances do bring out traits that would otherwise perhaps remain obscure or veiled. The processes of peer assessment mentioned above (7.2.1 and 7.2.2) therefore become equally applicable here in these 'extra routine' circumstances.

7.3. Pupil Assessment—Teacher Assessment
7.3.1   *Equal Responsibility and Transitions*
A point often celebrated in Waldorf's favour is its integrated curriculum. Integration in Waldorf is strengthened further through the fact that teachers of all ages meet regularly together once a week. Thus, although

the Kindergarten, Lower School and Upper School teachers often have separate pedagogical meetings in which teachers can work as a specialist research cluster concentrating on their own age groups, the transition from one department to another is made smooth by handover reports being given on each child. Also, such complete gatherings of teachers means that comment from former teachers (even right back in Kindergarten days) when assessing pupils' progress is permanently available.

7.3.2   *No Text Books*
That Waldorf schools are, in the main, text-book-free zones has already been referred to (7.1.3). It is self-evident that the day by day work done by pupils in main-lesson (and other) exercise books provides the teacher with immediate port-holes which look out a) onto their ability to assimilate and individualise the lesson content presented in class, and b) onto the pupil's power of fantasy, creative writing and other skills in its re-presentation.

7.3.3   *Check List*
Standard check lists of pupils' achievements as distilled from the broad-ranging Waldorf curriculum can give a kind of cross-section assessment picture of where each pupil stands at any given point, though it has to be borne in mind that many significant components within the pupil's nature cannot be quantified in this way. Important though such 'check list' snap-shots of the pupil may be, the Waldorf approach will not mistake such details as appear in them for anything other than symptoms of the pupil's deeper nature.

7.3.4   The Teacher's Preparation

Part of Steiner's advice to the teacher preparing lessons is to picture each pupil that is going to be taught the following day. This 'exercise' can be done in a variety of ways: by considering the class photograph, by recalling current behaviour or recent incidents that have cropped up in lessons, by working alphabetically down the register and so on. Whatever technical aid is preferred, however, the aim is the same: that in course of time a sufficiently in-depth impression of each pupil be developed for the teaching to be relevant, direct, efficient, supportive of the learning process and of fundamental value in the realm of assessment.

7.3.5   Child Study

Study of individual children is a regular item on the agenda of faculty meetings. It is conducted in various ways, with those present having recourse to photographs of the pupil (profile, facial, full length, 'in action'...), samples of the pupil's work (writing, drawing, painting, mathematics, modelling, handwork...), descriptions by teachers (the child's nature, family background, movement in eurythmy and gymnastics, sport, behaviour in class, relationship with other children) and some medical history by the school doctor (salient features of the pupil's physiology, diagnosis of weaknesses, medication and/or prescribed learning support or therapy ... where relevant). When this 'exercise' has been completed, discussion can then take place with the aim of finding ways of corporately supporting the pupil in the next stage of his or her development, through the different pedagogical approaches available subject by subject.

7.3.6   *Public Occasions*
Public occasions have been mentioned twice before (7.14, 7.2.4) as a significant element in Waldorf assessment. Most of what has already been said applies in the present context, too, though there is naturally a further dimension for the teacher whose initiative it has been to present the item for performance, in that he or she will from time to time have assigned a special role to a pupil or pupils. With such 'inside knowledge', the pupil's 'performance' will have greater significance for that teacher than for anyone else, in that he or she will be able to assess to what extent the pupil is measuring up to or exceeding expectations.

7.3.7   *Reports*
It has often been observed that the writing of reports is as much an exercise in self-knowledge for the teacher as it is an assessment of the pupil. Assuming there is truth in this, here it is a matter of seeing how much such an exercise can help the assessment process and thereby—precisely because of the enhanced awareness of the teacher both of self and pupil—contribute to the pupil's greater motivation.

7.3.8   *Learning Support*
In theory, through the depth of knowledge of children which is cultivated in Waldorf (see 7.3.5), teachers in the school should be in a good position to identify children's special educational needs. It goes without saying that the school has also to be well equipped staff-wise to put into effect any early intervention. Because of Waldorf's professed wide-ability range, teachers should be especially au fait with special educational needs. Moreover, through teachers having to be alert to the potential need for learning support, the assessment of *all* pupils is likely to

be the more accurate.

7.3.9   Report Verses

A vital task of the teacher according to Steiner was to 'remove obstacles' to learning. Such obstacles, of course, are peculiar to each child. Some weaknesses are very deep-seated. There are many means within the run-of-the-mill classroom setting for tackling this task.

In collaboration with a teacher from Hamburg, Steiner pioneered a new approach to this problem: the writing of a verse for each child to speak once a week. The verse contains elements—images, rhythms, sequences of sound etc., not totally dissimilar to what might be done in speech therapy—deemed to be of assistance in the task of 'removing obstacles'. The teacher's responsibility is a) the writing of the verse (based on diagnosis of obstacles that can be helped in this way); and b) the direction of the child's articulation whenever the verse is being 'formally' spoken.

7.3.10   Nurturing the Whole Child

Waldorf seeks to nurture the *whole* child—its physical nature, its temperament, its threefold psychological nature, its spiritual nature and its motorial, emotional and rational intelligences. The complexity of human nature with which the teacher is thus confronted, necessitates a systematic approach to assessing the proportionate strengths and weaknesses of each pupil. It should be added that though this takes time, not least through the collegial collaboration required, the broader-based pyramid of knowledge of the child that results, pays dividends in the matter of assessment as well as being continually beneficial in the minutiae of teaching.

7.3.11   Arts and Crafts

The prominence given to arts and crafts in Waldorf—they are not subjects that have suffered marginalisation, as in much educational practice in the West—ensures that they feature effectively in the overall picture gained of the child. The value of this is seen particularly when forming an overall picture of and evaluating each pupil's 'multiple intelligences' (the so-called G-factor).

7.3.12   3-Day Rhythm

With the intellect being only one strand in the process of learning, it behoves the teacher to be able to tap into other intelligences and 'skills'. A method built into the Waldorf main-lesson 'rhythm' from its inception is that of taking an item of study over the course of three days. This has two connected advantages. There is the more obvious one of continuity, deepened by (broadly) appealing to head, heart and hand in turn. Equally important, according to Steiner, is the continued work that goes on in the human psyche (albeit unconsciously) during the hours of sleep, followed the next morning by the 'Socratic' questioning and other forms of class discussion which the teacher can instigate. Through all the above, the teacher's insight into the pupil's assimilation of the subject is enhanced.

7.3.13   Phenomenological Approach to Science

While science taught as hypotheses proved by experiment is learnt by experiences and memorising, Waldorf science education purports to be more active insofar as its phenomenological approach, beginning by being concerned with the phenomenon, continues (on the second day, following the recall of the 'experiment') by getting the students themselves to find what 'laws' are at work in the phenomenon. This they do through their own power of thought. This exercise is done verbally in class, enabling the teacher to assess the readiness with which each pupil enters into and is engaged in this vital part of science education. Such a method contrasts strongly with, say, the assessment of whether a pupil can recall (reproduce on demand) chemical formulae: for it enables the teacher to assess the pupil's power and accuracy of observation, his ability to penetrate the phenomena through the development of autonomous thought, and his power to sustain a lively interest in the phenomena presented by the world as well as what those phenomena might be the expression of.

7.3.14 Integrated Curriculum

Due to the integrated curriculum in a Steiner school, the class teacher will have the advantage of being able to identify the student's strong points, connecting to them on occasion so that weaker points can be supplemented or strengthened (what is referred to as left and right brain thinking, for example) as well as supporting the pupil's self-esteem by 'soft-pedalling' sensitive areas or high-lighting achievement—whatever is most appropriate to the occasion. Specialist teachers will not have such a broad perspective: nevertheless, at regular teachers' meetings (apart from everyday staffroom contact) there are ample opportunities of keying into the class teacher's knowledge in order that a full assessment of the pupil can be achieved.

7.3.15 Tutor/Counselling

As already mentioned (7.1.8), in keeping with Steiner's emphasis upon being aware of and meeting the needs of each individual pupil from Class 10 (age 15/16), it is customary for each pupil to choose a personal mentor from among the teaching staff. Scheduled conversations with tutor/mentor and pupil enable the former to gain an overall picture of the pupil's development as well as keeping in touch with the pupil's more personal needs—supplementing the necessarily limited perspective gained by each individual specialist. The tutor hence acquires a deeper insight into where each pupil 'is at' at any given moment in his/her journey through the school. While it would be totally counter-productive if confidentialities assumed in such a relationship were breached, this arrangement obviously results in the personal tutor/mentor being in a strong position to advise in any staff discussion about the tutee.

7.3.16   Profile

All that has been said regarding reports (7.3.7) can be reiterated here. The profile calls for the highest degree of assessment and the ability to express succinctly those salient characteristics of the pupil's nature that will be helpful, for example, to prospective employees

7.4 Pupil Assessment—Parent Assessment

7.4.1   Spirito Psycho Somatic

Because Steiner conceives of the child as not only having a psycho-somatic dimension but also a spiritual one, it is essential to gain as many insights as possible into the full nature of the child, in order to assess how development is progressing on all three fronts. Though the teacher has continuous opportunity in the classroom of doing this, regular contact with parents is a strong, if ancillary, element of Waldorf education.

7.4.2 *No Text Books*

The child's own 'textbooks' (see 7.3.2 above) provide what is probably the most intimate and direct way that a Waldorf school has of assessing work in progress. Habits are established early in school, so that children complete work at home—albeit work of the kind that is more time-consuming in the early years as opposed to cognitionally demanding (drawing pictures, colouring geometrical constructions, collecting items for class projects, drawing maps, making copies of historical facsimiles etc.). Nevertheless, the opportunity is also there for the parents to keep themselves informed of their child's progress.

7.4.3 *Public Occasions*

Little more need be added to this point. Parents, in any case, tend to be less critical (and if anything somewhat doting, particularly with younger children) on these occasions. Nevertheless, the parent's is a different perspective and it would be an omission not to recognise the fact in garnering a full concept of Waldorf assessment.

7.4.4 *Parents' Evenings*

Regular parents' evenings (two or three p.a.) ensure that parents not only have the opportunity of seeing the 'written work' that pupils bring home, but also of seeing all their work as each year proceeds and of assessing progress through comparison with other pupils' work that is on show on these occasions. Opportunity for sharing impressions is also there through the more informal conversational part of such evenings.

8. Teacher Assessment[2]

8.1 Teacher Assessment—Self-Assessment

8.1.1   *Self-Knowledge*
          The gaining of teacher self-knowledge is a vital factor in
          Waldorf methodology, professionally acquired through
          various means.

8.1.2   *Preparation*
          Steiner set great store upon the teacher fully preparing
          lessons. Knowledge of the teacher's own boundaries,
          knowledge of the pupils to be taught (individuals and
          group), aspects of the subject that are particularly relevant
          to these pupils, methods of teaching that will get the
          subject across, as well as common-or-garden classroom
          management, are likely to be included in such preparation.

8.1.3   *No Notes*
          Preparation having been carried out methodically, Steiner
          saw the use of notes as not merely being superfluous in
          teaching, but a hindrance to the teacher's observation of
          how the pupils react to the material being presented as the
          lesson unfolds.

8.1.4   *Daily Review*
          Either as part of preparation, or at some other time, a
          systematic daily review of how lessons have gone forms
          part of the Waldorf method. This can be particularly
          effective if carried out in an 'overnight' way—i.e. before

---

[2]   The following notes have been kept briefer than those above dealing with pupil
       assessment. While pupil assessment could be—and frequently is—presented as
       something in its own right, the symbiotic relationship between teacher and
       pupil which is axiomatic to Waldorf requires that, in any document on pupil
       assessment, the teacher's position not be left altogether out of account.

and immediately following the hours of sleep. Apart from other benefits, this discipline is seen as having a supportive, cumulative effect in the teacher's self-assessment.

8.1.5   Reports
The writing of Waldorf reports receives more than cursory attention. As well as plain achievement, something of the pupil's inner progress should find reflection in what is said. This can only be done if the teacher has accompanied that progress fairly intimately throughout the year. Report writing is thus not only 'part of the day's work', it is a particularly potent opportunity for the teacher's self-assessment.

8.1.6   Studying Steiner
Though Steiner would probably be the last person one would consider arrogant, he did on one occasion (in the *Konferenzen*) upbraid the teachers for insufficient study of the basic educational lecture courses he had given prior to the school's opening. These, he maintained, gave the teacher—and this serves to underline the non-arrogance of his concern—self-sufficiency in teaching.

8.2 Teacher Assessment—Collegial Assessment
8.2.1   Faculty Meetings
In the weekly and often very extensive faculty meetings, space is regularly reserved for teachers to present their work (classroom or otherwise), followed by feedback from colleagues. Such feedback provides food for thought for the teacher and has the advantage—through being in the wider faculty with its degree of familiarity that builds up over long periods of collaboration—of coming both from

experienced and relatively new teachers. The former can present views and points that help to 'save reinventing the wheel'; the latter can speak 'unhindered by experience' about how the presentation strikes them from a creative and possibly contemporary' point of view.

8.2.2   *Study*
The study, referred to above (8.1.6) was intended as private study. Equally valuable is study within a professional body of colleagues. There are various ways of doing this which do not need elaborating here.

8.2.3   *Public Occasions*
Following public occasions, already several times mentioned in this paper, a review in faculty meetings (as well as, perhaps, privately) can help the teacher gain a true perspective of how his or her work stands in relation to what is seen to be 'centre court' Waldorf. This must, of course, include comment on and draw on insight into whatever is innovative in the teacher's work.

8.2.4   *Year Opening and Year Closing*
In the review of these events at staff gatherings, similar reflection and therefore assessment can take place as in 8.2.3.

8.2.5   *Waldorf Resources*
The numerous books, articles, magazines and other study material produced by the Waldorf movement not only help the new teacher gain a firm footing relatively quickly, but assist all teachers in assessing how their own work stands in relation to how the "achieving of Waldorf" fares in the wider world. This is not a matter of leaning on parrot-like emulation—though many good ideas and 'good practice'

will be stimulated by such resource material—but of being stimulated by 'thinking through' whatever is presented in written form by colleagues. Whether, after reading such material, the conclusion is positive or negative, and irrespective of the enjoyment gained from the reading, the value may be said to be in the inner questioning of and reflection upon the reader's own pedagogical practice.

8. 3. Teacher Assessment—External Assessment

8.3.1   Inspecting, Monitoring, Advising

From time to time, depending on regulations obtaining in any one country, the teacher may be visited officially as part of an inspection of the school. It may also happen that the school invites its own advisers who can perform a similar function, albeit and in all probability with a wider knowledge of Waldorf than an 'external' inspector is likely, by definition, to have. The value of all such visits will depend on both the observation skills and the communication skills of the 'visitor', as much as on the 'hearing' skills of the teacher in question and their willingness to take in what has to be offered as part of the ongoing process of self-assessment.

8.3.1   Autonomy

When an approach to education stands or falls on the autonomy of individual teachers, as is the case with Waldorf, it is vital in any form of external assessment of a teacher's 'performance' that this be done in ways that strengthen and not undermine that autonomy. Though the school can assist any State inspectorate, it cannot influence the above factor. However, with those external assessors, advisers, monitors and evaluators that the school *invites* into the classroom, this factor does come within their jurisdiction to a certain extent. Such an assessment will strengthen the individual's autonomy while at the same time, and equally, strengthening the school's confidence that its trust in that autonomy is justifiably placed.

Extracts from the Konferenzen re exams.

29 July 1920

There is the question of the leaving examination. This is not such an easy matter in view of the fact that if we were to work for State recognition of our Middle School we should actually be unfaithful to our principles. We would make ourselves dependent on the State, and we would no longer have the right to talk of a school that is independent of the State. We can only remain true to our principles if we simply refer children to the fact that they must take examinations themselves if they want to work for the State. They would have to take an exam at a State school to obtain the right to attend a university. As soon as we start having business with the State we become dependent on it. It will probably stipulate that an officially approved school inspector has to be present at least in exams. We cannot give them access to the real management of the school. If they want to look at the school, they may, if they hang around. But we cannot enter into real negotiations. We are not being untrue to our principles if the children who want to return to the old order of things take a State examination.

The founding of Class 9 only makes sense if we intend founding a truly independent High School in which case we shan't need to mind what decisions are taken about the leaving exam. In that eventuality we shall only have to consider the question of High School qualifications. That is the sort of question we will postpone. By then the situation may have changed to one in which recognition for this kind of High School is likely to be withheld.

31 January 1923

The best way to solve the exam question is by trying to prepare the pupils as well as possible and then going to the relevant examiners... Dealing with them on a personal basis is fairly useful on the whole, but it all depends on *how*. Even then you shouldn't deal with things the way you did in today's introduction, when you said we had decided to let our most charming colleague loose on certain people. I would rather suggest that the people who have no graces take lessons from those who have.

8 March 1923

[as the children are uneasy about their exams] ... difficulties will have arisen because the pupils were given so much in lecture form and have not taken an active enough part in the work, despite the fact that we have often spoken about it. They do not contribute enough themselves. So we must get the pupils to take an active part in Class 12. One cannot say they are not capable, but it does not remain in their memories sufficiently strongly for them to be able to stand up to exam nerves. They cannot get it across under exam conditions.

30 March 1923

The best thing would be if we could arrange it so that only those pupils go in for the Abitur who really want to do it. Perhaps there won't be so many of them after all. This problem of the Abitur is a difficult nut to crack.

24 April 1923

The trouble is we shall have to make compromises. We shall have to go to the length of getting the pupils through [Abitur]. It is 'frightful'.

25 April 1923

We shall simply have to say that in the final year we shall have to teach all the subjects taught in local secondary schools, and do them the way they do them. In fact I am already dreading the last half of the year when we shall have to stop everything else and concentrate entirely on the exam subjects... It is a real worry and I have finally decided that it is fundamentally useless to say much about the curriculum...

... if we could bring it about that our reports are a valid alternative, then, with our curriculum behind them, our pupils would easily be able to take up a professional study at university (author's emphasis). None of the things that make the Abitur ... such a misery are necessary for present-day professional study. People could specialise in 'Kolisko' chemistry; they would be initially shocked at all the formulae, but they could catch up on them.

3 May 1923

If we did not prepare the pupils for [Abitur] it would certainly lead to our having to close the top four classes. Our parents would not send us pupils. For the most part the parents think that the Waldorf School principles include the fact that their children can do the exams just the same as elsewhere, only that it ought to be ten times easier at the Waldorf School, [that] we make it easier for them by a kind of magic. ...Therefore I see no chance of doing anything else but accepting this compromise.

It will not be so terribly difficult to bring the pupils up to standard if we interrupt our Waldorf school principles by taking other subjects. It is not in the natural course of development for a pupil to know these things.

...on the whole our aim should be to obtain an understanding of the fact that we have to make a compromise.

...However, we shall never achieve this by using loopholes; we must stand by our principles and admit that we are making a compromise where necessary so that we show how absurd the whole thing is.

5 February 1924

...the school leaving exam ... is purely a matter of compromise.

(And later in response to a teacher saying that it was impossible to fulfil the curriculum of Classes 10, 11 or 12 if the final exams were to be taken in Class 12)... On the other hand the whole question of the final exam arose from a quite different point of view, namely that the pupils or their guardians wished them to take it. Has anything changed in this respect? The pupils are certainly unhappy; but pupils in other schools are also unhappy because they have to learn things they do not want to learn. What I mean is, surely what our pupils consider a hardship is felt by all 18/19 year-olds. The exam question is purely one of expedience. The question is whether we can risk telling people at the outset that we prepare for no final exams at all and that it is a private matter for each pupil to decide whether he will take it or not. That is how it is. For the future this matter could be settled on principle, but I do not think it is admissible that at this stage we decide to do it this year.

...What most of the parents wanted was that although they entrust the pupils to us we should give them the chance of going to university. Both the parents and the children themselves want that. The children were not originally of the opinion that it would be an agony. They were anxious to be able to take it. There is a very good chance of their giving it a try, but we shall not solve the problem merely by letting them go to other schools for their thirteenth year. The only question is whether we shall solve it in the highly problematic way we have discussed here before and which we then set aside; and this is, if we absolutely insist on keeping to the curriculum, whether we should not consider compensating for this by introducing preparatory coaching alongside the curriculum. We discarded this idea because we considered it very unpedagogical. The choice is whether we introduce coaching or neglect the curriculum. I think the wisest course would be not to hand over our pupils to another school. They would have to take an entrance exam anyway. But if we carry out the curriculum to the end of Class 12 we can spend a 13th year on exam coaching.

...The pupils who do not want to go to university must find a career without that. They will lead a useful life without the exam, for they can easily find all they need here. And those who plan to go to university can easily spend a further year growing a little bit stupid. ...We should have to appoint coaches for it. The staff would have to be increased yet again because of Class 13. If we appoint people like that and the college of teachers kept an eye on things it could be done.

27 March 1924

...the statistics seem to show that the bad results are very much connected with the fact that the pupils could not manage when it came to solving problems on their own because they were so used to solving problems as a group.

30 March 1923

If we are under the strain of Class 12 having to do the Abitur exam, we shall have to fulfil other obligations. The lessons would have to be extremely well focused. We must soon get down to the question of the Abitur. They will use a method of asking questions of the pupils that is aimed at catching them out.

The best thing would be if we could arrange it so that only those pupils go in for the Abitur who really want to do it. This problem of the Abitur is a difficult nut to crack. Perhaps there won't be so many of them, after all.

3 September 1924

This year we are not counting on an exam but on continuing with the Waldorf education. And next year we shall try to prepare for it ourselves. You heard the discussions today from which it is clear how attached the young people are to the Waldorf School. The present Class 12 would find it very uncongenial to have to take the exam this year. However objectionable it is we shall have to do coaching. The children certainly do love their teachers and their school. We shall not call them Class 13 but the "exam preparation class".

1994-2001

An Australian friend who once had dinner with Cecil Harwood and Marguerite Lundgren, as they were travelling from Rudolf Steiner House in Central London to stay at their their home in leafy Sussex for the weekend, told me of an amusing moment in the after-dinner conversation. With her inimitable mixture of choleric humour and uninhibited seriousness, Lundgren, apparently commenting on what literary heights Harwood might have scaled if only he had remained on his own after his first wife's (Daphne Olivier) death, flared up with: 'Silly old fool to marry a dancing girl!' Harwood, barely moving the pipe from his mouth, with that twinkle which was never far from his eye, and with that presence of mind which never seemed to fail him, retorted, 'Time will tell who is the fool.'

To see what time might be telling as I passed my seventh septennial phase, over which Saturn presides, I had several opportunities to look back, take stock, try to assess what life might be asking. Others, of course, were doing the same as the calendar announced the arrival of the year 2000.

It was to commemorate the turn of the millennium that I was invited to contribute an essay to a volume which saw the event as an opportunity to address contemporary issues, and making public the spiritually-scientific take on them. My contribution found a resonance in the United States of America and was reprinted in the *Journal for Anthroposophy*. The article was primarily concerned with literacy, at first sight hardly a gripping page-turner that could compete with grandiose firework displays and other millennium euphoria.

My own interest in the subject had begun in the 50s. Long before the research which came from Hungary in the 80s surfaced, showing how early approaches to literacy, *even in terms of literacy itself,* were counter-productive, Steiner had given guidance on how it would best be taught when the Waldorf School first opened its doors in September 1919, a method well documented in the secondary literature, as well as one he returned to frequently as a distinctive feature of Waldorf education. However, it was not until some five years later that his reasons for the 'gentle', pictorial approach became evident—and, conversely, the severe consequences for civilisation in general that resulted from an early introduction to writing and reading.

At the time, in view of the severity of his remarks, but not going deeply enough into the subject (and not having heard of the local education authorities' stipulations with which Steiner had had no alternative but to comply) I questioned friends at anthroposophical conferences or wherever I could corner them—Eileen Hutchins who was generally regarded as the language and literature authority in the British Waldorf Movement, and Jim Byford who was a class teacher at Michael Hall, amongst others—why the Rudolf Steiner schools in this country didn't modify the early advice Steiner gave with what he had to say in 1924. Being somewhat headstrong—not uncommon in one's 20s!—I was not totally convinced by their explanations and only later came to see the wisdom in what had become established and accepted Waldorf praxis. When I am reflecting on the situation I sometimes wonder whether it was my comparatively uneasy feeling about the teaching of literacy that contributed to my staying in the curative movement as long as I did, rather than make the change that I describe above, in '1959-1966'.

Be that as it may, for me it explains my early gut feeling that the thing to do was to put whatever *creative writing* skills I possessed at the disposal of the public, first and foremost in support of children's literacy—literacy not in its limited sense of being bound up with writing, reading and comprehension, but with *the word*. Albeit through the *printed* word, to help nurture the child's connection to the *living* language. Hence the work that went into the publishing of the two slender volumes of poems for class recitation, *Weft for the Rainbow* and *Meteor Showers and Us,* and the two readers, *Patter Paws the Fox* and *Trumpets of Happiness.* 'Children come first', was my guiding star. Time will tell if it was the best way of using the creative powers that destiny put at one's disposal. But I do treasure, and occasionally try to keep burnished, one tiny pip on the epaulette: a Waldorf teacher was telling her class of my forthcoming visit for their school's 21st birthday celebration. "Do you mean *the* Brien Masters?" asked one of the children—the class had recently been reciting one of my poems…

The Spirit or the Letter
On whose side is the teacher of literacy fighting?

Imagining myself in the shoes of the devil's advocate—which need not be a bad exercise, as long as one remembers how to untie the laces once the exercise is accomplished—I have sometimes wondered what would be the single most effective target to recommend to my 'client', in order that he achieve his evil designs.

Asking a panel of people with different backgrounds—agriculture, medicine, sport, organised religion, genetics etc.—to put themselves into the same shoes (cloven hooves?), would no doubt result in a revealing catalogue of replies. Being an educationalist, I shall attempt in this essay to confine myself to the sphere of education and, within that very extensive sphere, the theme of *literacy*. From the broader picture of literacy (what has been described as 'cultural memory')[1] to that of its narrower meaning (i.e. in the context of the three Rs), my aim will be to argue that this taken-for-granted acquisition in an educated person's mental portfolio might turn out to have been the spade that has been thrust into the hands of humanity, which it has been systematically yet unwittingly using to dig its own spiritual grave.

*

Of the comparatively few occasions on which Rudolf Steiner spoke specifically of its narrow meaning, I shall single out and comment on three. These were:

- during August 1919, when speaking to the teachers designate of the first Waldorf School;
- at the meeting with those same teachers, together with other

---

[1] see M. Rawson 'Writing and Cultural Memory' in *Steiner Education*, July 1998, Vol.32 No.2, pp.24-31, 42.

colleagues who had joined the school, on the 15 March 1922, i.e. after the Waldorf School had been running for two and a half years;

- in 1924, during the near year long sequence of lectures to members of the Anthroposophical Society on Karmic Relationships.

The first of these occasions comes as no surprise. One could hardly found a school—which was what Steiner was helping to do at the time—without substantive reference to literacy and numeracy. What Steiner had to say probably strikes the reader more for the *what* than the *whether* or *why:* for it is here that Steiner introduced the well-known Waldorf approach (swimming against what was to become a strong 20th century tide) of allowing the introduction to literacy to wait until entry into the Lower School (age 6+/7 years); and even then, going well out of his way to use innovative pictorial methodology while doing so. It does not need a specialist to realise that to swim against that same tide now, as it races at the turn of the millennium, requires more effort and conviction.

The second occasion is more complex. In March 1922 an inspector had just visited the Waldorf School and had clearly grasped but little of what the school was about. So at odds was his viewpoint with the Waldorf approach that Steiner good-naturedly teased a teacher, who was 'rejoicing over something the school inspector [had] approved of [with]: "You *will* have to pull your socks up".[2] During the ensuing discussion, two points arose which are particularly relevant here. More than once Steiner emphasised the importance of publishing afresh the distinctive features of the school—and it is clear that he did not simply mean a reprint of old material, but a new and lively way, that today could be classed as

---

[2]   R. Steiner *Conferences with the Teachers of the Waldorf School in Stuttgart,* Vol.2, p.51, Steiner Schools Fellowship Publications, Forest Row 1987.

good PR.[3] Of these distinctive features, the approach to literacy heads the list.[4] The other significant point was the way Steiner encouraged the teachers to make known the methodology pursued in the school, through giving public lectures. A number of short citations follows that were part of the aftermath of the inspector's visit.[5] 'A lot will depend on the Waldorf School Movement really containing what it should contain.' 'The spiritual aspect [of the education should] be really well represented in the world.' Near the close of the meeting Steiner ranged widely, summarising the tasks and indicating effective strategy: 'First of all you have to tell them that something is wrong with the world ... awaken interest in the educational problems of the times.' 'Convince the audience that we know our subject.' 'More intensive use must be made of our work.' 'We must establish a reputation.' 'Increase in interest only increases our responsibility.' In all of these, Steiner seems to be emphasising the importance of holding fast to what was central in Waldorf education without any trace of being deflected by 'orthodoxy'.[6]

So we have four main points:

a) we have a way of introducing children to literacy, clearly detailed by Steiner from the outset;

b) we have the fact that, among the distinctive features of the Waldorf School, literacy was high on Steiner's list of unshakables;

c) looking outward rather than merely into the classroom methodology, we have the fact that somewhere, wrapped up in this approach to literacy, was an urgency that had to do with

---

[3] The present essay, weaving as it does anecdote and straightforward argument, could be taken as an attempt to dress partially familiar concepts in new garb.

[4] R. Steiner, *Conferences with Teachers*, op. cit., p.53.

[5] Ibid., pp.58f.

[6] This is one incident among many where Steiner's vigilance over the independent nature of Waldorf education is asserted (q.v. *Freie* Waldorfschule).

the spiritual dimension of Waldorf education; and
d) that this spiritual dimension was sorely needed in general, the
   lack of it being somehow intrinsically connected with 'what
   was wrong' with the world. That is to say, the world problem
   was at root an *educational* problem.

While all this no doubt gave those concerned enough to be getting
on with, there remains the lingering feeling that, within the diffuse,
discursive and differentiated discussion at that meeting, there is
more in what Steiner is saying than meets the eye.

What the 'more' might be leads us to the third occasion that I
have singled out for comment: a reference to literacy which seems
to be of a very different nature from where we began in August
1919. On that earlier occasion one could take the inclusion of the
subject in a basic educational lecture cycle for granted; on this
occasion, certainly as regards its context, it could not have come as
more of a surprise. Yet the reference (which I shall quote presently)
largely appears to have escaped notice hitherto. The fact that Steiner
was not speaking about education but something quite different
(*Karmic Relationships*) may account for this. But why? Such a
remark could hardly have been made as an aside or as a mere
illustrative allusion: as we shall see it verges on the epoch-shaking.
Could the impact of the *content* of the Karma lectures—the
members of the Anthroposophical Society hearing, no doubt with
soul amazed, of the previous incarnations of prominent figures in
history, many not long since deceased—could that content have
eclipsed for them the immediate reality, as Steiner postulated it, not
to mention its harsh implications? Could a mood of sensationalism,
however slight, arising out of the *content* of the lectures, have
caused some of the *principles* at work behind karmic phenomena to
have escaped notice? Not that this is necessarily anything to be
ashamed of: most of us frequently see new implications in
'revisiting' Steiner that evaded us on first reading.

Whichever way it was, I intend to make the reference to literacy that occurs in the karma lectures the main thrust of my present enquiry. Furthermore, as it *is* to do with karma, it seems appropriate to begin by tracing a few of the karmic footsteps that led in this direction.

In the early 1960s, shortly after the first published translation of Steiner's lectures on karmic relationships were coming off the press,[7] my work in an anthroposophical curative home for adults led to the innovation in which the young adults in our care were guided during the second half of each morning through an extended course of 'study'. The first part of the morning, between breakfast and coffee, was given over to workshops, but it was felt that some of the morning hours, being manifestly best suited to 'head' work, should be put aside for learning. Thus a 'main-lesson' became part of the daily round lasting for some two hours.[8]

But what to teach? The ages of the 'young' adults ranged between 14 and 50, so there was no question of peeping over the Waldorf fence to see if the grass growing there had anything juicy to offer.[9] After some discussion amongst colleagues, it was determined that the year should be divided into three (allowing for a break in the summer season) and that one of these 'thirds' should be given over

---

[7]   R. Steiner *Karmic Relationships, Vol.I,* Anthroposophical Publishing Co., London 1955, lectures of 22 and 23 March 1924 are those referred to in this essay.

[8]   This was at Nutley Hall, Sussex, then known as Perevale. It was founded in 1959, two of the founder members (Misses M. Buckeridge and M. Bridger) having been trained at the Sunfield Children's Home in the 1930s. The latter was the first anthroposophical home of its kind in the UK putting into practice that approach to curative education that had been developed at the Sonnenhof in Switzerland under Dr Ita Wegman's medical supervision. Thus evolved, from the workshops, from the cultural life and from the social life that staff and 'residents' all shared, an interpretation of curative education that seemed justified in the way it met the needs of those concerned in harmony with Steiner's ideas.

[9]   The Waldorf age-related curriculum going up to Class 12 (age 18) does marginally overlap with this age group. However, four years out of an age range of 35 did not seem to justify any direct borrowing.

to biography, if possible led in such a way that it had a karmic ring to it. If Rudolf Steiner had emphasised the importance of studying concrete karma, why should this be confined to the non-handicapped? Through an in-depth biographical study and given an appropriate methodology, wouldn't it be good, we asked ourselves, to link handicapped and non-handicapped alike with the beings and impulses of 'great' individualities? Handicap, after all, is only a small segment of an individual's biography, if one looks at the individual through the telescope of reincarnation over millennia. Maybe more of us than we realise, or would outwardly care to admit, are handicapped anyhow. Certainly one would imagine that comparatively few of us have been able to detect any handicap lurking in the attractive garb of what we normally regard as one the indispensables of culture: literacy. But this is to beg the question with which we are concerned.

As a result of the above, through research in the wake of Steiner's karma lectures, it came about that an unusually deep and absorbing interest in Giuseppe Garibaldi (1807-1882), the liberator of Italy, was stirred. For, as I was considering *which* biography to take—awed, even daunted, by the reality that there are as many biographies as there are people!—by chance, I acquired a very dishevelled copy of the historian G.M. Trevelyan's *Garibaldi and the Thousand*[10] from one of my favourite haunts, a second- (ninth-, tenth-...) hand bookshop in the outhouse of a pub yard in a nearby town. (One cannot expect all biographical paths to keep to salubrious highways!)

But why should the book have caught my eye? By chance, in the late 1940s, I had met a member of the Trevelyan family on a bone-shaking Northumbrian country bus near Morpeth, where their family home was situated. The incident happened to be just when I was deep into Trevelyan's *English Social History*; and the memory of a

---

[10]   G.M. Trevelyan *Garibaldi and the Thousand,* Longmans, Green and Co., London 1909.

fellow traveller sitting in the next seat, chatting to me about the famous author, and coming out with remarks like 'Uncle George this; Uncle George that...' remained fresh in my mind. It was therefore the author rather than the subject who claimed attention among the peeling spines, the stained covers and the tattered, mildewy bindings of those discarded remnants of auctions, house-clearances and the like.

But I am not yet done with my 'by chances': for the decision to inaugurate the biographical 'third' of the year's main-lesson with Garibaldi was followed by another 'find'. In my preparatory research, I came across a reference to Garibaldi's autobiography. Some of the details of that discovery *have* faded; whatever diligence I may have had did not always stretch to annotations of that kind. However, the urge that was born to occupy myself with his autobiography, far from fading, was strangely impelling. Moreover, it intensified as my efforts to borrow or purchase a copy drew one inexplicable blank after another—first at the local library; then amongst friends whose strong connection with the karma lectures I imagined must have led them to acquire a shelf of supportive literature; then at antiquarian booksellers up and down the length of Charing Cross Road in London, which I scoured systematically, all to no avail.

At last during a summer visit to friends in Cheltenham, I heard (by chance?) of yet another book dealer in the town centre. Off I went and put my question to the proprietor. 'Ga...ri...baldi,' he repeated slowly. After seeming to be steeped for several seconds in reverie, he knelt down on the floor—I remember it being exactly on the spot where he stood at the moment of my asking him the question (though I am willing to grant that this may be artistic licence)—removed half a dozen books from the bottom shelf of one of his stuffed-tight, floor-to-ceiling bookcases, ducked over downwards and sideways to take a reassuring look at the back of the shelf, pressed his cheek against the spines of some handsome tomes higher up—very similar to the attitude of a milkmaid hand-milking her Friesian!—extended his hands and forearms into the space he had created and grimaced once or twice, before slowly, but deliberately, drawing forth no fewer than three chunky volumes that proved to be (once the dust of decades had been scattered with a breath) the mysteriously elusive *Autobiografia*.[11] After all those months of enquiring and traipsing around, I felt more like a witness watching a midwife in attendance at a birth than a mere customer buying books! Moreover, this feeling seemed strangely redolent (for those who know the incident) of the mood of coming-from-nowhere, materialising out of the blue, which was so palpable as Garibaldi and his 'noble thousand' descended from the monastery perched on the heights of Gibilrossa, down through the citrus groves above Palermo, in Sicily, much to the consternation of the Austrian militia, the forces of occupation which he was bent on overthrowing.[12]

On the one hand, the above account, the length of which may at first sight seem somewhat indulgent, may appear out of place here— too much of an anecdotal detour. On the other hand, leaving it intact in this way may serve as an example of how the *will* can be discovered to be the partner of a process which, though seemingly entirely under one's control, is simultaneously participating in something that has a larger orbit. Or words to that effect. This, I would suggest, is the aspect of will, albeit in miniature, that was playing into Garibaldi's biography as he walked the breath-taking tightrope, taut between life and death, upon which the story of his life seemed constantly to be poised, particularly in the 1840s/1850s.

*

Steiner's explanation of this remarkable biographical phenomenon is that Garibaldi had been an initiate in an incarnation that had occurred long before his life in 19th century Italy, and that *some* of the spiritual capacities from the former time filtered through and were evident in his 'madcap' yet somewhat miraculous adventures

---

[11]   G. Garibaldi *Autobiography,* Trans. A. Werner, Walter Smith and Innes, London 1889.

[12]   see Trevelyan, op. cit. Map III.

in his own country and the emerging republics of South America. But—and this is the crux of the matter—*not all*: some capacities had been filtered out. As a result of that filtering, his spiritual gifts resided principally in the *will* and not in his *consciousness*. But how had they come to be filtered out? In addressing what must have been his flabbergasted audience, Steiner infers that this was through education and in particular through being exposed to literacy at a young age. Indeed, though the theme of reincarnation is no longer as unfamiliar a one as it was in the 1920s, what he had to say then is still astonishing even to the extent, possibly, of having something of a bizarre ring about it for some readers:

> Now I come back [from considering the deeper significance of Garibaldi's path of life] to the question: Where are the earlier initiates? For certainly it will be said that they are not to be found. But, …—I shall have to say something paradoxical here!—if it were possible for a number of human beings to be born today at the age of 17 or 18, so that when they descended from the spiritual world they would in some way or other find and enter 17- or 18-year-old bodies, or if at least human beings could in some way be spared from going to school (as schools are constituted today), then you would find that those who were once initiates would be able to appear in the human being of the present day. But just as little as it is possible under the conditions obtaining on earth today for an initiate, when he needs bread, to nourish himself with a piece of ice, just as little is it possible for the wisdom of an older time to manifest directly, in the form that you would expect, in a body that has received education—in the present day accepted sense of the word—up to his 17th or 18th year. Nowhere in the world is this possible; at all events, nowhere in the civilised world.
>
> When, as is the custom today, a child is obliged to read

and write, it is torture for the soul that wants to develop and unfold in accordance with its own nature... It is necessary to say such a thing, paradoxical though it may sound.[13]

Thus, assuming Steiner's insight to be reliable, we may extrapolate: early exposure to literacy prevents individuals from bringing their spiritual gifts from the past to expression in the present time. And although this may not account for all the errors of the century through which we have ploughed and the end of whose furrow this book is 'marking',[14] the turn of the millennium offers an opportunity both poignant and pregnant for evaluation.

*

But how can the process of 'filtering out spiritual capacities' be understood? Having been alerted to the problem through the flight of Steiner's spiritual insight, can one approach it via a different route accessible to the average, more pedestrian turn of mind?

Surely the method of teaching literacy that Steiner evolved— about which, while avoiding being prescriptive, he was so adamant —must have been, or at least contained, a prophylactic against at least some of the *maleffects* of early literacy to which he points. Let us, therefore, look at how Steiner tackled the problem of literacy in education. But as a prelude to doing so, and before leaving the karma lectures, it should be noted that Steiner emphasised that the educationist could not ignore the trend of the day—e.g. by *not* teaching literacy when the children entered the first class (which was at age 7). Nor was it is justifiable deliberately to circumnavigate the problem—a sort of 20th century pied piper, setting up some educational establishment in a forgotten valley, say, in Papua New Guinea. Nevertheless, Steiner must have been faced with finding a compromise upon which far-reaching consequences hinged. The

---

[13]   R. Steiner *Karmic Relationships, Vol.I.,* op. cit. lecture of 23 March 1924.
[14]   *The Future is Now: Anthroposophy at the New Millennium.* Temple Lodge 1999.

solution to the problem that he advocated, so well known and widely practised in Steiner/Waldorf schools, is therefore examined in what follows.[15]

After a few preliminaries, such as choosing letters of the alphabet and deciding in what order they are to be introduced to the class, the Waldorf teacher needs to become active in certain creative spheres: in the first place, connected with *sound* and *form*. Through inwardly listening to the sound that the consonant 'makes' the teacher arrives at what might be termed the 'creative essence' of the letter. From that, and from the images arising from the words in which that essence is expressed (or, in which the sound is incorporated), the teacher moves from sound to form—from a creative *force* to something of a personified *image*. I am using the term broadly: personification usually implies a person. In a Waldorf teacher's introduction to a letter, inanimate objects may well assume a degree of personality. However, overriding this is the fact that a child's consciousness may well blur the edges between animate and inanimate more than we normally realise. Most people will not need to stop to think for long before recalling an example of this that they have witnessed.

To appreciate this 'creative essence' of a sound, let us take a common example: the sound *f* was clearly thought to be significant by our ancestral creators of language in words such as *fire, Feuer*/German, *fuego*/Spanish, *feu*/French, *flame, Flamme*/German, *fiammifero*/Italian (=match)... The gesture of flickering flames, flaring up, will-o'-the-wisping from the heart of a fire does seem to express the sound well and is a gesture that would lend itself to personification. However, given the sound *f* as a staring point, different individuals might choose other examples in which they feel intuitively that the *f* is a significant factor in the inner meaning of the word. *Fantasy, farce, farrier, father, feather, feminine, firm,*

---

[15]   see B. Masters 'What's the Problem? Steiner Education Theory and the Teaching of Literacy' in *Steiner Education* July 1998, Vol.32 No.2, pp.18-21 for a detailed and less philosophically ensconced account than the present one.

fervour, festival, fiancé, flight, foam, folly, fool, form, fortress, fruit, fun, funeral, fur ... are all food for thought in this respect. Not all of these will conjure forth an archetypal image that relates to the shape of *f* as readily, perhaps, as that of the flicker of flames. As it so happens, Steiner more than once chose *fish (Fisch* in German) as a ready-to-hand example for classroom use.[16] But he seemed happy with less animate instances, though to cite these would be peripheral to the present line of thought.

So the teacher has inwardly progressed from sound (force) to image (form). A step further in each direction now follows. Still at the 'hand' of the teacher, the personified image gains life and evolves into a story. From the story, which the teacher narrates to the class (another artistically cultivated activity, and in which the word beginning with the letter being taught is given prominence among the other *dramatis personae,* is extracted the shape (and name) of the letter.[17] Thus, through the abundance of the teacher's creativity, through which the child's first meeting with literacy is ushered in, the child is kept buoyant on the stream of the 'spirit' of the letter. This means that, in the longer term, when finally the *letter* of the letter is arrived at, the teacher is less liable to have to deal with the leaden and frequently traumatic struggle of learning to read (which unfortunately is increasingly the case, as the age of early learning is forced down younger and younger, often killing the appetite for literacy in the process). But the main point at issue is that the buoyancy deriving from the spirit of the letter remains an abiding factor in the child's soul.

It is self-evident from the above that, before the stage of (passive) reading is arrived at, the child has embarked on a journey of (active) writing, from which activity it gradually alights towards the more

---

[16]   Although giving ample scope, it should be noted that the above examples are restricted to where *f* occurs as the initial letter.

[17]   The intermediate steps taken by the children are pedagogical details that have been elaborated frequently by Steiner/Waldorf practitioners and in any case are less germane here.

cerebral occupation: reading. Emphasising that active point of embarkation, not even is the form of the letter experienced purely as something static on the page—a mere formality, such as the adult would normally take it to be. The shape of the letter will be run or acted, by individual children or in groups;[18] so that even when it reaches its final 'resting place'—a letter crayoned by the child on a piece of paper—the drawing/writing[19] is psychologically subtended by an active, realism-free attitude towards form that has been and is being nurtured all along through form-drawing,[20] where form for form's sake is what provides the motivation rather than some realistic end product. The letter is experienced not merely—not even primarily—through the clinical sense of sight, a black host of squiggly lines and curves—the printer's *font*—parading rank on rank in a school 'reader'; the letter lives in a *fount* of 'colour, movement, life, imagination, inspiration, dynamic form, vibrant orality...'

Thus, when the child reaches the first stage of 'reading', something of the inner soul disposing that characterises pre-literacy still prevails, even though literacy as such must needs more and more preside. The word SUN, for example, does not represent or resonate the shrivelled Copernican concept that we can neatly define as well as any dictionary, the measurable source of light and energy at the centre of our solar system that we mostly take for granted. Rather, it enjoys an echo of that which earlier peoples, through their vibrant empathy, felt was embodied to some extent by the three sounds S...U...N—and here we shall have to bypass the way that Steiner recommended dealing with the vowels. (In other parts of the

---

18   A description of this classroom activity is referred to by B. Henderson in 'Move along please: the need for movement in the teaching of literacy' in *Steiner Education* July 1998, Vol.32, No.1, pp.14-17.

19   see R. Steiner *The Child's Changing Consciousness*, Anthroposophic Press, New York, lecture of 18 April 1923.

20   see R. Steiner *Practical Advice to Teachers,* Rudolf Steiner Publishing Co., London 1937, lecture of 21 August 1919.

world different experiences of the sun have been 'inscribed' into language—e.g. *shemesh*/Hebrew; *aurinko*/Finnish; *ilyos*/Greek; *allunga, chintoo, tupelo, tonaleah, uuna, ykuko* / various Australian Aboriginal dialects!)[21] It is such echoes that have filled the child's soul through hearing and speaking the mother tongue up to this moment of its life. With Steiner's approach to literacy those echoes are not ever more efficiently vacuum-sealed off; they have a chance to vibrate on.[22] The breath of life still hovers over, wafts around the mummy that the spoken word becomes when encased within its sarcophagus of literacy.

And the corollary? Having concentrated mostly on how not to vacuum-seal off the child's spirituality through its meeting with literacy, so that the incarnating individual is endowed with the fruits of the past—however exalted or modest the child's genius may be— is there something, as well as avoiding the *vacuum*, that might prove a good *conductor* also to be found in Steiner's method?

*

Whoever may be in the wings, the two actors on stage in this morality play are the teacher and the child. Let us therefore take one more look at the scene, and in particular the role of the teacher.

In striving to discern the essence of the *sound* of the letter, the teacher is having to develop and exercise *Inspiration*. In striving to impart *being* (personification) to that essence which has been discerned, or discover being within it, the teacher is having to develop and exercise *Intuition*. And in striving to derive an *image* of that essential being, the focal point of the story that is subsequently drawable on the board and in the child's book, the teacher is having

---

[21]   see A.W. Reed *Aboriginal words of Australia,* Reed Books, Balgowlah, NSW 1965.

[22]   see R. Steiner *Adolescence: Ripe for What?* Tr. M. Stott, Steiner Schools Fellowship Publications, Forest Row 1996, lecture of 22 June 1922, in which Steiner hints at the fact that the teaching of literacy is tied up with the child's 'recapitulating' of the general consciousness experienced by humanity in former civilizations.

to develop and exercise *Imagination*. Thus, even if only at a very elementary level, in attempting to introduce literacy in this way, the teacher is having to aspire towards and activate within him- or herself those stages of consciousness described by Steiner as definite steps on the path to 'higher knowledge'.[23]

We may take it as empirical—thanks to the life work of Owen Barfield and others[24]—that these levels of higher knowledge were readily accessible to the human beings of ancient times, due to their pre-literal state of consciousness. We people of today have sacrificed this original, participative state as the price of freedom—and the child, being a child of today, is in the same boat. But—if I may risk a nautical analogy—whilst we 20th century adults, who have succumbed or are at least subject to, the materialist's paradigm, are stowed away deep in the hold of the boat, unable to gain sight of those spiritual horizons whence we have journeyed, the child still enjoys something of that vision (even if partially impeded) being somewhere up in the shrouds. Teacher and pupil in the same boat, therefore, yes! But different ranking: the adult's being is enshrouded with the sense-world below; the child to whatever extent (depending on the child's age), is still up-shrouded above—the dark 'light of common day' as against the still-irradiated 'trailing clouds of glory'.[25]

But do not let this innate difference in rank deter us from trying to gain insight. Rather let us consider the inner effort that the teacher has to make, outlined above, to *achieve* the Waldorf way[26] in the approach to literacy now by juxtaposing it alongside what Steiner

---

[23]   R. Steiner *Occult Science,* Anthroposophic Press, New York, 1950, Chapter V.

[24]   see Owen Barfield *Saving the Appearances*, Faber & Faber, London 1957, Chapters IV & XX.

[25]   Wordsworth not only divined this state but, of course, expressed it infinitely more poetically in his *Ode on Intimations of Immortality from Recollections of Early Childhood.*

[26]   B. Masters *An Appraisal of Steinerian Theory,* op. cit., pp.274-276.

termed the pedagogical law.[27] In that law he described how a higher member of the adult 'educates' (ostensibly through self-education: 'what you are' or are in process of becoming) that member of the child that is one stage lower. This is suggestive of the 'conductor' that we hoped to detect. As the child descends from *original participation*, it meets the teacher who makes the attempt to climb a rung or two towards *final participation*. Through this, literacy—that has been described as the watershed between spirit and world[28]—is no longer the drastic watershed that it would otherwise be. The teacher's efforts towards final participation, through the working of the educational law, are transformed in the child into the prophylactic which—while still permitting freedom to take root, unfold and thrive in the growing human being—enables the ego to bring into play that spirituality to which it is heir, by virtue of its own past.

This, it seems to me, is what by implication is divulged by Steiner through his observations on Garibaldi; this is why he set such high stakes on the *way* literacy should be taught in the Waldorf school; why he exhorted the teachers to hold tenaciously to the Waldorf way as a key feature of their praxis ... and why the devil's advocate's client will do all in his power to prevent it and bring about the opposite so that the human spirit is eclipsed with human beings forced to act, not out of their higher, but out of their lower, easily diverted, easily hi-jacked, easily manipulated, anti-cultural, anti-social, anti-brotherly, clouded selves. Freedom, yes, lenient, even permissive, lashings of it: *except* the freedom to climb up again towards the heights of final participation.

Within the spiritual arena in which we find ourselves at the turn of the millennium, there are, however, signs that the results of the

---

[27] R. Steiner *Curative Education,* Rudolf Steiner Press, Bristol 1993, lecture of 26 June 1924.

[28] see N. Skillen 'The Uses of Orality' in *Steiner Education, July 1998, Vol.32, No.2, pp.5-9.*

'advocate's' subversive advice are being identified.[29] The outcry
against early literacy led by Professor Josef Nagy, the Hungarian
educationalist, is a recent sign, even drawing forth a certain amount
of condemnation of early literacy (and early learning in general)
from within the 'establishment'.[30] Despite the fact that the reason for
the outcry only reached as far as under-achievement, it is
nonetheless welcome, for the first step must always be to identify
the clouds of obscurity before setting about dispersing them.

Not that this gives cause for complacency for, ironically, almost
to the day, a year later than the above article, a new 'reading plan'
was reported in the same newspaper by the same Education Editor.[31]
In it, the British Government's favouring of 'analytic phonics' as a
method of teaching literary is cited by a research team from St
Andrew's University, Scotland. The team found that a method
described as 'synthetic phonics' produced much faster, 'staggeringly
effective' results. This underlines the fact that the debate of whether
or not early learning is a desirable educational aim, is still likely to
take time before it comes to any prominent place on the agenda.
Doubly ironic, directly beneath that article, the newspaper printed
Article 26 of the Universal Declaration of Human Rights, marking
its 50th Anniversary, in which Clause (3) states: 'Parents have a prior
right to choose the kind of education that shall be given to their
children'.[32] Trebly ironic is the announcement at the foot of the
column that quotes the Article, that the proceeds of a pamphlet
reprinting the Declaration will go to the Medical Foundation for the
Care of *Victims of Torture* (my italics). Torture would, of course, be
the wrong term for what we are discussing here (even, perhaps, for

---

[29]   see J. Judd 'Children sent to formal schooling too early, says minister' in *The
        Independent,* 9 December 1997.
[30]   'Dispatches' on ITV's *Channel 4*, 29 January 1998.
[31]   see J. Judd 'New Reading Plan "staggeringly good"' in *The Independent*, 7
        December 1998.
[32]   Moreover, Clause (1) states that education should be 'free at least in the
        elementary and fundamental stages'.

the personal trauma experienced by many young children who are put through this particular mill). Nevertheless that should not tempt us to underestimate the consequences of teaching literacy— prematurely, seen from the spiritual standpoint.

Steiner is known to have waited until he was asked the 'right' question before revealing the results of his spiritual research. When we hear leading questions of such import being asked in our present time, it is surely imperative that those who have attempted to continue Steiner's work try and find the right form in which to share the results of what is known and has been achieved (both in an inner and outer sense) so that it can be recognised by contemporaries who are in the same boat—the boat that encompasses, enshrouds and enmeshes the human being down in the deepest hold of literacy— contemporaries nonetheless, in whose heart the future progress of humanity is also ready to leap at a chance.

2001-2008

When I began class teaching in the 60s I felt the need to connect with Northumberland. Mother gave the family a welcome holiday close to the River Tweed, during which, one day we visited the old family watermill and on another Bamburgh castle, a place that formed the centre of many a lesson I have given on Medieval history. On a later occasion, I spent time on my own, crossing over to Holy Island (Lindisfarne) for the first time in my life and there met the curator of the tiny museum in which the relics of the past that had been gathered on the island by archaeologists had helped him come to a concept of cosmic Christianity. On the return journey, I followed this essentially Celtic stream of Christianity to Durham cathedral. But it is not my purpose here to dwell on reminiscence. I am interested in looking, for the moment, at *patronage*.

The *Lindisfarne Gospels*, for instance, were the result of monks pouring their forces of dedication and devotion into their work—writing the priceless manuscripts of which many have survived the ravages of time and are to be found in museums all over the world. To bracket these works together with patronage is, I submit, to miss the point, however, for those who laboured in the heyday of the monastic orders—whether writing manuscripts in the cloisters, or caring for the sick, or serving at the altar, or tending cattle in the fields—did so to the 'glory of God', not out of any feeling of being employed by the Church as their patron in any modern sense.

Nevertheless, in due course, the Church was most certainly one of the great patrons of the arts, together of course with the aristocracy in whose hands the power of governance rested. As spirituality in culture dwindled and the Church lost its power, patronage shifted more exclusively to the aristocracy who, in turn losing power and wealth, lost the gift and privilege of being able to patronise the arts to anything like its former extent. This then shifted to institutions and organisations of one kind of another—universities, Guilds, and so on.

At the same time, there was an abundance of initiatives not connected with such institutions, due to the increase in the prominence of the individuality in Western culture. Writers and composers turned to publishers directly, first selling them their works outright and then, through exchanged contracts, having an on-going stake in the fortunes of each publication. This was the situation at the beginning of the 19th century. It is not for nothing, in the light of this, that one of my essays included here focuses on Beethoven, whose negotiations with his publishers are legion.

Now, 200 years later, the book trade is rapidly being overtaken by the effects of the internet. Not, perhaps, in the region of bestsellers but nevertheless in significant ways. The margin that the bookseller receives has shrunk. One publisher put it this way: We have to work much harder just to stand economically still. The cost of storage of publications that do not sell all that quickly, however deserving they might be, has rocketed and so print runs have gone down—again more work for less return. And this is compounded by the risk taken if the proposed title is unlikely to be 'commercial'—thus, again, giving the publisher insufficient income.

I can identify in my very, very small way with each of these stages. In the 50s I was asked by the vicar of the Anglican church where I was organist and choirmaster, to write articles for the church magazine while he had to lighten his load due to illness. The thought of the articles being commissioned could not have been further from my mind as I laboured to write them—the first writing in my life that had not been in the categories of thank you letters, or school/university essays/assignments, though to attribute what I was doing as being 'to the glory of God' would be presumptuous as well as anachronistic. My writing leap-frogged (or should it be frog-leapt?) over the aristocratic-patronage stage, not surprising really for someone born in 1931. But when it comes to patronage which is heir to the aristocracy I can furnish two major examples: the first was when Dr Earl Ogletree of the University of Chicago and I co-authored a major work on Steiner education. It came as far as publication stage when some sub-editor noticed that my chapters did not conform with American spelling. For some reason I didn't have the psychological appetite to go through the whole thing and change the chameleon's *colour*! Neither did I have the software at that point that would have 'perpetrated' the change at the click of a mouse. The manuscript is collecting indignant dust somewhere on one of my study shelves. Yet I have no regrets. The second stab academia took at me was more successful, resulting in my PhD thesis and the small handful of satellites (articles for academic journals) that came (and are still coming) my way as a result, the first ones being commissioned by the university's internal examiner (for the academic journal for which he was the editor) who, despite being widely regarded as a hard-headed protagonist of the first order for cut-and-dried logic, left all the questions at the viva that probed clinically into that side of the thesis to Dr Vivian Law of Cambridge (*an anthroposophist!*). Before that, came my appointment as editor of *Child and Man*—and I am inclined to think that the university's invitation to do advanced research into Steiner education, in the first place, partly resulted from it—the then longest journal for Steiner education in the world with an unbroken record, and enjoying a high reputation amongst anthroposophical journals.

The next step was the Beethoven step: find a publisher who is interested in publishing what you have produced. The first outcome of this approach was *The Waldorf Song Book* (Floris), a happy combination of dialogue between author/collector/composer and publisher, the latter, with his eye on uniqueness being one of the ingredients in healthy sales, persuading me to include a few old chestnuts (popular songs that would-be purchasers would identify with) at one end of the scale and—something I definitely would not have thought of myself—to include some songs in out-of-the-way languages—spice for the cultural taste buds. This resulted in Manx, Sanskrit and a few other songs. The second outcome—also successful in terms of being kept virtually continuously in print and presumably serving a need—was *Patter-Paws the Fox* (Temple Lodge), a first reader for Class 2, based on the fables with which a Class 2 child would normally be familiar.

Skipping over recent major publications, I come to the present: research I have been involved in concerning several of Steiner's indications which are either little known, ignored, too difficult to grasp or otherwise not heeded nor finding their place in Waldorf praxis. The conspiracy theorist in me—not a large part of my persona—leads me to conclude that as well as the other reasons, given above, for people moving into self-publishing, there are forces at work that would prevent a progressive spiritual stream from re-entering evolution. Steiner himself, after all, founded a publishing firm for his basic books on spiritual science—not that the rest of us can hold a candle to him. Nevertheless, examples come to mind: the most recent I have met is that of Dr Emil Páleš who, on meeting everything from disbelief, to ridicule, to downright opposition which even went as far as adversely influencing his professional position in life, decided to establish his own publishing company so that his 15-year-long, mathematically-based research into the archangel rhythms to which an ancient Babylonian calendar refers with almost disarming accuracy, could be brought to the public's attention and thus help to awaken Western consciousness to the reality of other worlds and their influence in many spheres of earthly life.

When the Steiner Schools Fellowship's (sic) *Newsletter* was forcibly taken over by a self-appointed editor in the 90s and used—as one his closest colleagues experienced it "for [his own] propaganda"—the conspiracy-theorist in me certainly wondered if there was anything in the colleague's perceptions. This is manifestly not the place to pursue such perceptions. The fact remains, however, that publishing research based on fairly remote indications of Steiner's is not a commercial proposition, which brings me back to the broad sequence of Church/Aristocracy/Institution as '

Patron'/Author seeking Publisher/Publisher commissioning/Self-publishing—a sequence which helps one to see the situation not as one of being faced with a brick wall, but as a publishing band-wagon on which many writers are jumping for one reason or another, fully recognising that not all titles will occasion a huge number of popping champagne corks.

I have already spoken about the 'time-sensitive' aspect of this. Following the advice of a friend who foresaw technical complications and advised *as a first run* something less technically ambitious (which meant virtually plain text), led to the present volume—with the essay on Beethoven from the *Golden Blade* included, since all the graphics connected with the musical quotations, through the expertise of Paul Breslaw, were already available electronically.

This was not the only change striding over the septennial doorstep, for on the teacher training front, things have taken a remarkable turn. It seemed wise—knock a nought or two off the annual flying miles—to discontinue the very long hauls (South Africa, Kazakhstan, and Israel) which had become annual events and, as I reluctantly closed that door, another door flung open (through Israeli connections!) leading to the training courses in the Canary Islands—La Gomera (2005-2007) and Gran Canaria (2007-2009).

At the same time, closer-to-home connections have sprung up: in the Czech Republic and in Slovakia (which have resulted from graduates of the London Waldorf Teacher Training Seminar) and a renewed connection in Finland (the link there dating back to my teacher-training square-bashing in Emerson College in the 70s. A 33-year-rhythm phenomenon?). It was this visit, this year, which happily coincided with research into one of Steiner's references regarding the fashioning of Europe. It seemed to shed new biographical light on the strong connections I made in Helsinki, Tallinn and Riga—through Markku Nunivirta, Judith Cristie and Dzintra Viluma (now a class teacher in Bologna)—all places situated on the Gulf that Steiner drew attention to in his lectures on the great Finnish epic, the *Kalevala*. The story is in the essay which follows, which perhaps could do with a sequel connecting, still more explicitly than does the essay, insight into the spiritual forming of Europe, through the qualities that came to birth in its most ancient Finnish 'race', with the vision of the future expressed, surprisingly, by Trinculo and Stefano in Shakespeare's last great comedy *The Tempest*. Such a sequel might enable present-day consciousness to see Europe not as the father of superior intellectuality, nor as the bunch of puppets hanging from the rail of a super-power over in the west, but as an epoch-sized stepping stone on which humanity is firmly treading as it crosses over the river of time from its distant past towards the unknown shore of its 6th epoch future.

On the Sands with Printless Foot
The Work of the Elements in the Landscape[1]

There are two types of ferries that sail across the stretch of water between Tenerife and La Gomera, two islands in the Canaries. There is the express type which knocks ten minutes off the hour's crossing, with the craft being a powerful, element-defying catamaran that is basically a colossal box that ploughs through the entire repertoire of the ocean's caprices unimpressed and through 99-point-something percent of its tirades unperturbed. And there is the older shipping company with its traditional type of ferry that has plied across the strait for decades, pitching and tossing, chugging and rolling in harmony with the dance of the waves. Passengers on this vessel frequently see dolphins calmly disporting themselves at a certain distance from the Tenerife shore. Passengers on the save-ten-minutes monster (and pay the not inconsiderable extra euros!) sadly never catch a glimpse of the playful creatures. For some reason known to nature, they keep their distance or dive for sanctuary in the Atlantic depths.

If, let us suppose, this were the only place in the world inhabited by dolphins and there were no records otherwise to prove their existence, and if—let us suppose further—the catamaran voyagers were strictly of a 'seeing's believing' turn of mind, for them dolphins (should they, by chance, hear mention of them) would be purely a figment of the 'slower' voyagers' imagination.

Like dolphins, fleetingly gliding into visibility, a similar phenomenon surfaced recently—and in an unexpected way. *The*

---

[1] A written version of a lecture of this title given on 20 May 2008 in Rudolf Steiner House, London as part of the Tuesday series *Etheric Earth*. As indicated in the blurb advertising the original lecture, the author's written works contain material relevant to the theme; some of this has been included here as the time constraints of the lecture did not permit it.

Shorter Oxford Dictionary[2] makes no mention of elementals per se whereas Roget's *Thesaurus of English Words and Phrases* teems with pixies, mermaids, hobgoblins, sylphs, trolls, leprechauns, elves, gnomes ... (I am resisting the temptation to list them all—and hope, through what I have to say as a whole, to avoid disappointing those elementals who are not specifically mentioned by name!)

So we have an intriguing phenomenon: an erudite dictionary that omits any reference to 'elementals', on the one hand, and a 'classical' compilation of outstanding comprehensiveness that lists them in profusion *and* includes the term 'elemental spirit' to boot. Clearly two layers of consciousness or belief systems are manifested here. The catamaran: not visible, therefore not mentioned. And its opposite: these beings were thus named and (giving the ubiquitousness of such references also in a host of languages the benefit of the doubt) were therefore visible at some point in the past.

One question which follows would be: was there a time when the earlier layer of consciousness was giving way to the later? Shakespeare's matter of fact treatment of the fairy world and the magic which it wielded in *A Midsummer Night's Dream* (1595) and his giving that world a more marked role in *The Tempest* (1611) would suggest that either he suspected that the consciousness of his contemporaries was on this cusp and/or that that was indeed the case. There is more than just a hint of this in the later play in which the villains of the peace are addressed accordingly by Ariel,[3] Prospero's 'tricksy spirit'.[4]

The overtones of the plot even suggest that villainy is somehow inexorably connected with the consciousness that sees the world purely as a composite of 'elements' in the chemical sense (hydrogen, oxygen, sulphur, zinc...), in strong contrast to Prospero's

---

[2]   The 1968 edition.
[3]   You are three men of sin, whom destiny, ... / That hath to instrument this lower
       world, / And what is in't,—the never-surfeited sea / Hath caused to belch up;
       Act III sc (iii) 54-57.
[4]   Act V sc (i) 236.

magnanimous, peace-making, conflict-resolving attitude which takes the elementals, working through the elements, into account in a paradigm which, on the one hand, was fading from view, but, on the other hand, was far-sightedly conscious that the new-fangled *exclusion* of the elemental world (of lesser spirits) would some not too distant day need to be consciously superseded by its rediscovery.

It was Isabel Wyatt, well-known as author of *The Seven-Year-Old Wonder Book,* who emphasised the central role that the play of the elements had on the familiar events of the 1066 Norman conquest of Britain.[5] First came the adverse winds keeping the Norman fleet in port. Then came the heat wave, an unconquerably strong ally in King Harold's favour (the last of the Saxon kings) in his defeat of the Norse invader Harald Hardrada at the Battle of Stamford Bridge. Finally the wind changed direction furthering the cause of William of Normandy and so bringing about the turn in the tide of events: the English Saxon dynasties were replaced by Normans.

In the opening paragraph of the editorial to the *Child and Man* with the theme 'Waldorf is it new?' the turning tide is used as a symbol for what is potentially ever-renewable.

> When the ebbing tide turns and begins to flow back again it brings about a variety of responses and reactions. The multitudinous life in the rock-pools stirs with animated anticipation; pilots in the harbour and humble fishermen converge on the quay-side in clouds of pungent pipe-smoke; the sun-bathing crowds on the beaches gather towels, thermos flasks and tubes of lotion and prepare to beat their retreat [...] And the sand-castles? Their hour has come, too. Presently, each one busily patted into sand-bucket, fondly tipped out and surmounted with a sprig of sea-weed or a little winkle, is washed into the horizontal oblivion of being mere sand again, the friendly winkle left

---

[5]   see Wyatt, I., 'The weather in 1066' in *The Golden Blade 1956,* pp.80-88.

high and dry on the tide-mark or else borne out into the deeper waters of the continental shelf.

Then, on the restored carpet of virgin beach, the whole merry-go-round can make its foot-prints anew: the hooves of the donkeys, the wheel-tracks of the ice-cream carts, the scuffled confusion left over from a game of beach-ball, or the delicate foot-print of a lonely sea-bird standing on one leg.

In the same vein, and now on a much higher plane of life, it is surely not for nothing that Shakespeare's last plays are set against/within a maritime context. The quickly changing tidal flow of events in *Pericles* is prodigious, often taking place on board ship, and must be a head-ache for any producer with limited imagination but a priceless gift to the one endowed with plenty. *Cymbeline's* turning tide of events is greatly influenced by the invading army landing on the coast of Wales. The Gulf of Corinth (en route to the Delphic Oracle), the island of Sicily set in mid-Mediterranean and Shakespeare's highly enigmatic 'coast of Bohemia' provide the plot of *Winter's Tale* with its main ports of call. And, at least for now, *The Tempest* speaks for itself. Can it be that Shakespeare was either consciously or otherwise commending to us a consciousness (paradigm) that—while needing to disembark on the dry land of the zinc/sulphur elements, and suffer the aridity of spirit-void, rational consciousness—prompted by such images, anticipated a time when the *ebbing* imagination of earlier ages would become the *flow* of a new insight?

Be that as it may and although this is not a Shakespearean-based study of the changing world view which prevailed at the beginning of the 17th century, he provides a convenient milestone to help us concentrate on, and limit our enquiry to, four main paradigms apropos the elements in the landscape.

•   The pre-Shakespearean elementals that Prospero's extra-

- sensory consciousness is aware of in the "hills, brooks, standing lakes and groves…"[6]
- The post-Shakespearean elements "of whom [the] sword is tempered".[7]
- The artist's feeling which leans away from, and hesitates to give carte blanche credence to the latter and which evokes something of the distant past whilst often also inching the awakening consciousness, still at a feeling level, towards the future.
- A future-oriented paradigm, not reliant only on pure feeling, represented by Goethe's Urpflanze-type thinking/seeing, Lovelace's Gaia-thinking and Steiner's anthroposophical, spiritually-scientific-investigatory thinking, all of which lead to advanced insight.

Folklore supports if not substantiates the first category, and for now I wish to make no further comment in this direction—though it is difficult to see how positivism considers it has dispensed with the overwhelming, millennia-long-valid volume of evidence with the mere brush of a so-called scientific hand.

The second category is what we would deem informs common knowledge today, the standpoint of most men in the street, with the ancient four elements of earth, water, air and fire having become straight-jacketed into neat 'scientific' explanations. (Earth)—the continents are shaped and positioned as shown in modern cartography, and all altitudes are specified as per the readings on the surveyor's theodolite. (Water)—the oceans exert an influence on the climate, and rainfall is engendered in a precise way, being precipitated according to principles which mostly can be forecast, while flowing back to the sea in accordance with the contours of the land combined with the perviousness of the soil and rock on which it

---

[6]   Act V sc (i) 34
[7]   Act III sc (ii) 63.

falls. (Air)—currents arise from global air pressure discrepancies. (Fire)—the seasonal variations of warmth and cold are directly the result of the annual tilting of the earth's axis and are predictable according to latitude, while other temperature differences are the result of the earth's atmosphere in relation to altitude—height above sea level. (We can, for example, when flying at 30,000ft. expect the outside temperature to register something in the region of -60°C; but go down to the Dead Sea at midday and temperatures will probably be in or above the upper 30s.) While acknowledging that the foregoing is little more than pocket science, it is perhaps a sufficient 'sop to Cerberus' for the present circumstances to allow us not to have to employ rocket science and therefore to move on.

For me, it is as if, in the third category (the artist's relationship to landscape) there is a link between the past—where the elementals were seen playing their part in the kingdoms of nature—and the future. Like a river flowing underground in a landscape that shows signs of karstification, only to emerge later to continue its course at ground level, the artist's descriptions of the landscape (be they in paint or via language) carry over something of the qualitative mood of the past towards a future human perception which will enjoy a resurgence of awareness of how the elements/elementals function behind the scenes.

Outstanding examples that come to mind are as follows. Born in the 1770s are the great Romantic English poets Wordsworth and Coleridge, alongside the English landscape painters Constable and Turner.[8] Turner's paintings for the owners of the great country houses who were his esteemed patrons tended to be of a particular style, the earthly part particularly (the stately home and its surrounding 'park' as distinct from the sky) being depicted representationally. A large body of his other work, to one degree or another wore thin, so to say, the veil between the sense-world and

---

[8]   Turner 1775-1851, Constable 1776-1837, Wordsworth 1770-1850, Coleridge 1772-1834.

the elemental world which sustained it. With Constable it would seem that his almost exclusive concern with the nature of his beloved home environment (the countryside around Dedham in Suffolk) and the clouds that sailed overhead in their majestic illusiveness, is telling us of an *etheric* connection he must have had with the landscape despite his known habit of sketching al fresco. In the case of Wordsworth, he pours his boyhood awareness of nature "apparelled in celestial light" into his unsurpassed *Intimations of Immortality on Recollections of Early Childhood*, an awareness which permeates his entire oeuvre in a variety of ways. In Coleridge's *Hymn before Sunrise over the Vale of Chamonix* (to take just one example from his poetry), the striking awe and vastness of nature, her indelible beauty and the impelling wonder of the beholding soul are proclaimed in each stanza in language that both expresses the poet's inner response and at the same time explores both in large and in fine detail the wondrous plethora of the sense-phenomena.

Inspired by the cataclysmic outpouring of phenomena that had clearly engulfed Coleridge, the author posed the questions: How might this look in post-Romantic language? Would the subject need to be as outwardly stunning? Can nature still open up an avenue in the modern soul—cf. "Awake, my soul! Not only passive praise / Thou owest! Not alone these swelling tears, / Mute thanks and secret ecstasy! Awake, / Voice of sweet song! Awake, my heart, awake! / Green vales and icy cliffs all join my hymn."—which leads to an experience of the divine? Though it cannot match Coleridge's grand Romantic outpouring, his *Autumn Sunrise over the Orwell* (though the inclusion of the word 'sunrise' was a mere coincidence) resulted from such an attempt.[9]

---

[9]   From Masters, B., 1989, *Meteor Showers and Us,* London: Temple Lodge Press, pp.48f.

...Tide was out:
A mill-pond stillness
Waded silently over the mud banks
And over the salt-marshes
With mist
Lingering like lost sheep
And the odd wader
Preening importantly
On a Persian carpet of light-filled ooze
Standing bemused
As if overlooked by the weather forecaster.

While the tide of sunrise
Washed
Washed from the east
In waves of jewelled light.

And the silver hush of the sky
Crescendoed
Into a cornucopia of morning radiance
Gliding full-sailed into every creek
Rolling among the low hills in fertile joy
Drooping mountainously over the gull-dappled plain
Hurdling like athlete over the undulations of birch and willow,
    furrow and stubble
Greening the fresh beards of winter wheat and the jaunty
    moustaches of weed upon the ploughed fields
Resting in quiet pools like lining in a nest...

To return to the Titans of Romanticism (and, of course, there were
many others): they stand sternly, as it were—even warningly—at the
entrance to the highway of materialism, their poetry and canvases
clearly indicating (a) that the highway is *one* way, and (b) that it
terminates—for them—in a highly distasteful cul-de-sac. The

engineers of that highway are still constructing the extension that will enable materialistic consciousness to penetrate further into matter—the irony of the age: to discover the elementals behind the elements.

Steiner could be described as something of a forerunner in this respect. He studied at the Vienna Polytechnic and absorbed a comprehensive range of scientific knowledge, such as it was in the late 1870s-1880s. Simultaneously (we have to assume) his research into the spiritual dimension of mineralogy, botany, chemistry, physics and so on must have been progressing apace. But with characteristic scientific discipline, he avoided going public until the research (a) had gone far enough, and (b) had reached a degree of certainty—nowadays we would probably label it as 'robust'. A tidemark in the research (outer and inner) is clearly reached in his being commissioned as editor to bring out the scientific writings of Goethe in the definitive complete Goethe edition (the *Sophien-Ausgabe*) produced in Weimar in 1890s.

It would seem that Steiner had to make a karmic decision at a certain point in his life: Would he richly unfold the results of his research for those eager to receive them, either in print or in lecture form?[10] Or would he be selective and substantiate his spiritual-scientific findings with data that resulted from empirical research, with which ordinary rational consciousness would feel comfortably at home? Life was clearly not long enough to do both. He chose the former course, with the hope (expectation?) that his followers would verify the indications he gave of the realities on the spiritual plane with more or less humdrum empirical corroboration.[11] This has happened in two senses. Followers in his anthroposophical footsteps have pursued very definite lines of investigation: medication for cancer and other diseases, agricultural methods which enliven the

---

[10]   see Steiner, R., *Man as Symphony of the Creative Word,* 19.10-11.11.1923 for the locus classicus of the research in which he discloses the characteristics and role of the elemental spirits.

generative forces in earth and her produce, and the influence of planetary forces in the rhythmic growth of plants are amongst the most well known. Fortunately (since those followers are also restricted in their capacities) there are those who are followers of Steiner in the chronological sense, whose concern for healthy human progress—which includes a holistic approach to ecology—is also leading in the same direction.[12]

In the context of the present study, I wish to refer to one particular theme that Steiner investigated—a pre-cursor of Gaia one might say, in that, if the earth is primarily an entity of *life* (top-down rationality), where and how does that manifest?

In the months following the outbreak of the first World War, Steiner spoke of how people, incarnating in different places, imbibe the spirituality of that place through the language, through customs and through the very landscape which the elements (the *four* elements) have formed and sustain. Moreover, his research suggests that between Gaia (not his word, but nevertheless encompassing the concept of the Life-Being of the entire globe) and the landscape, there exist three other influential powers. (i) Gaia manifests as mighty spiritual forces that govern large tracts of earth. (ii) Such a force or being works through the elemental spirits, i.e. in the etheric realm: undines, gnomes, sylphs etc. (see Roget rather than *The Oxford Shorter Dictionary* for at least nomenclature!). (iii) The elemental spirits are the servants of the great creators of air pressures, tidal flow, earth's altitudes and the mineral consistencies of which they are composed, warmth conditions and so on.

The value of Steiner's investigations at that time may well have

---

[11]   see Steiner, R., *Calendar of the Soul* for, I would suggest, a poetically expressed pathway by which modern consciousness can re-discover week by week its lost or diminishing connection with the spiritual realities at play behind the changing scene of the year's seasons. In this respect, it seems significant that Owen Barfield entitled his translation of the work *The Year Participated.*

[12]   An extensive library is of course building up in such fields.

been weighed against the world situation—nations at war and people's gut feelings of antipathy towards those of another (enemy) nationality coloured by all the disasters of war with, of course, the colour intensely and adversely influenced by the respective governments' propaganda. The present-day value of his investigations has veered in a different direction: towards our combined understanding of the planet and, hopefully, our attitude towards it as the *stage* upon which human evolution—integral to evolution as a whole—takes place, is enacted, proceeds.

To continue the metaphor: this gives us a backdrop for each phase of evolution as a scene in the 'mystery drama' of human consciousness. Steiner's procedure was to start by unfolding his view of the spiritual phenomena and only after that arrive at the landscape and the effect on its inhabitants. Here, it seems appropriate that I begin by first characterising the landscape and then use Steiner's spiritually achieved spyglass to look more deeply into it.

The major bulk of Europe is essentially back-boned by the Alps, with their W-E orientation, and with their appendages, so to say, as one travels east: the Dolomites, the Transylvanian Alps, the Velebit and Dinarske Planinas etc. South, they enjoy extending themselves into the peninsulas of Italy and Greece before diving into the Mediterranean. They sweep round on themselves at their eastern extremity in the Carpathians with an enough-is-enough kind of gesture, leaving an immense lake-ridden corridor free from mountainous heights to stretch from the Black Sea in the south, through the Ukraine, right up to the Baltic Sea in the north. They take their time, both in the west and the north, before becoming submerged by the Atlantic and the North Sea, thence descending to the continental shelf. Consequently, they spread out extensively into the north German plain and into the huge land-masses of France and the Iberian peninsular. At first sight, they appear to fragment in the north-west into the British Isles (and Faeroes)—though this is not a reflection of how the British feel it. If one went by that—their feeling of (certainly in the past, somewhat aloof John Bullism) independence from 'the continent'—one would have to view those islands as a somewhat separate feature.

Separate, too (though not separated by land as an island) are the Scandinavian countries. It is as if something else is happening 'up there' in the far north of Europe! Scandinavia presents the gesture of a colossal protuberance, jutting out, arm-like from the shoulder blade of Karelia in the north of Russia, that shoulder being Lapland, with Finland in the armpit; and with the unparalleled phenomenon of the Baltic Sea with its three wide-gaping gulfs (of Bothnia, Finland and Riga) pushing back its coast-fringed Baltic States; and with an indomitably determined neck thrusting its way round the Adam's Apple of Denmark!

One could argue that the EU has been inaugurated because of the way world economy is going. But it would be a sad day for Europe and its peoples if it denied the remarkably colourful idiosyncrasies of the nations which form it. Let us next characterise, therefore, a few of these, though somewhat symptomatically.

- Finland, the last country to retain a mythological epic, the *Kalevala*, and the 'best country in which to be educated today', according to the Pisa research of 2003.
- Norway, home of the Vikings, the 'father' of the Norsemen (q.v. Normandy, the Norman Conquest etc.); Norway, discoverer of North America long before Columbus, and at the same time guardian against the premature infiltration of American N-S forces into Europe; Norway, its towering peaks, taking the brunt of the surging watery force coming

from the western seas.[13]

- Sweden, with its balancing role and with its wary eye on Europe (e.g. the part it played in the Thirty Years War), and with its language still featuring on Finnish metro stations.
- The Baltic States—Estonia, Latvia and Lithuania—a unity in many ways, despite the differences in language, through their having retained their identity through thick and thin when occupied by neighbouring powers: Swedes, Nazis, Communists. Their deep connection with nature is manifest in their triennial folk song and dance festivals, which attract vast audiences and coach load upon coach load of participants in folk costume from all corners of the country. The numbers of both performers and audience rise well into the thousands.
- Hungary, with its immensely youthful forces, epitomising, could one say, the Slav forces which poured into Europe from Asia, at first constituting a threat but which were withdrawn.
- Russia and the Ukraine—precipitated from the 'devil' of Tsardom into the 'deep blue sea' of Bolshevism in the 20th century and now rediscovering and re-inventing their identity.
- Greece, resting on its laurels, still with the 'magic' world conjured forth by its classical treasures and antiquities.

---

[13] See Masters, B., 1983, 'Into the Fjord's Majesty' in *Weft for the Rainbow,* East Grinstead: The Lanthorn Press, for a description (in terms of the third paradigm) of Norway's unique position in the continent:Tide-slashed sentinel-skerries, / Spray anointed, guarding; / Treacherous rock-teeth, hungry; / Dream-hatched wrecks their feast-spread. / Guardians of calmer waters, / Joy-journeying through the gulf-surf, / Across the mouth-merged threshold, / By mellow moon illumined. Lady's mantle myriads, / Dawn-dewy droplets dancing, / Mercurial, jewelling, pearly. / Frost-white fjord-flanks fir-sloped, / Perpetual falls cascading, / Silver-spread sun-showered sparkling. / Majestic firmament blaze-throned, / High heavenly wonder—hill-hewn: / Victorious sun at midnight.

- Italy, despite its modern industries, basking in its undying, still avidly sought after, Renaissance cultural, artistic wealth.
- Germany, seriously bruised by the Thirty Years War and even after its belated unification, deflected by the World Wars from its unsurpassed tradition of the highest standards of craftsmanship and artistic and mental integrity.
- France, still buoyant from its Roi de Soleil splendour and the somewhat conflicting ricochets of threat in the guise of the French Revolution and the Napoleonic era.
- Spain, more than recoiling from civil war but with seemingly unfailing resources and resourcefulness as part of its gold-shored imperial past.
- Britain, boosted, blasted, warted and bloated from its one-time industrial supremacy, but as if never quite bereft of its green patchwork quilt of hedges, green fields and winding country lanes.

These characterisations provide a rather restricted view of the main features of Europe's 'countenance'. As a formative agent working on this countenance, Steiner identified an ancient and powerful spiritual force, surging from the ocean depths and extending its tentacles, so to speak, via the Gulfs of Riga, Finland and Bothnia into Europe from the north.[14] It conveyed etheric formative forces onto the land and into the people's constitution. It formed an ancient, albeit Post-Atlantean race (though as far as I am aware, Steiner does not relate it chronologically to his oft-elaborated sequence of Post-Atlantean epochs). The inner linguistic connection between Finnish, Estonian and Hungarian might find an explanation here, a facet of evolution which seems to have escaped orthodox scholarship.[15] The present-day Fins and their deep introspective soul-richness can be seen as a lingering memory of this race, vital to

---

[14]   9, 14, 15 November 1914—no English translation has been published.

the wellbeing of Europe.

Long before learning of Steiner's discoveries, I distinctly remember feeling this quality in the Finnish soul as something deeply congruent with the landscape. After one visit, I was anxious to convey this quality as having an inner connection to the purity and sanctity of early childhood.

> But as we look at the scene, it is the light that quickly claims attention: light that entrances and entertains, that quickens sight and soul with its splendour, its delicacy, its playfulness, its joy in being. At one moment it spotlights the white sails of a boat leaning its way into the shimmering waters; at the next it laughs with the pendulous birch twigs that frill and fan the blue-washed air; or trembles with the excited aspen leaves in the breath of early morning; drenches the nodding rowans with their reddening clusters of cheer-born berries; pauses at the enshrining threshold of dim twilight with which each towering conifer is dowager-clad; and rejoices in the bark-white trunks of the birches, soaring from the shore like royal sceptres, silver-lifted through the bird-songed canopy of green [...]
>
> When a child is born, those privileged to follow its early development become beholders of a metaphor of light [...] Towards the shore of earthly life, we are aware that an Ego is sailing. No parent needs telling that Divine Promise is navigating at the helm, as their new baby embarks on its voyage.[16]

---

[15] see the Finnish publication: Pirkko, Leino, 1991, *Kieleen mieltae—hyvaeae suomea,* Helsinki: Otava, p.18 for a map showing nineteen dialects/languages which are interrelated. Apart from Finnish, Estonian and Hungarian the author cites examples from well beyond the Ural Mountains.

[16] From Masters, B., 'Editorial Introduction' in *Steiner Education,* January 1996, p.2.

And, as those perceptions became intensified during a subsequent visit, I sought to follow the first play of elemental impressions (earth and water and light) into further ramifications (water and air in movement).

> The outlook from the windows was idyllic: after a little grassy area where the children could safely play, the ground sloped down towards a stretch of water, some hundred yards across. On it, a few tethered boats bobbed in what seemed like a paradoxical calm of ruffled stillness. Even when the temperature lolled on its baking plateau of 27°C, the leaves of the trees—both shores were wooded—flitted incessantly, making sounds as if the crinoline from a century's waltzes had been gathered together in a museum of rustling memories. On the near bank, the tall tree trunks, any one of which would have taken first prize in a schooner-mast competition, formed a kind of frame to the picture [...]
>   On the far bank, seen through this 'frame', the trunks were not directly visible, being blotted from sight by the overhead canopy of green. What could be seen was their reflection in the water: in one place sturdy pines advancing and retreating in a sleep-walk of eternal courtship, their cinnabar-red bark, molten in the algae-drifting surface; in another place, it was as if myriads of poplars had been Monet-wizarded from their canvas, hanging beside the Garden at Giverny, and swooshed onto an unstoppable, slow-motion video; in yet a third place, silver birches that merged into an inverted mirage of even more silvery wavelets, chased one another dreamily in the

rippling play of summer light [...][17]

Following the spiritual force at work there, from its southern limit (the Black Sea) we see it forming Europe, as it were through the back door. As the old order of Ancient Egypt receded, from the water it sputtered out the archipelago of Greek isles as host-heralds of the civilisation which was to become the cultural progenitor of Europe, fathering its philosophical and political thought, and mothering its artistic attainments in sculpture, dance, poetry, drama and architecture, both elements (art and philosophy) in its culture recognised by all as great zeniths in humanity's evolution.[18]

And when, via the explosion and implosion of the Roman Empire, that initial launch of Europe had run its course, and the precession of the equinoxes summoned forth the present 5th Post-Atlantean epoch—which Steiner dates from 1413—this great spiritual tide then moved the driving force of human evolution through great recapitulatory phases: that of the Sentient Soul (originally fashioned in Egypt) and that of the Intellectual or Rational Soul (the achievement of Greece and Rome to which we have just referred). The move, land-wise, flowed west—firstly to Italy and Spain (both surrounded by water on three sides, with Italy having the lesser ratio of land to sea) in which lands the recapitulated Sentient Soul found expression; and secondly to France whose task it was to bring the Intellectual Soul into a contemporary mode. France, bounded in the east by the Rhinelands and the Swiss Alps, and in the southwest by the Pyrenees, is an enormous land mass whose gesture culminates in the horn-like

---

[17]   from Masters, B., 'A Case of Motion Towards: What is the place of movement in Steinerian Education Theory? In the light of neuro-scientific research, to what extent does Motional Intelligence—MQ—deserve an equally valid place alongside IQ and EQ?' in *Early Childhood Development and Curriculum,* 1998.

[18]   The terms fathering and mothering are here meant of course as mere metaphors and bear no relationship to the formerly perceived roles of male and female in society.

peninsulas of Brest and Cherbourg which jut out and command the Bay of Biscay and the English Channel—entrances to Central Europe.

But before leaving France it is necessary to identify a pivotal element played by the French in Western consciousness. In the northwest, in Brittany, the ancient Celtic peoples predominated—in their language and in their customs. In common with kindred souls (Irish, Cornish, Welsh and Gaelic) a perception of elemental spirits had been retained by the Breton Celts. Though I have not as yet come across anecdotal evidence from Brittany, a teacher of mathematics in the Rudolf Steiner School of Edinburgh once commented in the early 60s that whenever he alluded to this faculty in class—the faculty known variously as the 'sixth sense' or simply as 'the sight'—there were always a few pupils who had acquaintances or relatives or a friend of a friend, whom they could cite as verifying the fact.

Herein lies France's pivotal position, for Steiner sees what he calls the (French) 'Romance impulse' as superseding this faculty. What existed in the spiritual heyday of Carnutum (the present-day Chartres) as vision on the etheric plane, discontinued. Even in the French 'Books of Hours', perhaps the pinnacle of the illuminated manuscript genre, exquisite though they are, there no longer exist the same spiritual connotations as are found, say, in the *Book of Kells* or the *Lindisfarne Gospels*.

The resultant consciousness paves the way for the next stage of development, which takes place in Britain. However, unlike the Isles of Greece, which seem to find their apotheosis in the Greek peninsula, the British Isles rise up in isolation from the continental mainland. Something of that defiant isolation can be particularly powerfully experienced in the south-west tip of Cornwall. On a small-scale map the acute-angled shape of its peninsular looks frail, as if it were a piece of protruding candy just waiting to be snapped off and snapped up. But in reality, stand somewhere close to sea level and you will feel the triumphant drama of a small island's defence against a mighty ocean's wrath, as comes across in the following passage.

> Into the rocky Cornish bay the Atlantic tide was prancing —a swelling surge of froth and foam, massive drifts of wind-whisked spray that lit up in fleeting rainbow-hued clouds, phalanxes of high-hoisted waves, sun-irradiated walls of deep aquamarine heaving and cresting and bursting into shattering displays of dashing white plumes, churning the shingle below, and flinging themselves against the barnacled slabs of jet black lava in unbridled ecstasy. The weather-beaten notice leaning against the coastguard's hut stated in sprawled chalk the precise minute of the forthcoming high tide; the exultant drench of spray, the wind-smitten cliff-face, the thundering breakers, the distant, dull booming of tide-shocked caverns and the shrieking mirth of gulls all proclaimed the hour to be a festival of unleashed forces, ploughing the endless furrow of time.[19]

Thus, as with the great ocean currents that circle the north Atlantic (clockwise: the Gulf Stream and the Canaries Current), the south Atlantic (anticlockwise: the Brazil and Benguela Currents), and similarly with the north and south Pacific, so here, in this *etheric* stream, humanity's cultural current emanates from the watery depths before spiralling in towards the British Isles. It is a spiralling which further modifies 'Romance' consciousness, nudging it *away* from a perception of the elementals. At the physical level it brings about a platform for change: the Consciousness Soul of the 5th Post-Atlantean epoch is born. The romantic element in English life could, perhaps, be seen as a kind of consolation for what was to follow. In particular, the Englishman's love of his garden (though even here,

---

[19]   From Masters, B., 'Editorial introduction' in *Child and Man,* January 1993, p.2.

tarmacing over for the purposes of car parking shows signs of divorcing him from that love) points to a certain ambivalence in the English make-up. On the one hand, the pragma of unleashed materialism holds bountiful sway; on the other hand, the care he gives his garden and the loyalty towards nature he displays in tenaciously securing National Trust properties for posterity (to give examples) remain as faint echoes of the Celtic past—the Arthurian *taming* of nature.[20]

Looking ahead even a step further, this great spiritual power has not only ushered in the present Post-Atlantean epoch but, again according to Steiner's research, is forming the landscape in preparation for the 6th epoch—on the great Russian plain, but not permitting it to be so flat as to be swamped by the watery forces to the extent that could bring about the next epoch prematurely.

Finally the question arises: Is there sometimes (in the fourth category) an artistic achievement which contains profound wisdom concerning the evolution of humanity in a form which is digestible for the consciousness which prevails at a certain point in time, but which will eventually be expressed more conceptually as consciousness advances? This is perhaps the highest goal to which art in all its forms can aspire; and I believe that Shakespeare, especially in his last plays, approaches that goal more and more discerningly.

The Tempest, to which reference has already been made, affords a prime example. Amongst the shipwrecked crew are popular characters, Trinculo and Stefano, who have an enigmatic streak. For an Elizabethan audience (though by 1611 the dynasty in England had become Stuart), they were first and foremost the comics. This means that their very appearance on stage would tend to open the soul in anticipation. Yet Shakespeare teams them up with the brute Caliban. In some ways he is even more enigmatic than the others.

---

[20]   see Masters, B., 2006, *Mozart: his musical style and his role in the development of human consciousness,* Forest Row: Temple Lodge Publishing, p.15.

For in his language he appears to identify with nature more intimately than anyone else in the play, yet in his sordidly desirous soul life he would rape the highest—as he sees it, the most superlative achievement—of nature: Prospero's daughter Miranda.

Had Prospero's command of the elements (who are symbolised by Ariel, the elemental whom his consciousness, and his alone, is aware of) not been equal to it, Caliban (with Trinculo and Stefano, recruited for the purpose) would undoubtedly have achieved his evil aim, having first murdered Miranda's father, Prospero himself. As it happens, the three of them are led a merry and mischievous dance by Ariel and their thwarted plot is made public, attracting a strange mixture of ridicule and condemnation.

But before Prospero sends them packing, their chastised consciousness (—is that what *conscience* is?) prompts them to utter words that hint at prophetically key qualities that could utopianise the future. Stefano, drunkenly staggering, belching and blurting, bursts out with "Every man shift for all the rest, and let no man take care of himself"; the very opposite of the malicious motivation which had driven Antonio to usurp his brother's dukedom in Milan and which had brought Sebastian to the very brink of murdering his own brother, also to gain a crown—his brother, Alonso, being the King of Naples.

Trinculo, the court jester identifies the senses ("If these be true spies which I wear in my head, here's a goodly sight.") (a) as 'etheric holes'—'wearing' them hardly sounds like something imbued with life; and (b) as having had the scales of the sense world removed, for he now views Prospero not as Caliban had portrayed him ("tyrant … sorcerer …")[21] but for his intrinsic worth, "goodly sight"—goodly sight in its more far-reaching meaning indicating one of the foundations upon which the next evolutionary epoch will be built.

Succumbing to the contagiously good-humoured mood at the end

---

[21] Act III sc (ii).

of the play, and in somewhat jocular vein, to conclude I am leaving the reader with a re-drawn map of Europe, allotting the countries (bearing in mind all that has been said above regarding the work of the elements in the landscape) to characters in *The Tempest*. While being tempted to leave the teasing task of doing this to the reader—who may, in any case, like to scribble a few ideas on the back of an envelope before reading further!—my suggestions follow.

- *Finland*, the Gonzalo of Europe—an ancient retainer of the king but at the same time speaking with the voice of conscience.
- *The Baltic States*, the Miranda of Europe—retaining something of the purity of earlier times, though not without an element of empathetic suffering.
- *Hungary*, the Ferdinand of Europe, bearer of youthful forces despite his initially fearing the worst.
- *Greece*, the Boatswain of Europe—he who recognises that the storm is threatening to annihilate past achievements.
- *Italy*, the Mariners of Europe—they who are inferior to, or at least less responsible than the Boatswain, but still 'in the same boat'.
- *Spain*, the Antonio of Europe—the one who bears the scar of having forcefully taken over the role of the duke (who admits to having lived too much in the past).
- *France*, the Sebastian of Europe—accent on the cerebral, sharp-witted and sometimes scheming.
- *Germany*, the Alonso of Europe—weighed down with the crown of rulership containing gems of a cultural past, whose purity is threatened by modern life.
- *England*, the Caliban of Europe—deformed through destiny, yet touchingly inspired by a childlike connection to nature.
- *Scandinavia and Ireland (and the so-called Celtic 'fringe')*, the Ariel of Europe—he and his spirits who retain the longest connection with developing human consciousness.

- *The Balkan States*, the Trinculo of Europe—colourful and attractive, motley-clad like a wise jester, a man of many parts, yet for the moment trapped between east and west, yet containing seeds in various forms for the future.
- *Western Russia* (i.e. the 'corridor' from St Petersburg to the Black Sea), the Stefano of Europe—the unlikely one who, at the very end of the play, has seen the light of the future, though still embroiled in habits which are self-demeaning and difficult to throw off.
- *The Fashioning Power, the Life-Being, surging up from the ocean depths*, the Prospero of Europe—the shaper of destiny, the dispenser of justice moderated by dignified humility, mercy and understanding.

If this seems something of an audacious interpretation of Shakespeare's late masterpiece—which it well may—may I plead its appearance in 1611, the year before the wedding of Frederick V, Elector Palatine and Princess Elizabeth, daughter of James I of England, (VI of Scotland) in 1612 the year immediately following, as support for the audacity. Some scholarship has even suggested that the masque in *The Tempest* was added to the play by Shakespeare when it was performed at the royal couple's nuptial ceremonies in London. The times were buzzing with the discovery of the tomb of Christian Rosenkreutz and publications (manifestos) that had 'appeared' out of the blue on the continent concerning Rosicrucianism. As the acclaimed Rosicrucian scholar, Frances Yates, comments, however, the author seems to be disassociating himself

> from the Rosicrucian mystery, which, by the time he [… was writing], had become dangerous, yet I do not think that this is the whole explanation of his use of the term *ludibrium*. A *ludibrium* could be a play, a comic fiction, and [...] Andreae thought highly of the theatre as a moral

and educative influence. The theatricality of the Rosicrucian movement, as revealed in Andreae's comments and allusions, is one of the most fascinating aspects of the whole affair.[22]

I realise of course that there is a multitude of other perspectives from which one can view Europe, but may I nevertheless commend the above, the outline of which was jotted down during the extra ten minutes spent on one of the slow Canarian ferries…!

---

[22] Yates, Frances A., 1972 *The Rosicrucian Enlightenment,* London: the ARK edition, 1986, p.50.